RECKONING WITH
RESTORATIVE JUSTICE

RECKONING WITH RESTORATIVE JUSTICE

HAWAIʻI WOMEN'S PRISON WRITING

Leanne Trapedo Sims

Duke University Press   *Durham and London*   2023

Project Editor: Liz Smith
Cover designed by Courtney Leigh Richardson
Typeset in Minion Pro and Helvetica Neue
by Westchester Publishing Services

COVER ART: *Kāhea*,
2019 (details).
Collagraph print,
15 in. × 55 in. ©
AbigailRomanchak.

Library of Congress Cataloging-in-Publication Data
Names: Trapedo Sims, Leanne, author.
Title: Reckoning with restorative justice : Hawai'i women's prison
writing / Leanne Trapedo Sims.
Description: Durham : Duke University Press, 2023. | Includes
bibliographical references and index.
Identifiers: LCCN 2022056210 (print)
LCCN 2022056211 (ebook)
ISBN 9781478025269 (paperback)
ISBN 9781478020370 (hardcover)
ISBN 9781478027362 (ebook)
Subjects: LCSH: Prisoners' writings, American—Hawaii—History
and criticism. | American literature—Hawaii—Women authors. |
Womenprisoners— Hawaii.|Americanlit erature—Hawaii—21st
century—History and criticism. | BISAC: SOCIAL SCIENCE /
Gender Studies | SOCIAL SCIENCE / Ethnic Studies / American /
Native American Studies
Classification: LCC PS508.P7 T737 2023 (print) | LCC PS508.P7
(ebook) | DDC 810.9/9287086927—dc23/eng/20230601
LC recordavailableathttps:// lccn.loc.gov/2022056210
LC ebookrec ordavailableathttps:// lccn.loc.gov/2022056211

For the beautiful women inside

& to
Vivacious Christine Wilcox, teacher, principal, mentor
For your wide heart
Who left the world far too soon

& to
Karen Newberry, who gifted me her life story
& who died on the outside

On the precipice of dawn: I lost my father to the pandemic
I dedicate this to you for your gift of compassion
~ Farrol Hyman Sims, MD

ACO	adult corrections officer
CCA	Corrections Corporation of America
CPS	child protection services
DPS	Department of Public Safety
FMC	Federal Medical Center
GVI	Grand Valley Institution for Women
HYCF	Hawai'i Youth Correctional Facility
IL-CHEP	Illinois Coalition for Higher Education in Prison
KPWP	Kailua Prison Writing Project
NCTIC	National Center for Trauma-Informed Care
NHIS	Nānākuli High and Intermediate School
OCCC	O'ahu Community Correctional Center
ROC	Restore Our Community
SHU	segregated housing unit (solitary confinement)
WCCC	Women's Community Correctional Center

A NOTE ON THE TEXT

I implement *inside women*, rather than *inmate* or *prisoner*, to avoid reducing the women to their crimes. Here, I acknowledge the influence of the inside women at Grand Valley Institution for Women (GVI), a medium-security prison in Kitchener, Ontario. I participated in a one-week intensive workshop at GVI with the women through the Walls to Bridges Collective in 2015. The inside women challenged academics and activists to avoid using stigmatizing language when referring to people in prison.

ACKNOWLEDGMENTS

I have learned that writing, seemingly a solitary process, is not a solitary journey. Two women have inspired me with their intellect, grace, and acumen: Elizabeth Colwill, mentor and friend, who read the manuscript with the eye of an owl, graceful and discerning; and Miranda Outman—editor at *Signs: Journal of Women in Culture and Society*.

As the conversation around prison abolition hurtles from the margins to the center in the midst of a global pandemic and the crisis of racial apartheid in the United States, I face a personal health crisis. I grapple with the limits of my own biological family, the surfaces of my skin, and the resilient ways in which intentional families live in locked-up spaces. The pain in facing one's mortality—the decay of the body—exacerbated by the exile from one's family of origin: a pressured abandonment in a world where so many on the margins are abandoned. I remember the words of one wise woman in my creative writing class at the sole women's prison in Hawai'i, Women's Community Correctional Center (WCCC), who interrogated the freedom of those on the outside. She said: "Just because you are on the outside of these walls—doesn't mean that you are free."

These past two years have indeed been exigent ones that have shattered the skin of democracy as we witness the disproportionate collateral effects that the pandemic has wreaked on people of color: Black communities, Indigenous communities, and those who are economically and politically precarious. The global pandemic has brought into clear vision the imperative for change: a systemic and structural revolution; an uprooting of nationalism and colonialism; an abolition of tyranny, white supremacy, and privilege. Without such change, we remain in the abyss of despair. As the underpinnings of abolition feminism summon: we are not free until we are all free. In their book *Abolition. Feminism. Now.*, Angela Davis, Gina Dent, Erica Meiners, and Beth Richie summon a radical reconstruction rather than a neoliberal reform. They proffer the predominant question that preoccupies contemporary abolitionists: "What would we have to change in our existing societies in order to render them less dependent on the putative security associated with carceral approaches to justice?"[1]

This book is a love letter to the inside women at WCCC, where I had the honor of facilitating creative writing classes and participating in the Kailua Prison Writing Project (KPWP). From 2012 to 2016 I was a feminist ethnographer—as contested as this category is within a carceral logic—guest, and creative writing teacher at WCCC as part of the KPWP, interviewing many of the inside women. I formed relationships with the women that persist today. While sitting in on the classes as a privileged guest from the "free" world and as a non-Indigenous and non–Pacific Islander woman, I found my own positionality as a white woman who has benefited from white privilege to be a troubled one. I spent years negotiating it, as both a feminist ethnographer and a facilitator, participating in classes taught by the director of the KPWP's creative writing program—Pat Clough—from 2012 to 2014; teaching my own poetry and performance lab (2015–16); and developing relationships over several terms that facilitated the interviews I conducted with the inside women.

These variegated relationships shape the terrain of my ensuing interpretations, which are representative not of all women's prison writing but of a singular women's prison in the Pacific. I have much gratitude and respect for the women I interviewed who shared their life stories with me. A big mahalo to Pat Clough and former warden Mark Kawika Patterson for allowing me to be a presence in the KPWP for years, as well as for facilitating the interviews with the inside women at WCCC.

So many others have held me along the way, among them my mentors and colleagues at the University of Hawai'i at Mānoa: Robert Perkinson, Vernadette Vicuña Gonzalez, Haunani-Kay Trask, Cynthia Franklin, Brandy Nālani McDougall, Meda Chesney-Lind, and Kapali Lyon. I especially thank Elizabeth Colwill, invaluable guide, who graciously gifted hundreds of hours to our conversations about women's life writing, the ethics of representation, and trauma. I am grateful to circles of activists, practitioners, writers, and editors: Honolulu prison activist Kat Brady and restorative justice attorney Lorenn Walker; my editors at Duke University Press, Gisela Fosado and Liz Smith; my lovely students at Northern New Mexico College, particularly Aaron Naranjo; other fierce activist students who have taught me along the way—Berenice Thompkins, Sophia Ventura-Cruess, and Kesha Jackson; my Knox College community; longtime friends in New York City; and recent friend (now family) Jonathan Arnon, with whom I was stranded during the

COVID-19 lockdown—I can never repay him for his generosity as my world imploded when I lost my father. Finally, my adorable and beloved fur friend, Daisy Arnon, who spent every night curled tight to my body, an example of the intuitive love in the feral world.

I extend gratitude to the American Association of University Women for the grant it awarded me in 2016. This support afforded me the time to write.

Much appreciation for *Signs: Journal of Women in Culture and Society* and the incisive conversations with its managing editor, Miranda Outman. The second chapter of this book appeared in the Autumn 2020 volume of *Signs* in a slightly altered form with the title "Reimagining Home: Redemption and Resistance in Hawai'i Women's Prison Writing." The fourth chapter appeared, in an altered form, in 2018 as the article "Love Letters: Performative and Biological Families in Hawai'i's Women's Prison," in a special issue of the journal *Frontiers: A Journal of Women Studies*.

I have been honored to participate in radical collectives around prison activism, abolition, and coalition building in various geographic loci—from Hawai'i to Philadelphia, Canada, Illinois, and Mexico. I am inspired by the perennial labor and love of these collectives: the Illinois Coalition of Higher Education in Prison; Illinois Humanities Envisioning Justice; the Coalition against Death by Incarceration; Vera In Our Backyards Initiative; the Walls to Bridges collective in Ontario; and the Hilo-based 'Ohana Ho'opakele. Thank you, Ronald Fujiyoshi and Kaleihau Kamauu, for inviting me up to Mauna Kea in December 2019 and allowing me to join your meeting at the Church of the Holy Cross in Hilo. Thank you to all of the warriors who have informed and shaped my thinking.

I owe gratitude to my mother, Lilian Trapedo Sims, with whom I have a complex and inextricable bond.

Finally, this book would not be possible without the consent and trust of the women. Much gratitude and love.

INTRODUCTION

The American Gulag and Indigenous
Incarceration in Hawaiʻi

Writing is my passion. Words are the way to know ecstasy. Without them life is
barren. . . . All my life I have been suffering for words. Words have been the source of
the pain and the way to heal. Struck as a child for talking, for speaking out of turn, for
being out of my place. Struck as a grown woman for not knowing when to shut up,
for not being willing to sacrifice words for desire. . . . There are many ways to be hit.
Pain is the price we pay to speak the truth.
~ bell hooks, *Wounds of Passion*

I write at a critical juncture within a circle of urgent conversations around
mass incarceration and what Ruth Wilson Gilmore coined the "prison
gulag."[1] Decarceration is no longer a fringe idea supported by radicals. In
a pandemic that has ravaged the globe—an aperture into the inequity and
apartheid state in the United States—we are compelled to act on decarceration. As a prison activist, abolitionist, and creative writing teacher in
incarcerated spaces, and someone who spent over a decade in Hawaiʻi, I
transport a unique lens to speak about the particularity of incarceration in
Hawaiʻi. Some activists may counter the contradiction in occupying dual locations: teaching in prisons and working for abolition. These scholars, theorists, and activists contend that any work connected to the carceral space is
an extension of state violence. I have had the privilege over several years to

participate in and facilitate creative writing classes within the carceral space, and my inside students attest to the power of transformational programming. Let us attend to those inside voices. Let us simultaneously attend to the ways in which "transformation can be coopted by or deeply embedded in notions of rehabilitation, treatment, and control—all carceral logics."[2] As inside writers astutely argue: "While often well intentioned in educational contexts, such discussions are often taken up by the general public as metamorphoses of 'prisoners' from 'uneducated' to 'educated,' 'deviant' to 're-formed,' and 'criminal' to 'citizen.' . . . [T]hese discourses of transformation can inadvertently result in saviorism, academic tourism, or outside people thinking that we're in need of redemption."[3]

Many outside students in the courses I have taught over the years, as well as many academics, consider themselves abolitionists without spending a day inside or meeting/communing with an inside person. Thus the ideological endorsement of abolition summons a particular privilege.

A Gendered Landscape

As a feminist ethnographer, I am suspicious of the distortion that quantitative data, particularly data aggregated by the state, leave in their wake. In the context of a gendered landscape, the data employ a binary approach to gender, which is illustrative of their limits.[4] There is a scholarly lacuna in the precarity of trans, queer, and nonbinary communities in the prison-industrial complex.

Women are entering prison at a staggering rate, yet they are anomalous subjects in our nation's gendered penal culture. According to statistical analysis from the Sentencing Project Research and Advocacy for Reform, the number of women in prison increased by more than 700 percent between 1980 and 2019, rising from a total of 26,378 in 1980 to 222,455 in 2019. The total count in 2020 was 152,854, a 30 percent reduction from the prior year—a substantial but inadequate downsizing due to the COVID-19 pandemic. Unfortunately, in 2021 many states began to increase the number of incarcerated women.[5] One-third of these women are imprisoned due to drug offenses, and they share significant histories of physical and sexual abuse and high rates of HIV infection.[6] Figure I.1 illuminates the sharp rise in the number of incarcerated women, particularly in state prisons, since 1980. Women are nonetheless miserably neglected in terms of prison program funding and in prison scholarship; infantilized and silenced, they are the "disappeared" of the prison population.[7]

Women's plight in the prison-industrial complex resounds within a broader, and disturbingly American, narrative: the disproportionate incarceration of people of color in our prison-industrial gulag. Women of color, Native Hawaiian women, and other Pacific Islander women are disproportionately incarcerated both nationally and in Hawaiʻi. Prisons in Hawaiʻi indicate an ongoing colonial relationship to the United States, which overthrew the Hawaiian Kingdom by force. As an occupied people, Native Hawaiians have been subject to systematic surveillance and discipline that persist in the contemporary Hawaiian carceral system.[8] While historical and contemporary prison literature addresses the Black male as the most marked body in the prison-industrial complex, my intervention highlights the testimony of women, including that of Native Hawaiian and other Pacific Islander women, who are overrepresented in Hawaiʻi's carceral landscape. Clearly, state violence is the malefactor in Hawaiʻi as the linkages of multiple forms of interpersonal violence and trauma with colonialism are palpable in the contemporary landscape: from economic gentrification and displacement to perpetual land and cultural theft.

From 2012 to 2015, I was a researcher, participant ethnographer, and guest, and in 2015–16 a creative writing teacher at the sole women's prison on Oʻahu—the Women's Community Correctional Center (WCCC) that warehouses approximately three hundred women of mixed security levels. This book, rooted in these experiences, addresses a scholarly lacuna in a tradition that privileges male prison writing by examining women's prison writing in two gender-responsive programs: the Kailua Prison Writing Project (KPWP) and its adjacent Prison Monologues.[9] The majority of women in my writing classes at WCCC represent a range of Pacific intersections, and the philosophy of the writing program itself is rooted in Hawaiian practices of hoʻoponopono (reconciliation and forgiveness) that resist state-sanctioned inscriptions on Indigenous bodies.[10] My work on expressivity (poetry, life writing, and performance) with the inside women counters the demarcation of a civic death for those incarcerated and emphasizes the specificity of inside women's voices in Hawaiʻi. The story that unfolds is a cartography—a bridge between social justice advocacy and scholarship that interrogates social justice failures in the contemporary carceral archipelago.

The inside women's diverse and multilayered experiences of trauma, as well as the nonviolent nature of many of their crimes, led me initially to perceive them solely as victims of the system. In fact, their poetry, prose, and interviews signal histories and self-understandings far more complex than the polarizing labels of "victim" or "perpetrator" convey. The types of trauma I observed in speaking to the women and listening to their narratives include childhood, familial, and sexual trauma; the social trauma of poverty and homelessness; the trauma of arrest and incarceration; the trauma of perpetrating a crime; the trauma (for Hawaiians) of living as a colonized people. Not all the incarcerated women are Hawaiians and thus colonized subjects, but the majority of women incarcerated in Hawai'i share memories of trauma rooted in dispossession, poverty, and violence. However, the particular violence experienced by Kanaka Maoli (Native Hawaiian) women is part of Indigenous dispossession under a settler colonial regime that is an ongoing form of domination set on eliminating Kānaka at large.[11]

According to the National Center for Trauma-Informed Care, an "inmate" at WCCC is more likely to be Native Hawaiian or part-Hawaiian (40 percent); to be a victim of child or sexual abuse (60 percent); to be convicted of either a felony drug charge (35 percent) or a property offense (36 percent); to have experienced violence in her life (80 percent); to have a history of substance abuse (95 percent) and mental health issues (33 percent); and

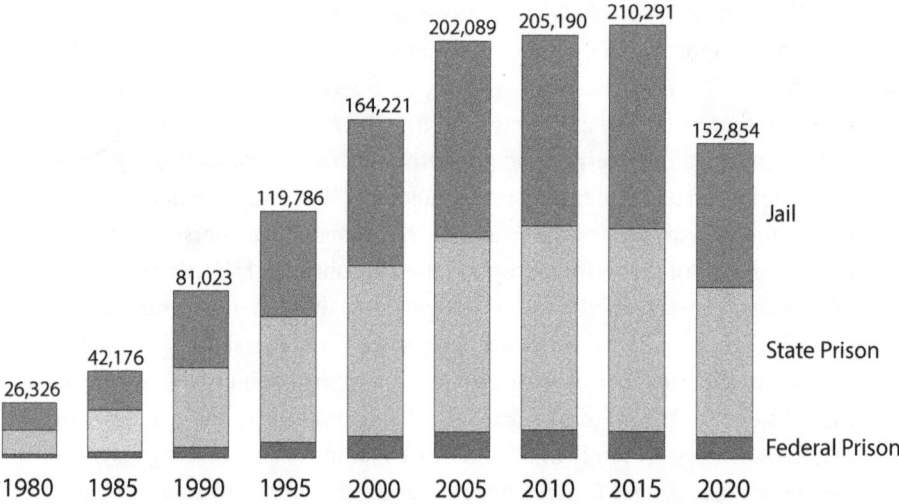

FIGURE I.1. **Rise in Women's Incarceration, 1980–2020.** The number of women in US prisons and jails has increased sharply since 1980. Source: The Sentencing Project, "Fact Sheet: Incarcerated Women and Girls," based on "Historical Corrections Statistics in the United States, 1850–1984," "Prison and Jail Inmates at Midyear" (1997–2020), and "Prisoners in 1980" through "Prisoners in 2020," US Bureau of Justice Statistics.

to be a mother of at least one child (60 percent).[12] Sixty percent of Native Hawaiian women at WCCC, 58 percent of women in prisons, and 80 percent of women in jails across the nation have children.[13] Two-thirds of mothers had custody of their children prior to entering prison. In Hawai'i, 44 percent of mothers who die in childbirth are Native Hawaiian and Pacific Islander, despite the fact that they constitute a smaller population of women in the state.[14] Many inside women thus face a particular gendered trauma due to the enforced rupture from their children.[15] Feminist prison scholar Beth Richie articulates the gendered trauma of incarcerated women:

> I cannot imagine a place where one might stand and have a clearer view of concentrated disadvantage based on racial, class, and gender inequality in the country than from inside the walls of a women's prison. There, behind the razor wire fences, concrete barricades, steel doors, metal bars, and thick plexiglas windows, nearly all of the manifestations of gender domination that feminist scholars and activists have traditionally concerned themselves with—exploited labor, inadequate healthcare, dangerous living conditions, physical violence, and sexual assault—are revealed at once. . . . The convergence of disadvantage, discrimination, and despair is staggering. In fact, it could be argued that prisons incarcerate a population of women who have experienced such a profound concentration of the most vicious forms of economic marginalization, institutionalized racism, and victimization that it can almost seem intentional or mundane.[16]

The nation-state's "get tough on crime" movement of the 1980s and 1990s and the War on Drugs campaign are largely responsible for the disproportionate rates of incarceration of Black, Latino, and Indigenous populations in the United States.[17] However, this ethos of punishment has been replaced in part by a contemporaneous national narrative that counters the devastating denial of Pell Grants to prisoners and encourages alliances between the university and the prison. Pell Grants for prisoners were reinstated nationwide in December 2020, reflective of the changing climate in penal reform yet ushering in some challenges to abolition.[18] Critical prison theorists Gillian Harkins and Erica R. Meiners trace the historical trajectory of the university-prison alliance in which they situate educational prison programs in one of two camps: redistributive justice predicated on human rights, and reformative justice based on moral and social reform.[19] The proliferation of educational prison initiatives that are both redistributive and reformative, such as the Inside-Out Prison Exchange Program and the Bard

Prison Initiative, has connected "innovative college-in-prison programs across the country" in the belief that "a liberal education can transform the lives of individual students and public institutions more successfully than the prevailing responses to crime and punishment."[20] These programs reflect current national debates that question prisons' ability to maximize resource expenditure, quell crime, and reduce recidivism, while incurring collateral damage to entire communities. The programming at wccc echoes these national reformist inclinations, yet it also takes inspiration from particular Hawaiian traditions of healing.

The wccc, under the leadership of its former warden Mark Kawika Patterson, was more in line with the prison reform movement than the state aggression expressed in the War on Drugs. In late 2008, as warden, Patterson implemented a trauma-informed care initiative at the facility. The program acknowledges women's histories of physical, sexual, and emotional abuse and the fact that their transgressions are primarily nonviolent. This initiative uses the framework of an Indigenous *pu'uhonua*, or a place of refuge.[21] According to the National Center for Trauma-Informed Care (NCTIC), "the spirit of pu'uhonua—the opportunity to heal and live a forgiven life—informs the vision that is changing the environment for both incarcerated women and staff at wccc."[22]

As Warden Patterson explained in an interview with professor and activist Dr. Eiko Kosasa, this marked space of *pu'uhonua* was utilized in ancient times as a traditional pathway to absolution and reconciliation. A Native Hawaiian who had committed a transgression that could in turn endanger his or her life was able to enter the *pu'uhonua*, where, as Patterson explained, "nobody could touch *him*."[23] When he became the acting warden at wccc in 2006, Patterson sought mentorship from his own minister from his school days at Kamehameha: "I asked him [his kahuna] can you please help me work out the place of our traditional pu'uhonua in our contemporary times and he answered, 'Kawika think of it this way—the women who come into your walls are like our people who came to the walls of the pu'uhonua. You need to embrace them and help them live a forgiven life.'" The programs within the trauma-informed care initiative that Patterson instituted address the various kinds of trauma experienced by the women inside, ranging from recent personal to collective historical trauma, including the 1893 overthrow of the Hawaiian Kingdom. According to the NCTIC, the impact of historical trauma is particularly disquieting for Native Hawaiian women, who are disproportionately represented among the prison population. The study correlates the devastation to Native Hawaiian culture in which women once played influential roles with a current state of precarity that produces "elevated suicide rates, substance abuse, mental health problems, coping mechanisms that appear self-sabotaging, unresolved grief, and physical ailments."[24] The trauma for Kanaka Maoli women as indigenous to Hawai'i is distinct from that of the other Pacific Islander women at WCCC. Pacific Islander is a marker for non-Hawaiian islanders, usually colonial migrants (American Samoans and Chamorros); immigrants (Western Samoans, Tongans); or those who hail from the former Trust Territory of the Pacific Islands and have legal standing to be in Hawai'i or the United States as part of their respective compacts of free association (the Republic of Belau, the Federated States of Micronesia, and the Republic of the Marshall Islands).[25]

As previously articulated, it is essential to witness that the violence that Native Hawaiian women experience is part of Indigenous dispossession under a settler colonial regime—an ongoing form of domination set on eliminating Kānaka at large, one way or another. This particularized violence is in distinct contrast to that of other racialized groups targeted for liquidation—because, unlike Kānaka Maoli, they are seen as part of surplus populations. Therefore, state violence is endemic to the trauma of Kanaka Maoli women because the multiple forms of interpersonal violence to which they are subjected are inextricable from the larger landscape of colonialism. Despite the persistent state violence perpetrated against Native Hawaiians, Native Hawaiian women have always resisted and have assumed central roles in the demilitarization of Hawai'i and the sovereignty movement. In *Nā Wāhine Koa: Hawaiian Women for Sovereignty and Demilitarization*, edited by Native Hawaiian scholar and activist Noelani Goodyear-Ka'ōpua, the narratives of the four wāhine koa (brave women) Moanike'ala Akaka, Maxine Kahaulelio, Terrilee Keko'olani-Raymond, and Loretta Ritte bear witness to the vital roles that Native Hawaiian women assume in the fight for unshackled futures.

Imagined by its founders as a place of refuge and transgression due to the then warden's envisioning of the WCCC as a *pu'uhonua*, the WCCC is a troubled site: a carceral landscape against a backdrop of colonialism, a space between hope and despair. My research illuminates the ways in which the KPWP, so warmly embraced by many inside women, remains embedded in a disciplinary system at the institutional, state, and national levels. That discipline takes both overt and covert forms, from the realities of sex with guards to the silencing—even within the KPWP—of women's intimate relationships with other women. My research holds in productive tension women's testimony of the immeasurable value of the KPWP and the ways in which the carceral and colonial regimes continue to impinge upon the women's lives. On the one hand, the KPWP—a composite of the biweekly creative writing classes, the Prison Monologues, and the biannual prison publication *Hulihia* (Transformation)—is a cathartic medium that effects change.[26] The women who write in an incarcerated space perform resistance, even as they confound the anticipations of readers familiar with an incarcerated male authorship. Yet, as I explore in the ensuing chapters, resistance necessarily runs against institutional constraint. If the creative writing classes function as a haven for the women, as the women themselves attest, they are never immune to institutional intrusions and fracture.

The Program

The Kailua Prison Writing Project traces its origins to 2003, when its director and founder, Pat Clough, in concert with *kumu* (teacher) 'Ilima Stern, began the first of the biweekly creative writing classes at the facility. Clough is committed to the KPWP as a program that is steeped in a particular location in the Pacific; however, she does not employ a Pacific Islander canon in her classrooms. At the same time, she has resisted joining a national online community not only because she desires to protect the women's identities and regards online learning as lacking in the personal connections so necessary in the incarcerated classroom but also because she realizes that the particularity of Hawai'i separates the KPWP from other national initiatives. In the *Hulihia* prison journal, Clough incorporates local artists and a confluence of languages (including Hawaiian Creole English), which collectively situate the journal in the particularized landscape of Hawai'i.

In 2008, Clough chose the Kailua Prison Writing Project as an umbrella name to encompass the prison publication, *Hulihia*, and its new public initiative, the Prison Monologues, rooted in therapeutic modalities that echo traditional Hawaiian practices of *pono* (social justice) and *ho'oponopono* (reconciliation and forgiveness). The program, via the Prison Monologues, soon grew into one of the "best received educational efforts in the system," reaching thousands of students in middle schools and high schools across the state.[27] The prison publication *Hulihia* was born from the writing classes, and in 2014 Clough planned to publish the tenth volume, with her biweekly creative writing classes reaching approximately six hundred women. Clough describes the KPWP and her collaboration with former warden Mark Kawika Patterson as a "magical confluence—a program that happened at the right place at the right time."[28] The program continued until 2014, when Clough decided to take a hiatus and Patterson left WCCC to take on a position at the Hawaiʻi Youth Correctional Facility (HYCF), which sits calculatedly in "the school-to-prison pipeline" design, directly across the highway from WCCC.[29] With their dual departure, the program faced attrition. The short life span of the KPWP reflects national trends concerning the fragility of prison programming due to a lack of funding and a lack of continuity among staff and the women inside. The COVID-19 pandemic largely obliterated prison programming.[30]

Clough sees the KPWP as a "vehicle for learning [that] replace[s] traumatic history with a believable future after years of criminal behavior, drug use, and incarceration" and as a direct antidote to recidivism. Her belief is reflective of a contemporary climate in which scholars, prison practitioners, and some carceral workers claim that education, and specifically writing, directly reduces recidivism. Clough envisions the program as an auxiliary to the inside women's traumatic stories and sanctifies the act of documentation—"writing it all down"—for its power to redeem and heal. In this sense, the KPWP resonates with other creative writing programs in American prisons whose evolution was inspired by the PEN Prison Writing Program founded in 1971 by a collective of professional writers.[31]

It is no coincidence that PEN America was founded in an era of penal policy reform—a period of cultural, literary, artistic, and political change.[32] The advent of prison writing programs was spearheaded by professional writers (mostly poets).[33] Since that time, the Justice Arts Coalition has been "building a nationwide collective of people who are committed to increasing opportunities for creative expression in carceral settings, amplifying the voices of those most impacted by mass incarceration."[34] The thematic preoccupations of women's writing in the WCCC reflect the reformist mindset of the 1970s and depart from the politically driven writing of the 1960s that condemned the nation-state.[35] Despite the WCCC's place-specific programming, it is rooted in broader national trends that are both reformist and politically driven.

The Prison Monologues—abbreviated theatrical performances of the women's narratives culled from the creative writing classes at WCCC—began as an experiment for fellow "inmates" and visitors inside the prison.[36] In 2008, a board member from La Pietra Hawaiʻi School for Girls, a private school on Oʻahu, came to the first *Hulihia* dedication in the courtyard of Maunawili "cottage" at WCCC.[37] Eight "inmates" from the creative writing class were invited to give a "dramatic presentation of their writings" at an assembly at La Pietra, which was prominently featured on local television and in print media. From this invitation, the Prison Monologues flourished: the "inside" program grew in size and expanded to the "outside," reaching not only students but also professional practitioners in the carceral turf: social workers, pastors, parole and probation officers, educators, and judges. More recently the Prison Monologues program was featured at national conferences on Oʻahu: those of the Office of Youth Services and the Hawaiʻi State Coalition against Domestic Violence; the Pacific Rim International Conference on Disability and Diversity; and the ʻAha Wahine Conference, a gathering of Native Hawaiian women from the community.[38] According to program publicity, "Nearing the end of 2012, the Prison Monologues had presented more than 40 programs at high schools, universities, [and] conferences on Oʻahu, Maui, and Hawaiʻi Island." Warden Patterson's decision to allow the women to travel in civilian clothes and fly to the outer islands suggests his allegiance both to the prison's potential as a "healing place" and to the women's ability to impact their audience. In the same way that Patterson envisions his work in the criminal "justice" system as a way of giving back to his own Native Hawaiian community, he imagines the Prison Monologues as an avenue for the inside women to give back to their communities and "live a forgiven life."[39]

Redemption is a premier character in the KPWP, and the women's testimony demonstrates that creative writing and performance can be transformative for the inside women who scribe and perform life writing, as well as for the audiences who witness the women's testimony. While many Americans may assume that the libertarian impulse of self-expression is a right, not a privilege, within the antidemocratic space of the prison that status of self-expression is ambiguous. In *The New Abolitionists: (Neo) Slave Narratives and Contemporary Prison Writings*, Joy James calls these antidemocratic loci, such as Abu Ghraib and Guantánamo Bay, "dead" spaces. Yet James argues that the state, despite its abusive excesses, incongruously provides the possibility of emancipation and redemption.[40] The cacophony of voices within the carceral institution reinforces exacting cultural scripts and forms of redemption, lending disciplinary effects to therapeutic rhetoric. The audiences for the Prison Monologues—from school groups to carceral and legal workers—are moved by and co-opted in the performance of authenticity. This book interrogates how speech performs as "an occasion for agency" and suggests that even if testimony speaks truth to power, it may likewise "speak untruth in the interests of power."[41] As the narrative unfolds, it becomes evident that it is our *kuleana* (communal responsibility) to understand the inside women's experience of testimony to and witnessing of national, institutional, and gendered violence as profoundly meaningful.

THE WARDEN'S TRAUMA-INFORMED CARE INITIATIVE

More than six feet three inches with a large, powerful frame, the former warden, Mark Kawika Patterson, favors lively aloha shirts and his large signature gold cross. He sports an effervescent smile and deep-set dimples. In 2019 Patterson was appointed by the Office of Hawaiian Affairs to lead the Hawai'i Correctional System Oversight Commission to oversee the state's Department of Public Safety. The commission was approved by the legislature "in what was initially hailed as a major corrections reform."[42] Warden Patterson, who has more than thirty years' experience working in the criminal "justice" system in Hawai'i and Nevada, ushered in many initiatives to WCCC based on an innovative circle pedagogy that embraces Indigenous programming.[43] Circle pedagogy references a way of knowing that is antithetical to linear systems of knowledge making. Those innovations include the cultivation of lo'i fields on the facility's grounds; the translation of turn-of-the-century Hawaiian newspapers from Hawaiian into English; talent nights; reentry and transition planning circles; and the employment of "life maps" at parole hearings.[44] The translation of turn-of-the-century newspapers from Hawaiian into English is an example of the politics of Patterson's programming situated in the pu'uhonua, which privileges Native Hawaiians and brings visibility to the resistance of everyday Hawaiians to Queen Lili'uokalani's overthrow, which has been written out of the historical record.[45]

Patterson's inventive programming emerged from a state of crisis in the Hawai'i prison system. As a result of litigation pending in 1991 against the State of Hawai'i regarding its conditions of confinement for women, the temporary WCCC was remodeled and subsequently completed in 1994 as the state's primary women's all-custody facility. Today, the facility "houses" pretrial and sentenced female "offenders," who are of maximum, medium, and minimum custody levels. At that time WCCC contained four separate structures: 'Olomana, Ka'ala, Maunawili, and Ahiki cottages.[46] Each cottage operates in accordance with the stipulations of specific programs and classification levels. The facility offers a fifty-bed, gender-responsive substance abuse therapeutic community, Ke Alaula (Breaking of a New Dawn).[47] Other programming includes cognitive-based curriculum, parenting and education classes, domestic violence treatment, day reporting, and electronic monitoring programs. The Project Bridge program is designed to "support female offenders in transitioning back to society through employment, education, and substance abuse treatment."[48] The Hina Mauka and Total Life Recovery (TLR) programs offer the women a path to recovery through access to spiritual transformation.[49] As 90 percent of the women's "crimes" are linked to substance abuse, and 75 percent of those women are victims of trauma, including domestic and sexual abuse, the former warden envisioned Hina Mauka—a program that targets substance abuse and promotes abstinence, in conjunction with spiritual transformation—as a pathway to the outside: "There isn't a single event of trauma that sent the women to prison, [rather] it is trauma that occurred over a long period of time, usually between the ages of 4–17. The women use substances to cope with their trauma. It is our job to break down the walls. Every one of my staff—from janitors to cooks to ACOS [adult corrections officers]—is trained to break down the walls [of trauma]."[50] In addition to offering in-facility programs, WCCC participates in many community service projects for state and county agencies and for nonprofit organizations.

At present there are plans to overhaul, expand, and modernize both the O'ahu Community Correctional Center (OCCC)—one of the three men's prisons on O'ahu and the largest facility in the state—and the WCCC, a subject of consternation debated by local community members and activists who call for a moratorium on prison growth in Hawai'i. Mirroring the neglect of women in the carceral landscape, there is more debate around the expansion of the male facility. The Hawai'i Department of Public Safety's November 2020 statement, titled "WCCC Improvements Moving Forward," outlines the department's plans that include the relocation of "female offenders from OCCC to the WCCC in Kailua, in order to improve living conditions while expanding treatment, rehabilitation services and access to family visitation." There is an emphasis on rehabilitation—one that dually summons the prison as an educational complex.[51]

Some of the "improvements" that the Department of Public Safety (DPS) proposes for WCCC include constructing a new housing unit and administration building; renovating the vacant Ho'okipa cottage and support building for housing and support purposes; and improving internal circulation, on-site parking, and ingress and egress from Kalaniana'ole Highway. According to a DPS bulletin, "The improvements at WCCC will be similar in scale and appearance to a community college campus with spaces devoted to administration, housing, visitation, inmate services, among others with improved visitor and employee parking near the WCCC entrance."[52] It will be curious to witness if the oversight commission and the fervent community support in favor of decarceration will halt this "recuperative" project.

Many of the writers in the Kailua Prison Writing Project were processed through Hina Mauka or Total Life Recovery, and the rhetoric from these programs lives in their writing. While many inside women attest to a shift in the culture of the prison with the piloting of a trauma-informed care approach and see Patterson as a visionary, others critique this movement as a strategy to satisfy political agendas and obtain funding. In a similar vein, Gillian Harkins and Erica R. Meiners articulate that it is difficult to track the goals and commitments of college-in-prison programs because all programs must operate according to the rules and expectations of the Department of Corrections: "This can often require public relations materials or program rationales that favor aims of public safety, reducing recidivism, and moral uplift over aims of educational equity and social justice, regardless of the actual operating principles of the program on the ground."[53] In promotional materials, the KPWP appears almost as a holiday camp, replete with reformist and redemptive expectations that fuel a colonial imaginary. Consider, for instance, the bucolic and idyllic description of women at WCCC in "Creating a Place of Healing and Forgiveness: The Trauma-Informed Care Initiative at the Women's Community Correctional Center of Hawaiʻi": "A group of women in green work clothes poses for the camera, smiling broadly, proudly displaying a six-foot wreath they crafted from flowers and foliage grown on the grounds. Nearby, women tend rows of hydroponic salad greens and herbs grown for the facility's kitchen, while others clear brush by a rushing stream. In the welding shop, an artist works on a large sculpture of an orchid. Women living in an open unit whose walls are painted brightly with tropical birds and flowers prepare for their jobs in the community."[54] This text presents the prison as an open, rather than an enclosed, space—one in harmony with nature and replete with smiling women. Tessa informed me that this re-presentation of the prison as a harmonious and healing space was the template presented to visitors but was, in her view, discordant with the reality of the prison.

One can also see a delicate politics of representation at work in the highly successful Prison Monologues program, as part of and sustained by the KPWP. Whereas Pat Clough believed in the distinctive nature of a writing program in Hawaiʻi, the warden's initiative further developed this notion of "distinctiveness" by highlighting Indigenous ways of knowing. Although

Patterson faced condemnation by the Office of Hawaiian Affairs and Hawaiian sovereignty groups for his positing of the prison—an anti-Indigenous space—as a *puʻuhonua*, his visibility and success as a prison administrator, his legibility in the Native Hawaiian community, and his public presence at TED Talks and other political forums positioned the Prison Monologues program as an authentic vehicle of restorative justice.

The politics of the program were shaped by Patterson's own perspective but also, in a sense, led to its demise. According to local prison scholars and activists, Patterson combatted professional jealousy, in a dis-eased system that does not look favorably on humanitarian feats. Clough explains that Patterson left WCCC because he felt he could accomplish more as an administrator at HYCF. In her words, "Mark always wanted to do work that would connect Women's with the youth correctional facility." As part of the larger national narrative of the "school-to-prison pipeline," HYCF tragically serves as a feeder program to WCCC.[55]

The State

According to the Prison Policy Initiative's 2023 report, Hawaiʻi has an incarceration rate of 439 per 100,000 people, which includes prisons, jails, immigration detention, and juvenile justice facilities. This speaks to the bleak reality that Hawaiʻi locks up a higher percentage of its people than almost any democracy on earth.[56] Taking into account probation and parole, more than 25,000 Hawaiians are under the supervision of the criminal legal system.[57]

Interrogating prisons in Hawaiʻi poses unique questions endemic to their location. Despite the fact that the program draws on Hawaiian healing practices, it is crucial to keep in mind that the state follows national patterns of incarceration in profoundly disturbing ways. According to local Oʻahu feminist criminologist Meda Chesney-Lind and prison advocate Kat Brady, Hawaiʻi has followed the national trend not only in the overrepresentation of people of color but also in its castigatory and disproportionate imprisonment of parole violators and nonviolent offenders. The writers note that Hawaiʻi is fifth in the nation in its incarceration of repeat drug offenders.[58] Its pattern of imprisonment has a particular emphasis on Indigenous incarceration. Native Hawaiians are also significantly more likely to get diabetes, receive inferior education, face homelessness—Kānaka Maoli constitute 60 percent of the state's indigent population living on beaches and sidewalks—and suffer from the collateral ailments of poverty. These devastations reflect the continuation of colonialism in Hawaiʻi.

Although they represent only 21 percent of the state's population, Native Hawaiians constitute 39 percent of the adult incarcerated population, more than any other racial group.[59] Native Hawaiian women are more likely than their male counterparts to be overrepresented in the prison-industrial complex: 44 percent of incarcerated women are Native Hawaiian, compared with 37 percent of incarcerated men.[60] According to a report titled *The Disparate Treatment of Native Hawaiians in the Criminal Justice System*: "Given the 709 percent increase in the incarceration rate in Hawai'i over the last 30 years compared to the 262 percent increase in the national incarceration rate, it is worth considering that the increase in the incarceration rate of Native Hawaiians over the same time frame is greater than that for any other racial or ethnic group in the United States."[61] According to the report by the Prison Policy Initiative titled "Hawai'i Incarceration Rates by Race/Ethnicity, 2010," the rates of Native Hawaiians in prison are probably underestimated, due to the mixed racial identities in Hawai'i and the vagaries of racial self-declaration.[62] Figure I.2 demonstrates both the overincarceration of Native Hawaiians in the state's criminal legal system and the confluence of racialized identities.

The overrepresentation of Native Hawaiians in the state's incarceration statistics follows a genealogy of national and global discrimination against Indigenous people in the criminal legal system. In the 1970s, many Native American women in the United States were granted parole only if they agreed to acquiesce to the nation's systematic sterilization program.[63] Critics have characterized Indigenous and Pacific Island communities as "unseen victims of a broken U.S. justice system."[64] Since 2010, the number of Native Americans incarcerated in federal prisons has increased by 27 percent. According to 2019 data from the Bureau of Justice Statistics, Native Americans in the United States are incarcerated at over twice the rate of whites.[65] In a 2014 *Guardian* article, reporters Nick Evershed and Helen Davidson expose the rate of Indigenous imprisonment in Australia as thirteen times greater than the non-Indigenous incarceration rate.[66] The Bureau of Statistics offers sobering statistics that show the number of Indigenous Australians in prison has grown by more than 80 percent in ten years.[67] In *Women of Color and Feminism*, Maythee Rojas provides data that indicate Native Americans are twice as likely to be victims of violent crime as any other group. Domestic violence on reservations is a dire problem, and homicide, according to Amnesty International, was the third-highest cause of death among Native American women in 2005–6.[68] Prominent Native legal scholar Sarah Deer—citizen of the Muscogee (Creek) Nation—reveals that 90 percent of sexual crimes in Indian Country are perpetrated by outsiders.[69]

There is no federal prison in Hawaiʻi. Hawaiʻi's state prisons that fall under the jurisdiction of the Department of Public Safety include the Hālawa Correctional Facility, which comprises a special-needs facility and a medium-security facility; the Waiawa Correctional Facility—a 334-bed, minimum-security male prison; the Kulani Correctional Facility near Hilo that warehouses two hundred men and was reopened in 2014 to mitigate some of the mainland transfers; the Women's Community Correctional Center; and the Oʻahu Community Correctional Center. The OCCC is the largest jail facility in the state of Hawaiʻi and is situated on sixteen acres in the urban Honolulu neighborhood of Kalihi. The 950-bed facility houses pretrial detainees, and this is where most of the women at WCCC are housed prior to their trials. Currently there is debate about the planning and design of a proposed new Oʻahu jail, expected to cost $525 million, to replace the crumbling OCCC.[70]

According to the Department of Public Safety website, several correctional facilities on the US mainland are contracted to house Hawaiʻi's prisoners in order to allay overcrowding. Red Rock Correctional Center and Saguaro Correctional Center, both located in Eloy, Arizona, are the most common destinations. Indeed, approximately one-third of Hawaiʻi's more than six thousand prison inmates have been transferred to private prisons on the mainland run by CoreCivic, formerly the Corrections Corporation of America (CCA). In 2010, the Office of Hawaiian Affairs released a report titled *The Disparate Treatment of Native Hawaiians in the Criminal Justice System*, which confirmed that Native Hawaiians are disproportionately sent to out-of-state prisons.[71] According to the Marshall Project, a leading news organization that promotes national attention to mass incarceration, "Hawaii first began sending prisoners en masse to mainland prisons in 1995, when it secured beds in a privately run Texas facility. Over the years, Hawaii expanded the practice, shipping thousands of prisoners to 14 facilities across eight states. Today, under a $30-million-a-year contract with CCA, the state sends all its overflow prisoners to Saguaro, which was opened just for Hawaii in 2007, with a blessings ceremony performed by Hawaiian 'cultural advisors' flown in from the islands. There are 1,391 prisoners from Hawaii housed at Saguaro, and last year [2015] they had 2,798 in-person visits."[72]

Prison transfers are not unique to the prison-industrial complex, but the geographic placement of Hawaiʻi as an island in the middle of the Pacific amplifies the exile that Hawaiian prisoners face. One of the unique ethical

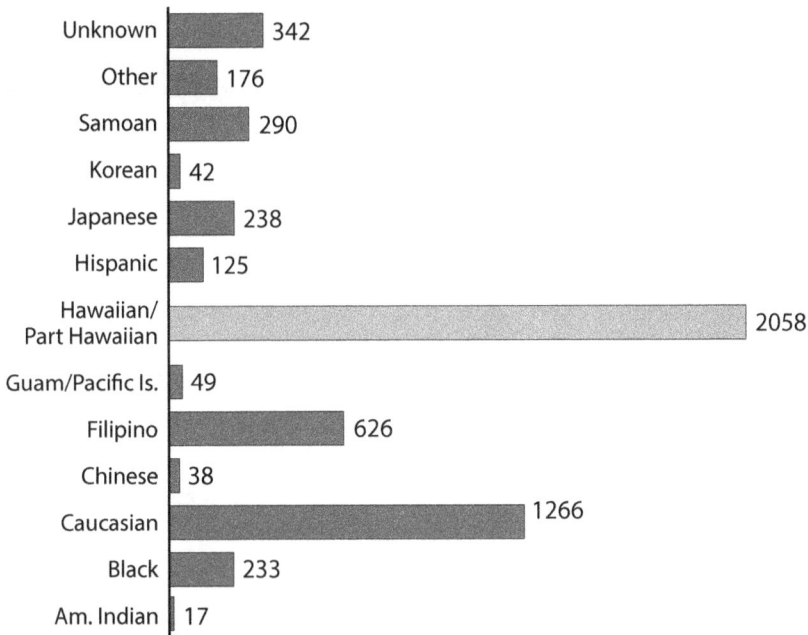

FIGURE I.2. **Hawai'i Prison Population by Ethnicity.** Overincarceration of Native Hawaiians in the state's criminal legal system. Source: *Creating Better Outcomes, Safer Communities: Final Report of the House Concurrent Resolution 85 Task Force on Prison Reform to the Hawai'i Legislature*, based on Hawai'i Department of Public Safety, System Wide End of Month Data, July 2018.

and logistical problems that incarcerated Hawaiians encounter in the plight of prison transfers is a racial "misfiling." Hawaiians, sometimes a composite of multiple ethnicities, are not easily "legible" on the mainland, which has led to further stigmatization and at times brutality within the prisons.[73]

There are economic incentives for states that accept prisoners from Hawai'i, as well as large savings for the Department of Public Safety. Yet even some carceral administrators, such as the director of the Idaho Department of Corrections, understand that "any time you move inmates away from the people who can support them, away from where they're going to actually re-enter society, [I have to say] it is flat-out correctional malpractice."[74] Hawai'i pays CoreCivic about $70 a day to house each inmate at Saguaro, compared with an average of $140 a day for an inmate at any of the four prisons back home.[75] The incarcerated population in Hawai'i is predominantly a low-security risk—a fact particularly true of the women—yet prisoners are deported to mainland medium-security prisons. Local research unveiled that most women in prison are nonviolent and should rather be serving their prison terms in gender-responsive, community-based programs in their home state.[76] The relocation to the remote and rural mainland prisons for Hawaiʻi's female inmates was a dire reality prior to 2016 as there was and still is only one overcrowded women's prison in the state. In 2016, former governor Neil Abercrombie mandated bringing all of Hawaiʻi's women who were incarcerated on the mainland back to Hawaiʻi; this urgent return was fueled by the persistent rape of the women by guards in the mainland prisons.[77]

While the male prison population in Hawaiʻi doubled between 1985 and 1995, the female population tripled, largely due to the sentencing and incarceration of female nonviolent first-time drug offenders. These statistics reveal that despite the rapid increase in the number of women who are incarcerated, they are neglected in programming, health care, and research in what is still perceived as a primarily male carceral space. Women in Hawaiʻi's prisons suffer a lack of female correctional officers, gender-responsive community-based programs, and rehabilitation programs.[78] Warden Patterson's trauma-informed care initiative, which was developed to address these gender inequities, focused on "reducing the use of restraints and isolation . . . since these interventions are likely to re-traumatize women who are trauma survivors and cause trauma responses in women who had not previously experienced trauma."[79]

The Nation

The carceral landscape in America as a whole remains a contested space. Many prison scholars argue that the skyrocketing rates of incarceration, the proliferation of multimillion-dollar industrial supermax prisons, the militant war against drugs, and the overrepresentation of minorities in the prisons represent an economic and racial crisis in America—a crisis that contradicts the myth of America as a benevolent democracy. Penal theorists argue that the contemporary climate is one of retribution and criminalization, evident in the expansion of the prison-industrial complex and its overtures to Dwight Eisenhower's military-industrial complex. According to the 2023 Prison Policy Initiative report, the American criminal legal system "hold[s] almost 2 million people in 1,566 state prisons, 98 federal prisons, 3,116 local jails, 1,323 juvenile correctional facilities, 181 immigration detention facilities, and 80 Indian country jails, as well as in military prisons, civil commitment centers, state psychiatric hospitals, and prisons in the

US territories."[80] Chesney-Lind and Brady note that the United States imprisons one out of one hundred citizens, establishing it as the world's largest incarcerator.[81] The shocking warehousing of US citizens in the nation's prisons or jails—a 500 percent increase over the past thirty-five years—and the disproportionate representation of nonwhite bodies among the incarcerated reflect the persistent racial and economic apartheid that exists in the United States.[82] According to a Prison Policy Initiative report titled *Mass Incarceration: The Whole Pie 2023*, Black people constitute 38 percent of the incarcerated population, despite representing only 12 percent of the total US population. Furthermore, there are 803,000 individuals on parole and a staggering 2.9 million individuals on probation. The Prison Policy Initiative cautions policy makers against mandating "alternatives to incarceration," such as probation, which potentially facilitates an extended criminalization of people who are not a threat to public safety.[83]

Scholars, including me, argue that the prison system has been designed to replace the earlier form of Black chattel slavery and functions today as an institutional, "sanctioned" arm to discipline minority populations. According to the Sentencing Project, more than 60 percent of the people in prison are now racial and ethnic minorities. One in every ten African American men in their thirties is in prison or jail on any given day in the United States. The disparate impact of the War on Drugs eventuates in disturbing realities: two-thirds of all individuals in prison for drug offenses are people of color.[84] According to the Bureau of Justice Statistics, as of 2020 the rate of imprisonment of African American women (65 per 100,000) was 1.7 times the rate of white women (38 per 100,000).[85] The rate of Latina women (48 per 100,000) was 1.3 times the rate of white women.[86]

Even more bleakly, the statistics fail to show any correlation between the gargantuan prison-industrial complex and diminishing crime and recidivism rates. Many theorists argue that media coverage commands public opinion, which is vulnerable to bloated and counterfeit statistics.[87] The critics claim that the correlation between crime and the expansion of the carceral system is fabricated as statistics confirm a marked decrease in crime rates since the 1990s. There are devastating collateral consequences that perpetuate the effects of incarceration long after release. According to a 2018 Sentencing Project report, increasingly stringent laws and policies restrict people with a felony conviction—particularly convictions for drug offenses—from access to employment, welfare benefits, public housing, and student loans for higher education. Such collateral penalties pose barriers to social and economic advancement.[88]

In American society, the prison-industrial complex is viewed as a masculine space because men are disproportionately represented in its confines. Although there are many more men in prison than women, the rate of growth for women in prison since 1980 is double that of men. As of May 2022, one million women were under the supervision of the criminal legal system.[89] The increases in prison spending are concomitant with the escalation in the imprisonment of women. According to Meda Chesney-Lind and Lisa Pasko, the nationwide incarceration of women has increased sixfold in the past two decades due to factors other than a shift in the nature of women's crimes. Researchers of these trends have noted that the criminal legal system has become tougher on women at every level of decision-making, from arrests to sentencing to parole determinations—particularly for Black women.[90]

Contemporary terminology, such as the War against Crime and War on Drugs, posits the prison-industrial complex within a masculinist landscape of battle. As of 2019, 53 percent of women confined in state and federal institutions are Black, Latina, Native American, or Asian.[91] Men and women exhibit different patterns toward drug use: women tend to engage in self-injurious behaviors and are more susceptible to drug addiction as a means of escape, whereas men tend to externalize pain via violence. The bulk of women in prison are incarcerated for nonviolent drug or property offenses, with drug offenses as the dominant liability for female incarceration. Women drug offenders, particularly those of color, are far more liable to be arrested, convicted, and incarcerated than they were prior to the War on Drugs.[92] Luana Ross and Deena Rymhs argue that women of color, particularly Indigenous women disenfranchised from land, are twofold victims in the prison-industrial complex.[93]

Women's Prison Writing

The genres of prison writing and autobiography hail from gendered literary traditions that privilege political exile and resistance over rehabilitative domestic exile. Scholarship on incarcerated writing tends to highlight men's misadventures while it maligns women as "cultural outlaws" because inside women, more than their male counterparts, are judged as violating dominant social and gendered norms. My reference to domestic exile reflects how the women's writing at WCCC expresses a longing to repair exile from family, society, and community. Incarcerated writing showcases preoccupations with borders—spatial, geographic, somatic, gendered, and linguistic—and both vilifies the prison as a Hadean inferno and celebrates it as a pathway to self-edification. In light of the ambiguous nature of carceral writing, penal theorists and creative writers have pointed to the intrinsic contradiction in the legal assignation of a "civic death" and the act of writing. If prisoners are civically "dead," their voices are accoutrements of an extended death and in that sense can be perceived as impossible voices. It is easy to see why legislatures, penal administrators, and the criminal legal system at large are invested in disciplining and patrolling the voices of those who are incarcerated. The very act of writing from a dead space and under the classification of a noncitizen is beleaguered. This type of civic death in America has its roots in the constitutional civic death of the slave.[94]

In this book, I examine the contradictions rife in this locked-up space and explore the ways in which healing might nonetheless transpire within a prison setting. The chapters that unfold reside at the nexus of critical literacy, feminist ethnography, and performances of trauma in a borderland space—the prison—that resist simplistic receptions. Drawing on qualitative methodologies such as interviews and participant observation, as well as on discourse analysis and penal, literary, performance, and trauma theory, my research not only interrogates the intersection of race and gender in contemporary literary texts but also emphasizes how women's prison writing redefines the literary.[95] Particular tropes distinguish women's from men's prison writing, with women's writing rooted in their specific experiences of sexual and domestic violence, their unique positioning as cultural outlaws, and the policing of women's writing that demands rehabilitative and domestic outcomes. In *Mohawk Interruptus: Political Life across the Borders of Settler States*, Audra Simpson names the Indian stories as "alternatives . . . to the dominant discourses of literature and history only in that they are Indian stories, and Indian stories haven't mattered much." These "hidden transcripts" are similar to many of the hidden narratives of women's prison writing in Hawai'i.[96]

Despite the steady flow of scholarship on creative writing programs in male prisons, women's prison writing suffers a drought.[97] Part of this absence is due to the lack of funding for enrichment programming and the asymmetrical access to educational opportunities in women's prisons compared to men's prisons. The editors of *Women Prisoners: A Forgotten Population* argue that incarcerated women are recipients of meager programs because their crimes are not *sufficiently* violent—an underachievement in crime—and because they more passively accept substandard conditions in prison.[98] This assumption of women's "passive" acceptance is a gendered stereotype that essentializes women's "nature," and thus victimizes women.

Several prison scholars and writers have refracted the prison-industrial complex through the lenses of race, gender, sexuality, and class.[99] Their approaches and methodological interventions are wide-ranging—ethnography, historiography, feminist criminology, sociology, autobiography, and literary criticism.[100] In writing this book, I have found inspiration in their work, as well as in anthologies such as *Wall Tappings: An International Anthology of Women's Prison Writings, 200 A.D. to the Present; Razor Wire Women: Prisoners, Activists, Scholars, and Artists*; and *Women, Writing, and Prison: Activists, Scholars, and Writers Speak Out.*[101] These gender-responsive collections focus on women's writing from inside the prison space and foreground the involvement of the inside women in all aspects of artistic creation. Visually, thematically, and ideologically, they resist the hierarchy inherent in many anthologies, as they showcase process in concert with product. *Razor Wire Women*, a collage of disquieting images, testimony, and intersectional theorizing, explores expressivity both inside and outside the prison-industrial complex. The anthologies reveal that the experience of imprisonment not only affects the individual woman but also injures the entire family and extended community. The autobiographical writing of inside women—unlike men's single-authored work—often appears in edited anthologies, offering a window on women's communal writing practices and on the politics of collaborative autobiographies in which the editor reframes or mediates the narratives.[102] Ashley Lucas, one of the editors of *Razor Wire Women*, insists that the women behind the razor wire—artists and writers—have the power to flesh out the missing details of their lives as countertexts to the nation-state's injurious and pathological phenotypes. As Lucas argues, the state concocts biographies based on a missing limb, a scar, a tattoo—visual evidence of the women in parts. Feminist academicians and practitioners like Lucas, by contrast, celebrate the women inside who "share their lives in art and poetry in brash celebration and utterances."[103]

Despite its cosmetics of complicity with the nation-state, the writing produced in the Kailua Prison Writing Project forms an archive of resistance.[104] The women's poetry generated in the project borrows from the tradition of prison autobiography—from Martin Luther King Jr.'s canonical "Letter from Birmingham Jail" to Angela Davis's *Autobiography*. Genres of carceral writing include testimony, testimonio, witness, apologia, confession, and conversion narratives, all of which occur across various writing forms: poetry, autobiography, memoir, political manifesto, and fiction. Davis's autobiography, an apologia (a defense of her political life), indicts the legal system and the revolutionary Black Panther Party for stripping women of political agency.

Autobiography as resistance, as deployed by Martin Luther King Jr. and extended by revolutionaries such as the Black Panthers, has today been refracted through prison reform. Women's writing in the prison journal *Hulihia* performs dissent in its ability to reimagine and forge new multifaceted identities, yet it is simultaneously institutionalized as an alternative avenue for rehabilitation. Women's voices chosen for *Hulihia* are less overtly critical of the nation-state than was Davis's autobiography, but they nonetheless resist female passivity, the American Dream, and the carceral state. The women's opposition is animated in the forms, styles, and themes of their presentations. Women in my creative writing classes occasionally offer well-articulated appraisals of national and state corruption. In these ways, women's narratives of trauma perform as counternarratives to a civic death.

The inside women's writing is a radical genre because of its demand for what Deena Rymhs calls a "second hearing"—a demand for society, rather than the incarcerated, to change. Many prison programs consist of cognitive classes that ignore the reality of social, political, and economic disenfranchisement and insist that prisoners account for their actions, take responsibility for the violence they have "created," and transform *themselves*. By contrast, Indigenous carceral writing, argues Rymhs, summons an "alternate hearing" or "second hearing" for the incarcerated: one that disputes the legal and judicial parameters that are circumscribed by the courts and the penal system.[105] The second hearings expose the failings of the criminal legal system and work as a form of apologia by affording the prisoner the occasion to rewrite or refashion her life history through autobiography. The reader, witness to the histories of abuse, poverty, and racism, is correspondingly able to reframe her own perceptions of guilt. Here, criminality is reassigned from solely on the individual to include society and its negligent apparatuses as the writers "maneuver around . . . the constraints that the law places on self-representation."[106] I argue that in using the framework of literacy as a moral and cultural affirmation of belonging, the entombed prison (a dystopian space) becomes a utopian one, as illiterate subjects transform themselves into literate subjects. The restorative justice circles implemented by attorney Lorenn Walker at wccc, the life-planning maps for parole hearings generated by the women inside, as well as the kpwp itself are examples of alternate hearings and avenues through which a woman can symbolically write herself back into society.[107]

Unsurprisingly, trauma narratives emerge as a dominant genre within the kpwp. The trauma narratives of inside women are deeply marked by gender, both because of the women's real experiences of personal trauma and abuse, and because of the modeling of certain scripts that authorize women's stories of victimization rather than political protest. The literary canon that Clough implements in her classes does not model trauma narratives, as her archive primarily consists of triumphant, or "heroic," narratives that mirror what Clough perceives as the women's own heroic journeys. Yet due to the personal nature of creative writing and the fact that we tend to write what we know, Clough does not necessarily control the themes that emerge in her students' writing. The Prison Monologues' tripartite scheme of "Who We Were," "Prison Life," and "Reflections" more directly lends itself to the production of trauma narratives. The Prison Monologues is rooted in a tradition of atonement for crime(s), and its very structure requires women to take responsibility for the ways they have injured others.

In *Reading Autobiography: A Guide for Interpreting Life Narratives*, Sidonie Smith and Julia Watson posit "that there is a growing audience for life writing focused on grief and mourning," which coheres with the assignation of the civically dead. These authors argue that "life writing in its multiple genres is foundational to the formation of Western subjects, Western cultures, and Western concepts of nation, as well as to ongoing projects of exploration, colonization, imperialism, and now globalization." In our "contemporary culture of self-help," they claim, "personal narratives of debasement and recovery as models for conversion, survival, and self transformation" carry considerable currency.[108] Thus, Smith and Watson suggest, writers of traumatic narratives appeal to modern readers because they "mine the discontinuities, mobility, and transcultural hybridity of subjects-in-process."[109] Perhaps this reassembling of the human is desirable in our contemporary era of commodification in which product is reified over process. In this sense, narratives of trauma nourish our sense of cultural and communal loss in an industrialized, global, and media-dominated world.

Methodology and Archive

In *Women, Writing, and Prison: Activists, Scholars, and Writers Speak Out*, the practitioner scholars, who bridge activism and scholarship, caution against prison programs that operate from a deficiency and redemptive (rehabilitative) model that assumes the "inmates" need to change or that the facilitators can "save" lives.[110] These dominant models divert American society from addressing its endemic racial, political, and gendered violence. My experience as a creative writing instructor in a women's prison in Honolulu has taught me the importance of a critical self-reflectivity that grants greater latitude to the women themselves, fortifying lateral rather than hierarchical alliances.

The fraught trajectory of outsider ethnographers conveying disenfranchised voices is politically charged. Eve Tuck, a Native Alaskan academic, cautions outsider "communities, researchers, and educators" who work in Indigenous communities "to reconsider the long-term impact of 'damage-centered' research—research that intends to document peoples' pain and brokenness to hold those in power accountable for their oppression." Tuck critiques the deficit model for its reliance on a flawed "theory of change"— one utilized to "leverage reparations or resources for marginalized communities," while reinscribing "a one-dimensional notion of these people as depleted, ruined, and hopeless." Tuck "urges communities to institute a moratorium on damage-centered research to reformulate the ways research is framed and conducted and to reimagine how findings might be used by, for, and with communities."[111] Clearly, using this collaborative model—one concerned with "understanding complexity, contradiction, and the self-determination of lived lives"—is fraught in an incarcerated setting.[112] Tuck compellingly unveils the violences that researchers perpetrate on Indigenous communities—"finger-shaped bruises on our pulse points"—with "characterizations [that] frame our communities as sites of disinvestment and dispossession; . . . spaces saturated in the fantasies of outsiders."[113]

When I sat in on the classes as a privileged guest from the "free" world and as a non-Indigenous and non–Pacific Islander woman, my own positionality as a hybrid (inside-out) body was an obstacle I spent years negotiating as both participant ethnographer and facilitator.[114] Participating in Clough's creative writing classes and developing relationships over several terms facilitated the interviews that I conducted with the inside women. These variegated relationships shape the terrain of my ensuing interpretations. As a facilitator in an incarcerated space, I employ autoethnography as a reflective practice to consider the process of transformation involved in reverse ethnography for both ethnographers and collaborators. Autoethnography is a mobile site that encourages an intersectional way of seeing and engaging with the carceral culture and is a useful tool for examining a space where unjust systems and processes are identified and interrogated.[115]

One of the integral components of feminist ethnography situated within a collaborative model is the ethical responsibility to exchange work with the community. Reading and writing in interaction with "subjects" is a central aspect of life writing and feminist ethnography. Feminist ethnography insists on a working through of relationships across boundaries of differential power—in the case of my research, the borders between those inside and outside. It was also difficult for me to share the manuscript for this book with Pat Clough, the director of the KPWP. Due to my own experience as an educator, I am aware that opening up one's classroom to a guest involves vulnerability, particularly if a critical lens is employed. Yet critique is an essential component of academic work. Prior to submitting my manuscript to Clough, I reread each chapter, imagining her as my reader. This altered lens allowed me to rethink my initial critique. One feminist methodological praxis I incorporate here is the use of parenthetical notes to Clough that perform as an invitation to an extended conversation: an invitation that echoes circle pedagogy or Indigenous epistemologies. The responses from Clough, which I incorporate throughout, confirm the unique and transformational journey that we undertook together and reinforce the process of feminist ethnography: its collaborative nature, vulnerability, and limitations. Her response likewise employs the personal and the political:

> I'm not sure how to respond appropriately to such extensive analysis and storytelling. I think we both knew when we were talking, that our conversations mattered—mattered most because I was "unpacking" a program that grew from no plan, no particular curriculum. Since I was teaching in a new space, I figured I'd have to become an explorer and explore I did! The writing, the women themselves became deeply important to me. I didn't know that would happen. You seem to have captured much of that personal connection that unfolded for so many—first with their relationship with themselves and then with the witnesses to that unfolding—the other students and me.[116]

Sharing the work with the women inside also proved to be complicated. Just as the KPWP itself is vulnerable to attrition, by the time I was ready to share my work, many of the women inside had been paroled and inevitably had moved on to their lives outside. One woman with whom I had a close relationship died quite unexpectedly. One of the principal Prison Monologues women was extradited to another country, and others were difficult to reach. As the KPWP project folded and my contacts—Clough and the former warden—departed, access to the inside was limited.

Throughout the book, I use pseudonyms to protect the identities of the women and the teenagers. There are numerous ethical questions about the inclusion of high school youth who, like the inside women, constitute a vulnerable population. Clough and the Nānākuli students' English teacher, Christine Wilcox, provided me with all the correspondence between the women and the teenagers at two Title I high schools on Honolulu's leeward side—Nānākuli and Kapolei—and gave me permission to publish their words. Wilcox tragically passed away from a glioblastoma in 2017, and although her absence leaves a gaping wound, memories of her endurance, spirit, and love of her students abide. In chapter 2, I implement the inside women's authentic names to accompany their published poetry to preserve and honor their authorship. The selection of pseudonyms in other chapters was fraught with complexity. I attempted to select names that cohere with the ethnicity of particular women; however, this resulted in an overrepresentation of Hawaiian and Pacific Islander names when in reality many of the women had assimilated "American" names. (In hindsight, this feels like a racial typecasting.)

I deliberately chose to begin and end each chapter with the women's voices, and chapter 4 with the teenagers' voices. In an homage to Kelly Oliver's articulation of witnessing as a radical act of "seeing otherwise" that summons mutual vulnerabilities across hierarchical divides, I desire the reader to experience the "stand-alone" text without my interruptions.[117] These unimpeded texts authentically reflect the testimony of the inside women and the teenagers. At the same time, I also conduct close readings of their poetry, as a writerly and methodological choice that foregrounds the women's testimony.

The following is a narrative that transported me to my inquiry, inspirations, and insights, which I offer as a gesture toward autoethnography. My personal genealogy is inextricable from a history of colonization. From a young age, growing up as a white person in apartheid in South Africa, I was aware of the devastation of economic, social, and political disenfranchisement. Far from our leafy suburb in Johannesburg—St. Andrews—sprawled the dilapidated shacks of Soweto, not unlike some of the public housing projects marking the Grand Concourse in the Bronx, where I worked years later as an HIV educator and activist, or the homeless shelters in which I taught creative writing.

When my family immigrated to Milwaukee in the late 1970s after the turbulence of the Soweto uprising, I found myself at the University of Wisconsin–Madison, where I became involved in the divestiture and feminist/queer movements. My early academic formations were nurtured by Black feminist scholars. I found home in grassroots activism, which has informed both my academic research trajectory and my passion for community activism. For two decades I taught in the school-to-prison pipeline in multiple geographic and cultural loci. As a New York City teaching fellow, and later as a supervisor of educators in Hawai'i, I witnessed the limitations and violence(s) embedded in programs like Teach for America that displace local teachers.

Feminist carceral theorists and practitioners articulate the need for those working in prisons to be mindful of the expected narratives of inside women. Teaching writing in the prison, like teaching in all classrooms in the "free" world, is a besieged act—one that insists on a grappling with ethical dilemmas. Some of the ethical critical praxis that informs my approach as a facilitator of incarcerated and "free" classrooms is as follows: the circle pedagogy praxis of the Walls to Bridges Collective in Kitchener, Ontario; the Inside-Out circles in the United States as part of the Inside-Out Prison Exchange Program; and the testimony of feminist creative writing practitioners in the prisons.[118] These nontraditional or decolonizing pedagogical models insist on an ethical critical literacy praxis that resists the tendency toward enforced confessionals in the classroom. This approach reinforces what feminist prison writing practitioners Wendy Wolters Hinshaw and Tobi Jacobi identify as the necessary ingredients for an ethical critical literacy praxis that supports and sponsors inside women's contributions to their own self-representations, builds critical literacy about prison conditions both inside and outside, accelerates tactical redistribution of power, and creates solidarity across privilege.[119]

In the summer of 2015, I was awarded funding to attend the Walls to Bridges Prison Facilitator program in Kitchener, Ontario, in concert with the Faculty of Social Work at Wilfrid Laurier University. The program is a five-day intensive training with primarily Canadian academicians and Indigenous activists at a women's multilevel-security federal prison: Grand Valley Institution for Women. I was trained in the logistics and ethics of establishing a pilot program, based on the Inside-Out program, which was originated by Lori Pompa at Temple University in Philadelphia. As the Daniel J. Logan Assistant Professor of Peace and Justice at Knox College, I am currently embarking on such a program with the Henry C. Hill Correctional Center in Galesburg, Illinois. The Walls to Bridges model offers "inside" and "outside" students the opportunity to embark on a semester-long seminar together within an incarcerated space, which works to reduce and interrogate stereotypes that cripple society in that it subverts hierarchies as "nontraditional" students educate "traditional" students and vice versa.[120] The weekly classes incorporate a circle pedagogy that foregrounds Indigenous epistemologies and collaborative dialogue aimed to foster egalitarian and collective learning. In *Turning Teaching Inside Out: A Pedagogy of Transformation for Community-Based Education*, editor Simone Weil Davis, who brought Inside-Out to Canada, articulates its radical pedagogical space as a dyssynchronous site of discomfort that embraces a politics of poetics and critically dismantles the hierarchies embedded in higher educational institutions designed to privilege status quo rewards.[121]

I began my research in Hawai'i with the idea that I needed to learn from and listen to the women inside not only for their personal stories but also for the silences that lie behind them. As a guest in the writing classes, I became a part of this writing community, witnessing and at times sharing in the personal and familial narratives that extended far beyond writing. The relationships I developed in the writing classes facilitated the formal, taped interviews that I initiated at the prison in April and May 2013 and led to the invitation to teach creative writing.[122] From the summer of 2015 to May 2016, I taught my own creative writing class at the facility, with ten women enrolled. Class impressions and informal conversations with the women in my class, as well as the writing generated from the classes, have all informed and deepened my work.

Feminist prison scholar Lori B. Girshick articulates the fraught role that trust plays in ethnographic work within a carceral setting. Girshick is inspired by Kathleen Duff and Cynthia Coll's innovative interviewing protocol while conducting her own interviews with the inside women at Black Mountain Correctional Center for Women, which establishes a feminist lineage of carceral ethnographic work.[123] Duff and Coll focus on the process of exchange that led to authentic group dialogue—one that shifted the framework of power from why inside women should talk to ethnographers to one in which the women would "allow us to listen to them."[124] In a similar spirit, I designed semistructured interview questions, which I used as a guide to frame the interviews without allowing the questions to impede the flow of what we refer to in Hawai'i as "talk story." Personal narratives resist linear trajectories; thus I privileged a circuitous aesthetic and drew on feminist ethnography in search of a methodology that interrogates the hierarchy between interviewer and informant.[125]

My method sample consists of one-on-one interviews with seventeen women from Clough's beginner and intermediate writing classes, some of whom were also in the Prison Monologues program. I additionally had extensive and repeated conversations with three women from my own writing class from 2016 to 2017. The beginner class typically services twenty women, and the intermediate/advanced class enrolls thirteen women, many of whom have taken Clough's class three to five times.[126] For three terms from 2012 to 2014, I attended the biweekly writing classes and taught four creative writing classes at the facility as a guest teacher. I have detailed field notes from the classes that I attended as a guest and participant ethnographer.[127] I conducted fourteen formal, taped interviews at the facility in the intake section and in an assigned visitor's office in the spring of 2013. Those interviews were arranged by the administration and lasted between 60 and 180 minutes. For the most part, I felt comfortable and at liberty to take my time during the interviews. Only once did a guard intrude when I had closed the door; he told me I needed to leave the door ajar. In 2014, I conducted three interviews with women who are past participants in both the creative writing classes and the Prison Monologues and who are now on parole. One of my former students has now been released and invited me to visit her in her transitional housing program, Women's Way, and participate as an active member in her Huikahi circle.[128] The demographics of the women whom I interviewed both formally and informally include women who range from their early twenties to their late fifties; one Black woman from the mainland (the only self-professed practicing Muslim in the prison); five white women from the mainland; and fourteen women all born in Hawai'i and from Filipina, Japanese-Hawaiian, Chinese-Hawaiian, Portuguese, Puerto Rican, Samoan, or Indigenous backgrounds. Three of the women are former Prison Monologuers, all of whom have been recently paroled.[129] From 2012 to 2013, I attended twenty Prison Monologues performances that included presentations at schools, residential treatments, community colleges, conferences, and events with audiences that ranged from intimate gatherings with forty people to an audience of fifteen hundred at Roosevelt High School. I informally spoke with some of the audience members who shared their overwhelmingly positive impressions of the performances with me.

I also analyze audience assessment conducted after the Prison Monologues presentations, based on correspondence between the new Prison Monologues Lab and the Nānākuli High School sixth-period English class (March 2014) and the Kapolei High School students.[130] Sources include the index cards designed by the students that outline their questions for the women about prison life, the women's responses, the English teacher's evaluation and correspondence, Clough's letter to the class, and formal student evaluation sheets from the Youth Challenge Center—a residential "boot camp" for juveniles at Barber's Point—and from the Bobby Benson Treatment Program in Kahuku. I also interviewed women who were active in the creative writing classes and who at the time constituted a peer-generated performance group on the outside, Voices from the Inside. These peer-mediated writing and performance groups are illustrative of contemporary pedagogical praxis that attempts to subvert traditional hierarchies of epistemological power structures.

In the following pages, I take the reader on a journey through this book's five chapters and the epilogue. Most of the chapters begin with an inside woman's life story, and chapter 4 begins with a teenager's autobiography. I foreground the written testimony of the inside women and the students as a political tool to counter the civic death of the carceral space, particularly one located in the larger colonized landscape of Hawai'i. In searching for ways to honor the trust involved in offering personal testimony, I have benefited from scholarship that highlights the voices of Native Hawaiians and Pacific Islanders such as *Nā Wāhine Koa: Hawaiian Women for Sovereignty and Demilitarization*, edited by Noelani Goodyear-Ka'ōpua; Ty P. Kāwika Tengan's *Native Men Remade: Gender and Nation in Contemporary Hawai'i*; and Katherine Irwin and Karen Umemoto's *Jacked Up and Unjust: Pacific Islander Teens Confront Violent Legacies*. In "Shifting Ground: Translating Lives and Life Writing in Hawai'i," the introduction to a special issue of *Biography*, coeditors Cynthia Franklin and Miriam Fuchs articulate the praxis of linguistic translation and its power to transport to the "surface 'buried lives,'" as it pertains to Pacific Islanders.[131]

Chapter 1, "Pedagogy and Process," begins with the complicated classroom space in which the Kailua Prison Writing Project is situated. Simultaneously resistant to and complicit with dominant carceral tropes, this program's refusal of the therapeutic script lives alongside the embrace of the therapeutic. Here the reader witnesses an assortment of pedagogies: those performed in the Tuesday and Friday classes aligned with the KPWP's philosophy, and those performed by repeated institutional intrusions. The second chapter, "'Home': Trauma and Desire," moves from the mediated and communal space of the disembodied classroom to proffer a close literary analysis of the writing generated in *Hulihia VII: Writings from Prison and Beyond: "Home."* As writing subverts the state-sanctioned imposition of a civic death, so do the polyvocal poems in the prison publication repel reductive notions of home and emancipatory narratives. The *Hulihia* writings appear on the surface to diverge from the political, but, as I argue, the women's critique lives in the omissions, ellipses, eccentric grammatical usages, and counterperformativity of their writing.

Chapters 3 and 4 turn to the complex relationships between performance and audience. Chapter 3, "The Stage Away from the Page," moves from text-based testimony and performance to the public performances of the Prison Monologues program. Utilizing the lens of performance studies, I analyze the slippage between performativity and life writing, exploring the model of reform behind the Prison Monologues project and the tensions between the "sacredness of testimony" and the "commodification and consumption of testimonial discourse."[132] I explore the quandary of redemption sponsored by the state as both censoring and productive, interrogating how the state exercises the performances for legitimacy. Patterson and WCCC are the recipients of much public praise for the KPWP, and for the Prison Monologues in particular, which reinforces the redemptive notion of the "prison as a healing place." Chapter 4, "Love Letters," is a participatory, performative dialogic between the Prison Monologues and the students at Nānākuli High School and Kapolei High School. In this chapter, I analyze high school students' reactions to female prisoner monologues in Hawai'i and frame these dialogues as Native Hawaiian epistemologies. This unique archive showcases a participatory life-writing exchange and the avenues in which trauma itself performs as the dialogic. By reading and analyzing the students' life-writing texts, which are direct responses to the narratives of memory, pain, and abuse of the inside women, I explore the nature of witnessing and attend to the cacophony of testimonies evoked. In this sense, unlike in the narratives about home in chapter 2, pain is sutured and testimony is restorative because of its corroborating "live" audience. As we uncover, spectacular bodies are fashioned, but, more prominently, a spectacular healing is performed.

At the end of 2019, I returned to Hawai'i to present an excerpt of "Love Letters" at the yearly national and international American Studies Association conference, where I was a panelist on the "Kanaka Maoli Childhood" panel sponsored by the Child and Youth Studies Caucus. Chapter 5, "Postrelease and Affective Writers," is informed by the interviews I conduct with one of the core Prison Monologuers, Reiko, who is now a student at Chaminade University; Nicole Fernandez, a prison administrator; Judge Karen Radius, who started the Girls Court in Hawai'i; Kat Brady, a longtime prison abolitionist and activist; Lorenn Walker, a restorative justice attorney; and Noriko Namiki, CEO of YWCA O'ahu and director of Fernhurst, which is one of the parole reentry locales that services released women from WCCC.

A few of the women are back inside.

It doesn't end when the class ends. It continues.

~ Kailani

1 PEDAGOGY AND PROCESS

Governmental Seduction

Look into my eyes and tell me what it is you see
Concede your mind to intertwine with my fantasy
Let me seduce your spirit and allow my soul to lead
Us to a place of style and grace beyond what you believe.

Open up your heart and feel me tell you all about it
Bring your body close to mine but be careful not to crowd it
This world is open to you, baby, till the day you doubt it
Let me play with your emotions until you can't live without it.

I'll make your greed insatiable
I'll feed you what's not edible
I'll claim it as incredible
You'll never want to let it go.

But listen even deeper and let's have a conversation
Watch a little closer as I infiltrate your nation

See through conspiracies, religion and FDA *with education*
And when you start to understand, sedate with medication.

So close your eyes and start to dream, I'll rush to meet you there
Embrace my empty promises. Desensitize your cares
Then inebriate with poisons when it's more than you can bear
Uniformity is key to every prey that I ensnare.[1]

~ Allyson

Ripe with misalliances, Allyson's poem "Governmental Seduction" exemplifies the tension that resides within the Kailua Prison Writing Project (KPWP). The classroom, I argue, performs concurrently as a healing and a disciplinary space in which the reinscription and rejection of programmatic and institutional neoliberal narratives coexist.[2] While this incarcerated classroom may share tropes and pedagogical praxes with other prison classrooms in the United States, it is not representative of them. As we experience the class itself and its multifarious interruptions, we attend to a community of writers that counters but never escapes the constraints of prison life.[3] To watch these classroom performances unfold is to confront a viewer's series of anxious questions. In what context is writing either liberating or therapeutic? If writing works as reinjury, then how can it be simultaneously transformative? Writing as self-discovery is a redemptive script and is embroidered into the program philosophy.[4] Similarly, it is a recurrent theme in the literature by arts practitioners working in the prisons, as well as in the women's writings. *How do we find ourselves through writing?* The question assumes a reverence for the arts as a means of catharsis and healing. Yet can writing heal?

As educators, we all struggle with the classroom as a troubled space, rife with spoken and unspoken hierarchies, power dynamics, and vested interpersonal relationships. Feminist critic and educator bell hooks posits the classroom as an erotic space and conjoins epistemological passion with erotic passion. Classrooms can be spaces of violence, of love, and of consummate potential. If classrooms are indeed challenging sites, imagine the institutional classroom in an extended institution—the locked-up/locked-down landscape of a prison. I spent four years in one particular prison classroom, in one particular penal facility. The narratives of the classroom that I share in this chapter are imbued with the essence of a specific classroom community. The actors in Pat Clough's beginning and intermediate/advanced creative writing classes that convene for two hours on Tuesday and Friday mornings shift from term to term, although there are many repeat takers who reappear in the advanced class. The teacher, Clough, remains constant. My own creative writing class, the Poetry and Performance Lab, radically departs from Clough's literary archive. Informed by spoken word and the performativity of life stories, it unveils the ways in which textual choices can inform students' writing.

The KPWP is both resistant to and complicit with dominant carceral tropes. Incarcerated classrooms and those in the "free" world are volatile sites, out of which emerge pedagogical encounters and relationships that are impossible to enclose.[5] What transpires in any classroom always exceeds the boundaries of narrative infiltrations—those of the educator/institution, as well as the interpersonal exchanges that flow between the participants and writers in the classroom. The women in the creative writing classes at the Women's Community Correctional Center (WCCC) form a community of witnesses who elude, and at times claim, redemptive scripts. A facilitator can elicit acts of imagination in a pedagogical space, but the direction in which imagination blooms cannot be harnessed.

This chapter describes an assortment of pedagogies: those in Pat Clough's Tuesday and Friday classroom space; those guided by the KPWP's philosophy; and those performed by the institutional intrusions. I use the concept of "witness" not in any religious sense—although, as Clough articulates, the act of witnessing is one imbued with "honor"—but rather to emphasize that the witnessing process is a liberatory and revelatory one.[6] Carceral workers, particularly prison guards, frequently assess prison arts programming as frivolous or threatening, and arts practitioners find that they must balance their allegiances to those inside—their students—with their accommodation to the powers that be within the institution. External forces, both ideological and institutional, inevitably infiltrate, and in fact structure, the classroom space. Positioning the reader of this chapter as a witness encourages a direct engagement with the roles that Clough and the inside women in the creative writing classes inhabit. These pedagogies, the programmatic guiding philosophy, and the institutional intrusions ultimately fail to contain the moments of witnessing, spontaneity, and improvisation in the classroom. These living scripts persist despite the institutional constraints.

I ARRIVE AT TUESDAY'S advanced writing class at WCCC on February 19, 2013. Kailani, a charismatic woman with short, spiky gray hair and dimples confides: "I see everyone's spirit today. Some dim and some bright." Pat Clough, director of the KPWP and creative writing teacher, begins the class by asking the women to listen to the Indigo Girls' song "I Bit the Better Bug" and freewrite associations to the lyrics, including their own moods, reflections, and thoughts.[7] She usually begins with a writing prompt, but this alternate modality is experiential and sensory. At the end of the session, Clough asks the thirteen women to say one thing they took away from the class that day. The words spill out like burnished stones: "spirit" and "inspired." It is my turn. "Meditative," I blurt. "What did you say—potato?" asks one woman, Tatiana, with disheveled fibrous gray hair and spectacles, who frequently thinks outside of the box. "No, meditative," I repeat. But what I really wanted to say was "pain."

I BEGIN WITH A creative re-creation of the classroom that allows the reader to witness from the multiple standpoints of students and teacher the transformations conceived in the classroom space. These transformations occur through a host of narrative scripts—therapeutic, Christian, familial/maternal—and via interpersonal relationships among the inside participants of the classroom, as well as between the women and Clough. These narratives and pedagogies, even as they are corrective, offer specific scripts for healing. Affect, empathy, and voyeurism are ingredients that complicate therapeutic contracts, and the institutionalized carceral narrative inflects/infects the pedagogical space. The carceral structure interrupts—inflicting heterogeneous assaults and suffering. In this way, the macro institution disciplines the possibilities of transformation and informs the ways in which women encode trauma in writing.

This chapter conveys the particularities of two days in Clough's Friday advanced writing class to foreground the construction of programmatic narratives of redemption and rehabilitation—narratives that sit uneasily alongside discomforting institutional intrusions. The women themselves shape the narratives as they forge alliances, bonds, and meaning via their spontaneous interactions in the classroom space. The classes perform congruently and discordantly with ethical critical literacy praxis. One programmatic harnessing and healing effect is the conflation of the writing program with therapy. Diverse—and often incompatible—healing modalities fall under the term *therapeutic*. There is therapy as the sacred, therapy as the secular, and therapy as the familiar American-based twelve-step program, evident in the Hina Mauka and Total Life Recovery programs from which many of the writers come. Additionally, there are methods of constraining therapy—enactments of violence to the therapeutic, and a disciplining of the therapeutic.[8] The experience of healing that may occur through witnessing and participating in a writing community considered "sacred" by many of its participants is a theme that infuses the pedagogical space.[9] Inside women utilize the term *healing* to refer to the writing process, and their relationship with one another and with Clough. Clough herself refers to the classroom as a "cocoon" where she and the women together create transformative work even as she takes care to distinguish her own pedagogical practice from therapy:

> Mark Patterson and I spoke regularly during those years and he informed me that there was some concern that I was dabbling in therapy with the women without any training/credential to do so. As far as my classes were concerned, I monitored very closely the kind of situations that sometimes came up when the women cried or got angry at someone else in class for saying something hurtful. In hindsight, I became more "firm" and more aware of how quickly some personalities could spin out of control. In the 12 years of the program, no one went to the clinic or to suicide watch as a result of my class, no one was hurt in class and there were no reports that I was doing any psychological damage.[10]

What, precisely, the inside women mean by *healing* is decidedly subjective, individual, and difficult to evaluate. Each experience is unique and congruent with a woman's personal experiences, her history, and the reasons for her incarceration. Processes of healing differ depending on where the injury occurred: in the institution, within the families of origin, or as a result of colonial violence. Most inside women have experienced multiple forms of trauma, and many—though not all—testify to the transformative potential of the KPWP. This book explores women's testimony of how a creative writing program might actually "heal." I remain conscious throughout of the limitations of any particular institutional project that purports to ameliorate trauma, and conscious of the constraints and violence inflicted by incarceration itself. Trauma endures; healing is a process without a definitive end point. Yet these realities do not invalidate many women's testimony that underscores how the creative writing classes, the sharing of community, and the act of self-expression are profoundly meaningful. Rather than imposing my own definition of healing, I have relied on the testimonies that the women shared with me.

I return here to that February morning from Clough's advanced writing class. Today the class is held in the larger space shared with the facility's education "department," which houses a supervised computer lab, rather than in the smaller, mildewy room where we usually meet.[11] Ten women of various ages and races (haole, Native Hawaiian, hapa) are present.[12] There is a whiteboard on which Clough begins to write the date and agenda for the day. This could be any classroom on the continent. *But it is not.* I am reminded of this as I look around at the inside women all dressed by the state in their prison uniforms. Many of the women are distinguished by creative markings of tattoos that reference past relationships and cultural origins—and they are wearing thick white socks with their *slippas* because it is a chilly day for Hawai'i. The women are late today. They are frequently detained on work lines, at parole hearings, by administrative infractions, or simply because the adult correction officer (ACO) refuses to call them to class.[13]

Clough, like any successful pedagogue, has multiple rituals embroidered into the fabric of her classes. She initiates the class by asking the women to pull out a word from the koa bowl that is a perpetual character in her classes.[14] Someone draws the word *Wai Wai* from the koa bowl and writes it on the board; it is translated by one of the Native Hawaiian speakers as "without water there is no prosperity."[15] This summoned quote resonates with life both inside and outside, confirming carceral theorists' analysis of the prison as a microcosm of American culture. In the one-on-one interviews I conduct at the facility, the women frequently voice that the writing classes have "saved their lives." This redemptive narrative articulates a utopian enclave—the pedagogical—wherein a sacrosanct community is performed and reenacted within the dystopia of incarceration. The heralding by the inside women of the creative writing classes as a utopian space is troublesome because of the institutional intrusions that disrupt and alter the classroom and the power hierarchies enacted in the classroom context. The censorship of the women's life narratives and women's corresponding performances of self in the ensuing prison publication, *Hulihia* (Transformation), also complicate any reading of the writing program as simply "liberating" the voice.[16] Theme, content, form, and canon, as well as the editorial process and even the beloved relationship the inside students have with Clough, both enable and constrain the possibilities of the classroom space.

The classes are in effect inextricable from their institutional setting. Although the women attest that the creative writing classes function as a haven, the pedagogical setting is never immune to institutional intrusion and fracture. In the incarcerated classroom, we witness narratives of healing coupled with violence that lurks under the shadow of the institution. The small education rooms in which we usually meet are no bigger than ten by twelve feet, with drab floors and desks that reek of mold. Divided by a glass partition, the rooms construct a persistent surveillance across multiple borders: institutional, systemic, and programmatic.[17] Today the women in the adjacent class, seemingly bored, peer into Clough's class in which the women are mostly engaged. Their eyes pierce the glass enviously. Violence and contradiction contaminate the "utopian" pedagogical space. The women are active agents in that they both resist and comply with the dis-ease. The tissue box is a persistent accoutrement, alongside the koa bowl, a bunch of dog-eared dictionaries, and a container with pens adorned with colorful flowers. I often resort to using one of these pens, albeit reluctantly, as the smell of mold is pungent. In setting up my own guidelines in the classroom, I opt against the Kleenex box. In a letter to me, Clough justifies her choice to utilize the Kleenex box in her classrooms and its role in the healing process:

> Writing freed the women to tell us about their hidden pain, about their traumas—the beatings and rapes, betrayals, standing in doorways getting high, leaving their children, knowing they were gay—all after repeated rapes at the hands of an uncle or stepfather. That's why the Kleenex box. They would comfort each other in class and learn for the first time that their pain was the same. They did that out loud often after reading/listening to something raw and fresh and new. There were class periods where all we did was listen to each other, when the written word needed elaboration or opened up more that needed to be said. We—in that classroom—represented hope. Healing came from release and we gave it time to develop together. You could feel it. It was a privilege.[18]

Two women join the class belatedly: now a total of twelve women are present. One woman, Imani, arrives in her signature white kitchen outfit, stained with oil spots, after her encounter with the parole board. No one needs to ask how the meeting went. She is trembling and in tears. Clough walks quietly behind her, places her firm hands on Imani's shoulders, and passes her a tissue. Trauma can enter the classroom in a myriad of ways: the reading of a poem that chronicles a woman's suffering, the looming shadow of a guard "escorting" a woman in chains, a barking loudspeaker that banishes the women to the head count in the yard. In Imani's case, the women are dynamic actors in the therapeutic script, passing the Kleenex box in a circle of shared compassion that requires no signal.[19] Oftentimes laughter functions as an accompaniment to pain or a "you go, girl" shoutout when a poem is especially poignant or applicable to the inside women's lives. In this way, an archive of feelings, affect, verbiage, and gestures is present in the classroom as a moral and emotional guide. The archive of feelings in this pedagogical landscape overwhelms the textual archive.

Pat Clough is wearing all white today. A white running shirt hugs her taut body and sinewy arms. Her short blond hair frames an angular face, slightly weathered from time spent on beaches or pursuing other outdoor activities. An avid marathoner, she is in phenomenal condition for a woman in her late sixties. Clough was a recent import from California to Kailua, the town adjacent to the women's prison nestled against the Koʻolau Mountains between Kailua and Waimānalo—homestead land.[20] Kailua was once a sleepy beach town, and many of its inhabitants have actively protested the gentrification of the neighborhood. With the acquisition of a Whole Foods and a Target, the town is losing some of its charm. Busloads of affluent Japanese tourists and those seeking a fantasy wedding on the beach descend on the town.[21] The tourists, and perhaps even some of Kailua's inhabitants, are unaware of their proximity to the women's prison. Clough's own introduction to the prison was haphazard. On a typical sunny day in 2003, she was running in her new neighborhood when she spotted women in orange jumpsuits on a work line. She approached them and discovered that they were "inmates" from wccc. A few weeks later, the persistent Clough visited the prison with an offer to start a creative writing program. An English high school teacher who was raised in the school system by nuns, Clough is a combination of no-nonsense, inspiring mentor and benevolent mother for the women. The women I interviewed unanimously sang her praises and expressed their admiration for her stalwart care and her genuine demeanor.

Clough frequently writes the prefaces and includes some of her own poetry in the *Hulihia* volumes, an approach that coheres with feminist anthologies of prison writing that attempt to dismantle boundaries between those inside and outside. Her writing assignments and textual explorations follow a "workshop model," although the editorial process is hers alone.[22] Peer feedback in terms of critique is rare in Clough's class because she never initiates it, which positions her as the sole critic of the women's writing. When I shared the manuscript for this book with Clough, she responded to my critique about the lack of peer feedback in her classes. Here, I provide her response in my commitment to a feminist ethnography and to illustrate how we all are influenced by our training, past memories, and subjectivities: "They [the women] learned how to critique—not by saying simply, 'oh that's really good,' rather with tears, laughter—the kind of unspoken critique that I think meant more to the writers than an analysis they were only just learning how to do for themselves."[23]

Today the class is meeting in the main education center that is shared with administrators and houses the computer "lab," rather than in the small, dank room where we typically meet. Students do not have access to the internet in the facility, and their computer access in the relatively clean lab is monitored. A facilitator needs to set up a supervised "study hall" for the women ahead of time if they require a typed "homework" assignment.[24] The inside assistants in the lab are helpful. Dressed in the standard red T-shirt and blue pants that signify their minimum-custody status, one woman, Connie, in her fifties, loves to "talk story" with me.[25] Connie was born in Mozambique and feels an affinity with me because I was born in South Africa. The assumptions and intersections of personal geographies are marked in the ties of kinship we form, however preposterous and fictive, across oceans and as migrants. Each week Connie helpfully asks if I need copies. When I sub for Clough on a few occasions, Connie assists me with copying the roster for the day. When word arrives that she has finally received parole after months of waiting, we learn that the parole board is extraditing her to Portugal, colonizer of Mozambique. Connie speaks Portuguese from her childhood in Mozambique, but she lacks any personal connections to Portugal; furthermore, her daughter lives in the United States.[26] This displaced exile is one of the many absurd regulations that occur in a world rooted in a colonial imaginary.

Race plays out rather differently at the WCCC. The women in my creative writing class, some of whom are Samoan, openly discuss the racial hierarchies that they perceive at the facility. In their view, the Samoan women receive preferential treatment because most of the ACOs are Samoan, and many of the inside women are related to the guards. As Vailea remarked: "Everyone's someone's cousin or aunty here." The women express that after the Samoans, the Native Hawaiians are recipients of more privileges than the rest of the general population, followed by all the mixed races and finally the haole (white). This is an inversion of the racial hierarchies that women who are incarcerated typically face.

Clough utilizes *The Diary of Anne Frank* as a pivotal text in her classes: an outsider text to the oeuvre of a white American masculinity—Ernest Hemingway, Robert Frost, and T. S. Eliot—that she typically employs. However, Anne Frank certainly falls into what Clough articulates as a heroic narrative, which she envisions as resounding with the women's "own heroic journeys":

I did use mainland and European writers extensively such as Hemingway and Frost and Maya Angelou. Plays such as *Raisin in the Sun* and *The Miracle Worker*, *The Diary of Anne Frank*, novels like *Old Man and the Sea*, *To Kill a Mockingbird* became templates for excellent writing but more importantly of heroic character—people overcoming enormous obstacles closely described, painfully lived. I learned the women responded to these large "prompts" and began to find themselves within their own heroic journeys.

I firmly believed that reading was central to writing and that the women needed to move beyond James Patterson and his plots in order to discover good writing. We developed a library at the facility of all kinds of literature both white and European and Pacific Rim. The women knew they had to read and I do think it helped them express themselves with growing authenticity.[27]

A Jewish Dutch teenager and Holocaust victim, Anne Frank may seem a curious choice, albeit one canonized in many high school curricula. She made her way into this curriculum after Clough traveled to Amsterdam, where she made a pilgrimage to the Anne Frank House. She returned with photos from the museum, which she shares with her students and uses as artwork in *Hulihia*, alongside the women's writerly engagement with Anne Frank's daily affirmation: "Work, love, courage and hope / make me good and help me cope." This affirmation is performed as a mantra in the classroom throughout the term. Here, the personal auto/biography of the facilitator intermingles with the life stories performed by the collective inside writers in *Hulihia*.

Clough spends much time developing a relationship between the protagonist, Anne Frank, and the women. She is passionate about the ways in which Anne's incarceration in an attic is a meaningful echo for her students—one that resonates in specific ways for the Native Hawaiian women. Anne's experience as a prisoner in her own house within a political landscape of terror resounds with the imprisonment of Queen Liliʻuokalani—the last ruler of the Hawaiian Kingdom—in the rooms fashioned as a cell in her home, the ʻIolani Palace:

> Perhaps the starkest example of the centrality of punishment in the Hawaiian experience of colonialism is the imprisonment of Queen Liliʻuokalani. The queen actually spent a considerable period of time in prison and would write about her experience in vivid detail in her memoir, *Hawaiʻi's Story by Hawaiʻi's Queen*.
>
> After a failed attempt to challenge the coup that had removed her from her throne, Queen Liliʻuokalani was arrested on January 16, 1895, and imprisoned in a cell crafted out of rooms in ʻIolani Palace. She described the cell from memory:

There was a large, airy, uncarpeted room with a single bed in one corner. The other furniture consisted of one sofa, a small square table, one single common chair, an iron safe, a bureau, a chiffonier, and a cupboard, intended for eatables, made of wood with wire screening to allow the circulation of the air through the food. Some of these articles may have been added during the days of my imprisonment.[28]

Both Anne Frank and Queen Liliʻuokalani crafted their personal autobiographies while incarcerated. Anne's diary and Queen Liliʻuokalani's memoir and her song "Aloha ʻOe," or "Farewell to Thee," are resistant texts, enshrined in a specific historical and literary canon.

At one point, Clough exuberantly exclaims, *"Become* Anne." This literary and psychic transubstantiation with a historical figure in a text, someone who lived and suffered a wrongful discriminatory incarceration, is rich fodder from which to generate writing. Clough hands back the homework pieces in response to the prompt "Stillness." They are bereft of comments. "You didn't do anything wrong," she tells the women. "I just want more meat! In poetry analysis, we look at people who did it really well, in terms of conveying their feelings. Analysis is never just about wandering around in a pool of tears. We need our mind. Good poetry carries us into someone else's shoes; usually we are [moving around in] our own. Let's apply our own truths to a quote by Anne Frank. It is good discipline. Like running the five hundred yard dash."

These appraisals are examples of Clough's indebtedness to a "good discipline"—perhaps the good discipline imprinted on the young Clough by a cluster of nuns. Clough's moral script summons the women to a "pick yourself up by the bootstraps" ideology in which the therapeutic extends the corrective gesture. Her maternal love is harnessed via an American nononsense antipathy to self-pity. Wallowing in self-pity is not an option in Clough's classes. But then there is the Kleenex box. Classroom spaces are ripe with paradox.

Clough's "good discipline" points to the complexity of literature and arts programming in a carceral setting and to the contested philosophy of a benevolent literacy. Prison writing scholar Patrick Berry discusses the moral bind that literacy practitioners face in the prisons due to their deep belief in the "power of literacy to improve individuals' lives socially, economically and personally"—beliefs that are not always harmonious with the experiences of students from marginalized communities.[29] Berry argues that these practitioners are "immersed in a popular culture that cherishes narrative links between literacy and economic advancement (and further, between such advancement and a 'good life')."[30] In this way, literacy programming in prisons can resemble acts of colonization.[31] By contrast, Megan Sweeney takes to task critics who, in their disembodied abstract musings, refuse to acknowledge the self-growth of those inside and the hope that arts programming can offer. Sweeney cites celebrity "inmate" and prison abolitionist Angela Davis and longtime prison writing practitioner Susan Nagelson, who recognize the institutional space as potentially one of self-growth despite their political investment in demolishing the system.[32]

A Detour into Form

Writerly form works in the classes as an ironic savior because the women undeniably privilege content over structure. Nonetheless, the women are able to relate to the form of the nineteen-line villanelle: a grammar of constraint. At first, the women "divine" their villanelles, which are not bona fide villanelles but rather approximations, without instruction about the form.[33] The ritual of repetition and the constraint of the form are familiar to the women; they are able to create effective villanelles without much guidance. In this way, writing is demystified, and it ultimately presents as a vehicle of expressivity. Clough discusses the ways in which curriculum building and lesson plans demand improvisation: "It was all experimentation as I got to know the women and experience what they weren't getting in other prison programming. Adapting was constant. Literary forms emerged in my own research, like the villanelle, which I almost dismissed but decided to try and oh my, how they responded to the villanelle as a form for finding what was hiding."[34]

In a conversation with Clough, Kailani explains that form can sometimes be an obstacle to expression: "I have to remove the barrier. I was in a writing frenzy. Always writing in bullets. Keeping me shut out from my own feelings and also from reaching other people." Clough responds to the power inherent in form, instructing Kailani, "You broke your structure because it wasn't serving you." Clough's pedagogies thus remain flexible enough to accommodate different needs. Hyacinth—a calm woman in her fifties and a serial participant in Clough's advanced classes—articulated in an interview that she finds significance in prescribed forms: "Ms. Pat is genuine. I have taken her class about five times and I learn something new each time. I accomplished something I never thought I could, like my villanelle that was published in *Hulihia IX: Writings from Prison, Conversations with Myself*."

The repeating refrain "There is a place past grief," in Pamela's villanelle, published in *Hulihia IX*, functions as a hermetic seal for the author's anguish and offers a byway to an imagined space, liberated from trauma:

There is a place past grief.

I've become aware that my game face does not suit me,
that it's a mask that is fake and boring.
When I find myself in a still place knowing that I've come up short,
there—I hear a whisper.

There is a place past grief.

It's a place where I don't feel smothered,
where kind words, tender mercies
and hollow sympathies don't feed my pain.
Like dousing a flame with propane,
it's a place where I am not faking it to make it.

There is a place past grief.

It's a place where it's safe to begin to heal,
Where the whispers begin to talk to my soul,
Where sadness is exchanged for soothing memories.
I cannot wait for it to come to me.
I must choose to journey there with a change of thought,
change of heart, change of will.

Out of stillness, a higher voice calls
"There is a place past grief."
I am meant to go on.

~ Pamela

The pedagogical space of the classroom is heralded by the women as intimate, safe, and separate from the rest of the facility, and the women speak about the disconnect between what "you write on the page" and "what you do back in the dorm." This subtheme circulates frequently in the classroom and resurfaces in the one-on-one interviews I conduct at the facility. Women who fail to uphold the code of honor outside of the classroom stand accused of betraying the "beloved community"—a code rooted in the spiritual indoctrination and institutionalized morality that is reinforced in the creative writing classes, in the prison programming—particularly the Total Life Recovery and Hina Mauka programs—and within the larger institution.

The gravity and dedication with which most of the women invest themselves in the writing classes, particularly the repeat participants, are striking. For many of the women, writing functions as an evolutionary narrative of freedom that allows them to access past memories and corresponding traumas and record them as a continuous living document, which, even though painful, serves as a guide to a "life worth living." In this sense, writing is a radical and therapeutic process. In our two-hour interview, Lahela conveys how the discipline of writing and reading—a restraint of form—tethers her to a present rather than dwelling on her past and keeps her intellectually and emotionally resilient. Twenty-three-year-old Lahela, with short, wavy onyx hair that frames her expressive eyes, reveals, "I have been institutionalized my whole life." Lahela, who is gay, grew up homeless on a West Side beach with her two gay sisters after their mother's suicide. One of her sisters, to whom she is very close, was sentenced with Lahela for the same crime and has been shuffled in and out of the segregated housing unit. Lahela has a fierce intellect and a propensity toward brooding introspection. She reads the dictionary obsessively and loves to audition new words in class. She claims the institution as her "teacher"—a pedagogical guide—a sentiment that dominates carceral testimony: "We all have our breaking points sitting in prison. My breakthrough is my goal. My mind is a sponge. I want to soak up everything the place has to offer me." Other women, such as Gemmi, a powerfully built woman from Big Island (the island of Hawai'i) with a large and confrontational dragon tattoo on her face, refers to writing itself as a painful document of memory—a guide that is both a constraint and an opening: "I have perfected the art of hating my past so much. I have to let it go, but never forget it, because it pushes me forward."

Although Clough privileges the particularity of the individual narrative and the experiences of her student writers, the communal stories that occur as improvisation in the classroom create a corresponding community of witnesses. In this sense, the power of spontaneous communal narratives disrupts the form of the expectant pedagogical script that Clough sets up. The inside writers narrate their loci of origin, which are simultaneously communal and individual. Clough prizes this individualism in both the form and the texts. As mentioned earlier, the canon that she implements in the classroom is composed of writers such as Hemingway and Frost, who overcame adversity by their adherence to individualism. Pacific stories of origin are discordant with the masculine narrative of individual striving and achievement that Clough highlights through her choice of Western canonical texts because, like the women themselves, many Pacific narratives celebrate community over individualism. However, to represent these communal narratives of origin as diametrically opposed to individualistic ones bears the burden of an essentialist nostalgia. David Milward, a Cree scholar and activist, argues for the power of restorative justice because it "facilitates more constructive responses to Indigenous crime and addresses its root by compelling the offender to face up to the harm caused, to persuade the offender to willingly make right for the harm, to set the offender on a path of emotional and spiritual healing, to guide the offender to living a more productive life, and to inculcate traditional values in the offender."[35] However, Milward cautions against employing utopic binaries that idealize Indigenous systems of justice because many Indigenous communities employed harsh and brutal modes of punishment.[36]

Clough persistently instructs the women, both in preparation for publication in *Hulihia* and within the Prison Monologues, that the power of writing lives in the specificity of the details. Any good writer knows that fertile writing lives in the details; yet, curiously, the erotic and romantic "private" particulars are invisible in Clough's classroom culture and within the *Hulihia* publications. Despite an absence of these details in print and performance, the women in class serve as witnesses to and cowriters of the other participants' private life stories, including stories of rape, self-mutilation, mental illness, drug addiction, and wives, as they participate in the witnessing of each other's vulnerable histories.

As the communal takes precedence over the individual, a community of writers gradually emerges in the classroom in ways that elude censorship. Feminist poet Adrienne Rich attests to the power intrinsic to a sacred community of writers that is communal without smothering the particular.[37] Although trauma is the sheathing of the women's writings, it does not obscure the intimate and variant details that embrace humor and difference. Ann Folwell Stanford, evoking Gloria Anzaldúa's notion of "dangerous writing," argues that prison writing, "scripted from the front lines of battle for psychic, spiritual, and even physical survival," is particularly dangerous because it "proclaims a 'we' within the confines of prison walls and disrupts the individualistic discourse and practice on which any system of oppression is dependent."[38] In this sense, the "we" is a consolidated corpus, a counter to the obliteration that the institution seeks to impose, and the women inside, not unlike the revolutionary writers of the 1960s, engage in treacherous acts as they pick up their pens.

Many feminist creative writing practitioners in the prisons resist the demand for sensational narratives of pain from the women inside.[39] In *Soft*

Weapons: Autobiography in Transit, Gillian Whitlock critiques the narratives of atrocity and abjection that we in the West extracted from Afghans after September 11, 2001. Whitlock renders a chilling scene in which a group of "well-meaning" Western feminists disrobe an Afghan female survivor of the Taliban on *The Oprah Winfrey Show* before a large American audience. This imperial gesture enshrined the United States as "savior" in a blatant mistranslation of Afghan culture.[40] Philippe Lejeune argues against the mercenary character of spectacular narratives by insisting on the function of autobiography as a pact between author and reader that "integrates a concept of both [an] implied and actual (flesh-and-blood) reader into the meaning making of autobiographical writing."[41] Confounding the pact between author and audience are autobiographical narratives of trauma, such as those of the inside women at WCCC—testimonial narratives that perform simultaneously as "real-life" stories and as fiction. In the charged and fragile space of performing their life stories, the inside women's auto/biographies hold invented stories, fabricated stories, hyperbolic stories, misremembered stories, stories of the everyday, heroic stories, and stories of despair.

Incarcerated writers are "outlaw" writers because of their somatic state-sanctioned exile from society. Caren Kaplan's theory of the outlaw illuminates the power within a collective practice of testimony and witnessing in an incarcerated classroom setting.[42] In the creative writing classes at WCCC, the women testify before each other, drawing from an archive of written and oral texts—an outlaw practice itself—and the ensuing acts of witness transform the process and meaning of the very pedagogies employed. In this classroom community, women write simultaneously against and within the identification of "outlaws" by proffering life stories that challenge and confirm their audience's expectations. The audience in this instance consists of their peers, Clough, and those they hope to reach outside, if their work is published. Stories of pain and abuse emerge alongside those of hope and humor; in this way, the women defy the institution's, the state's, and the nation's insistence on a depraved criminality.[43]

Life writing, particularly by women who are disenfranchised from publishing and modes of production, performs as a diasporic document—a stateless location, from which women who write about the "I" perform a multiplicity of identities. That diasporic document is even more crippling when marked by the space of diaspora: the homelessness of the prison-industrial complex. Recording trauma via writing is complicated, particularly for marginalized writers who are dispossessed of a legitimate status with which to voice their "crime," due to disenfranchised gender, race, and sexuality subjectivities.[44] The prison as a house of the state disorders this writerly and somatic exile, as Lori Pompa, founder of the Inside-Out Prison Exchange Program and a criminal justice instructor at Temple University, explains: "The setting from whence they come and to which they return each day is authoritarian and oppressive. It is an environment that is antithetical to what is necessary for a productive, creative educational process."[45]

Pompa and Patrick Berry point to an incongruity between prison creative writing programs as potentially liberatory and edifying (with their potential to defy corporeal and psychic limitations) and the essential character of the prison as a punitive site. Berry delineates the vitality and restraints of carceral writing: "The prison environment creates distinct spatial and temporal boundaries that shape literate practice. Inmates are told when to eat, when to sleep, and sometimes even when to write. Writing under such constraints, and sometimes in defiance of them, inmate students often produce narratives of freedom, movement, and transformation. Their narratives, read as both artifact and activity, demonstrate how language is used to move beyond obstacles."[46]

THE NEXT ADVANCED class a week later addresses moments of spontaneous dissent by the inside women to pedagogical scripts. I arrive at Clough's class on a typically gorgeous Hawaiian day. Ten women are present. Clough begins the class with an excerpt from *A Room of One's Own*, but she doesn't mention Virginia Woolf. Someone picks the word ʻoluʻolu (kindness) from the koa bowl. The women offer a host of responses that approximate a call-and-response litany to ʻoluʻolu. As Clough explains, "Once you touch a person's heart, you leave a lasting imprint that no one else can erase. Impression, memory, mark. I like the way it sounds." She approaches the board, where she writes her prompt for the day: "Creative Writing: to create, 'to bring into being.'" She then faces the class and asks: "What does it mean 'to bring into being'?"

Clough elucidates the process of creation: "A unique print/fingerprint. Our genetic imprint from our ancestors is lasting and permanent. It can't be swiped or lost." The women relate to the example of a fingerprint. They nod with enthusiasm. They have all been processed through the criminal legal system. They have surrendered their fingerprints. Denise goes to the board. She calls out dramatically: "Noelani: to mold something; to bring into existence. Create something out of nothing; give birth/make real." Clough says: "Please read your poem. *Make the visitors touch and smell your poem.*" The reference to "visitors" evokes the import of an audience for Clough, whether it is an audience for *Hulihia*, the Prison Monologues, or a reading in the creative writing class. Clough is indebted to the sensory: a sensorium of specific words.

Even as the women embrace the therapeutic pedagogies and the "good" discipline encouraged by Clough, their acts of dissent disrupt the classroom space at curious moments and assume various displays. Today Clough addresses the grammar violations in the homework as an example of her commitment to a good discipline and to generating proficient writers. Clough is a stringent grammarian and insists that the women turn to the dictionary centerpieces when they encounter unfamiliar words. The women also are allowed to check out the dictionaries from the library and take them back to their dorms for homework assignments, which is one of the few privileges they look forward to, even though the dictionaries are tattered and smell of mold. The women do not like the grammar exercises.

At times Clough's insistence on an orthodox grammatical structure appears contrary to the narratives of pain that fill the classroom. This tension between the aesthetic surfaces of writing and the foremost need to address narratives of horror is one of the ethical conundrums of being a facilitator in an incarcerated space.[47] The writing class at times resembles an emergency room, and the facilitator is faced with the dilemma of which wound to address first. In this sense, the refusal of the therapeutic script lives alongside the embrace of the therapeutic.

After a disturbing narrative of pain, Clough returns to her lesson, stating: "From the homework I see that many of you are not aware of complete sentences. As an example, when to use commas instead of periods." She then writes the following on the whiteboard:

An example of a noun is a television
A verb: falling (an action)
Adjective: a black square (what it looks like: the details)
Adverb: slowly (describes how it is falling)

Clough invites someone to approach the board and provide an example of a verb, adjective, and adverb. Tatiana, who is about sixty years old and reed thin, with uncombed gray hair and glasses, and who appears to be heavily medicated, fails to follow Clough's directive; instead, in an eccentric and spontaneous response to the grammar lecture, she shouts out, "Friendly triangle!" Tatiana's response is defiant. Clough responds with uncharacteristic emotion: "Where does that come from!?" Tatiana has bipolar disorder, and I like her offering. Clough continues: "Words are provocative, like punching a hole in the wall." Tatiana lowers her outstretched arm disconcertedly. Clough continues with the grammar exercise, as some of the women look out the window at the activity in the yard where the loudspeaker, violent and jarring, grunts the incomprehensible. Typically, the women are riveted to Clough's words and her lessons, but grammar in classrooms, whether inside or outside, is not captivating material. At many moments during the class, Tatiana resists the therapeutic script via her nonlinear and disjointed responses.

Competing lineaments of power crisscross in this exacting incarcerated classroom. Tatiana is not the only woman whose interventions alter the scripted pedagogies. Marge, a tall, athletic white woman with a weathered face and intense green eyes, always proffers insightful and philosophical contributions to the class, unless she is in a funk. Marge is reading Tolstoy's *War and Peace*, *The Little Prince*, and *The Essential Rumi*, which she first read in a Maui jail in her twenties (she is now in her forties)—all simultaneously. She is an avid reader with an extensive vocabulary. I wonder if Marge has been in prison most of her life.

Marge exclaims: "PROVOCATIVE!!" And that ends the grammar exercise for the day.

Poems on Stillness: *I don't speak to nobody. I am shut in here*

Moving on, Clough asks the women to turn to the assignment for the day— poems on stillness, which the women transported to the class like talismans. A woman with thick black hair and Elvira-esque bangs, perhaps in her early forties, cries unrestrainedly. The age spots on her high cheeks move: "I don't speak to nobody. I am shut in *here.*" Her hands fly to her chest: a spontaneous arabesque of pain. "But this writing it made me alive. Before I was dead. I went searching for what to say. I had so many papers. And inside I found *me.* I don't share myself with anyone." She exchanges "papers" for pieces of her fragmented identities: memories and recollections that she desperately desires to cohere into a unified self. The writing that transports the women back from the dead to the living authenticates the writing process as a site of rescue.

Voyeurism is a thorny part of witnessing testimony for the synchronized "nourishment" amid "horror and sorrow" that it provides for both the witness and the orator. The voyeuristic audience is saved from the pain of their own banal lives by testimony in which catharsis and pain are simultaneously "performed." The women's life stories/confessions/autobiographies provoke both dismay and sympathy for any audience. But in the witnessing of the systemic and personal brutality of the women's lives lie moments of embarrassment and shame that lurk as interlopers in the classroom. The witness as voyeur—whether Clough, myself, or the other women in the class—transforms the dynamics of the pedagogical encounter.

Allyson, the author of this chapter's opening poem, "Governmental Seduction," which arises from the Poetry and Performance Lab that I teach on Friday afternoon, confesses that she despises the expected performance of trauma narratives, particularly those in the process groups: "The women cling to their stories of trauma and use them as a crutch. The same things happened to me when I was fifteen. But now I need to move on." Allyson does not disclose the "thing" that happened to her as a teenager, but the inference is rape or incest, a tragically common violence in the women's lives. She resists what she describes as sensational narratives that dominate the prison's culture: "I don't want everyone to know the details of my life. . . . I prefer to have deeper conversations." In opposition to Clough's emphasis on the details, Allyson dismisses the details as banal. For Allyson, the definition of "deep" extends beyond the personal and beyond trauma. Although she has spent much of her life on the mainland, Allyson was born in Honolulu and has an elaborate Hawaiian name—Uluwehi Kamaliʻi Wahine Onālani—loosely translated as "Festively Adorned Princess of the Heavens." She laughs sardonically: "I bet my mother regrets naming me that . . . she probably shakes her head that I turned out nothing like my name." Allyson views the routine performances of trauma as heroic—and often fabricated—performances of self. The culture of the facility breeds a performativity of pain: the telling and retelling of trauma narratives.

Institutional Intrusions

The carceral structure inevitably intrudes, inflicting grief and suffering that interrupt the testimony underway in the classroom. As the women discuss stillness and poetry, a guard's immense shadow occupies the window space. His shoulders are as wide as a truck, and he is "herding" a woman in an orange jumpsuit, restrained by leg and belly chains, to her destination. The arresting image of his broad shoulders, bollo head, and impenetrable sunglasses shielding his eyes intrudes into the comfort, pathos, and laughter that infuse the classroom space.[48] The brutal thud of the chains is a sensory disruption of the classroom utopia. These institutional secular and habitual intersessions encumber the writing space. The brutal moment retreats, and Kelly offers up her stillness poem:

A child waiting to sneak up on a butterfly
Finding our own truth
Intimidation of authority
An honest assessment of the disaster
The remains of what's left

Serendipity exists in many classrooms. Kelly reads her poem, a testament to authoritarian intimidation, at the precise instant the shadow of the ACO obscures the classroom space both literally and metaphorically. Kelly's depiction of a child sneaking up on a butterfly resides disharmoniously with the ashes of disaster. Melancholy sits heavy in the classroom today.

Kristin Bumiller, a professor and Inside-Out instructor in economic and social institutions at Amherst College, argues that jail itself can function as a text.[49] She recalls that while leading a discussion in the Hampshire Jail and House of Corrections on the bureaucratic authority of a uniform, the serendipitous appearance of a guard in her classroom corporealized the symbol of power under discussion: "As [Bumiller] spoke, a prison guard, dressed in uniform, entered the room and stood behind her to take the first of the afternoon's two head counts. The class laughed. 'I thought it was one of those perfect learning moments,' Bumiller says. 'It's one of those things that create clarity by concrete example. Sometimes, the situation or the scene itself becomes an opportunity to learn something about how power operates, without putting the inside students on the spot and having them tell their story.'"[50]

In a similar vein, I attended a restorative justice circle at WCCC in the summer of 2016. In attendance to hear the women's stories were Judge Steven Alm—who had sentenced several of the inside women—a few lawyers, a parole and "imprisoned person" advocate, a federal court pretrial selection chief, members of People's Fund and Hawai'i Friends, and a few university folks. The sounds of a guard disciplining a woman infringed on the inviolability of the testimony: "YOU, you get back to your cottage NOW!" The explosions stand in stark contrast to the laughter and tears in the restorative justice circle. I look around the room, my hands shaking, but the inside women register neither shock nor dread—a testament to carceral culture.

The fragmented, interrupted narratives in the classroom constitute a composite and communal autobiography about pain, or what Miriam Fuchs refers to as "catastrophic narratives." Since the space of the classroom is a space of witness, the testimony of each individual woman, layered upon the previous woman's testimony, forms a communal autobiography that supersedes individual linear lessons. Fuchs posits that following the tradition of female autobiographers, the scribes and subjects of catastrophic narratives "wrote partial life stories rather than teleological unities, illustrating ways that women have produced narratives that address conditions over which they lose control or never had control."[51] The narratives-in-part that are performed in the WCCC classes cohere in uncanny ways to catastrophic narratives.

> I love T. S. Eliot. He is one of my favorite poets. His poetry will awe you. A rhapsody. His poetry is not meant to be about stillness. It is fidgety and perplexing.
>
> ~ Pamela

Pamela astounds me with her original analysis and alacrity. She has a vast vocabulary and keen ability for literary criticism; she has taken Clough's class more than five times. As the only practicing Muslim in the prison, Pamela has administrative permission to be "ministered" to individually. One day I notice an atypical sight for our cultural location in Hawai'i. A man with a yarmulke (skullcap) and tzitzit (knotted ritual fringes worn by Orthodox Jewish males) is checking in at the guard station. I uncover later that he is a messianic Jewish minister who, strangely, is brought to the prison once a week to speak to Pamela about being a Muslim. Pamela is African American and Native American. In our interview, she discloses that her grandmother is dying on a reservation back home, and that Pamela is struggling to acquire permission to attend the funeral. *Pamela never gets to say goodbye to her grandmother.*

Writing performs as a personal archive of the past and literally documents life's forgotten or repressed details—*details in hiding.* When Brooke refers to poetry as "an adventure like a treasure hunt," it is because writing disinters memories, and the excavation allows for a particular type of transformation. Danika flings a catalog of words toward the center of the table—an outcome of Clough's homage to the dictionary. Danika's body is always moving. She emotes: "I have discovered a teenager: Anne. I am hopeful in silence that another day is worth living. I have learnt so much about myself here. I am soon getting out. . . . I learnt that I don't always have to fight for everyone's rights and my own rights. In fact, I don't have to be *right.* I don't always need to speak. I am a verbal person. I can be a listener. It's OK to be a listener and hear what other people have to say to me." Danika's insistence "I am soon getting out of here" is a repeated "hopeful" narrative that appears like an incantation in many of the classes. The performance of self in a pedagogical setting is intricate, as the process always engages unspoken negotiations between the individual and the community, one that allows and disallows for tacit identities, personalities, and roles.

Clough ends her lesson by asking the women: "What do you hear?" The women answer: "Being still won't hurt me." Clough frequently writes herself into the community of incarcerated women writers, testament to the vulnerability and influence of facilitating a writing class for inside students: "*We have been unpacking self-defeat without knowing it through our poems on grief, waiting, and stillness. There is a discipline in this. You have shared your concrete experiences in writing. So where are you going next? Who are we now?*" (my emphasis). The "we" additionally marks a space of belonging as part of a community of writers within the classroom and beyond the prison: *Who are we now after we write?*

I think of the byway between discipline and disciple, a divide that Clough inhabits. Shoshana Felman affirms the fractured character of testimonial narratives and situates testimony as a performative speech act that is "idiosyncratic," "strange"—a "radicality" of the poetic. Her vision provides a framework in which to read the "strangeness" in the circular conversations (testimonial narratives) that perform as "liveness" in the creative writing classes.[52] Clough's insertion of herself into the frames of her pedagogy resounds with Norman K. Denzin's performative autoethnography as both a restriction and an opening, which subverts "liveness" and reinscribes it onto textual and pedagogical performances.[53] Its ethical autonomies and constraints unveil the pedagogical space as at no time immune to the institutional one. Roger I. Simon, Sharon Rosenberg, and Claudia Eppert instruct the reader on "remembrance as a means for ethical learning," arguing that ethical pedagogy "move[s] toward . . . a critical and risk-laden learning that seeks to accomplish a shift of one's ego boundaries, that displaces engagements with the past and contemporary relations with others out of the narrow, inescapably violent and violative confines of the 'I,' to a receptivity to others."[54] This "live" receptivity and violence inscribes the creative writing classes at WCCC as performances "between hope and despair."

Ultimately, Clough's classroom and her engagement with an ethical pedagogical praxis exemplify both the power and the limitations of performative autoethnography. Affective connections are omnipresent between teachers and students within incarcerated classrooms, as they are within classrooms in the "free" world. As Patrick Berry argues, we need to challenge the "polarizing rhetoric about what literacy can and cannot deliver, arriving at more nuanced and ethical ways of understanding literacy and possibility in an age of mass incarceration."[55] Books such as *Razor Wire Women: Prisoners, Activists, Scholars, and Artists*; *Wall Tappings: An International Anthology of Women's Prison Writings 200 A.D. to the Present*; and *Women, Writing, and Prison: Activists, Scholars, and Writers Speak Out* are the few carceral anthologies that pay close attention to women's words behind the concertina wire. *Women, Writing, and Prison* reminds us to interrogate the "romantic notions of the writing teacher or workshop facilitator as transformative agent or savior."[56] As facilitators of creative writing in incarcerated spaces, we must be vigilant about the institutional, systemic, and pedagogical dilemmas that coexist in the classroom, even as we observe the power of the written word—explosive in its capacity to inspire transformation for those who are excluded from the privileges of citizenship, as well as for those who are privileged to witness the voyage.

The Stuck-Up Blues

I was taught to be kind and know that everyone's equal
I was raised not to judge or humiliate people
I was told we're all different in our very own way
And informed that a smile can make someone's day—
But then I messed up and got locked in this hell
With know-it-all people who can't even spell
And some are so fat that they fight over fans
And use bathrooms, then walk out without washing hands.
I see people around me that gossip all grim
And write statements, then smile, like it wasn't them.
I see girls trying to take the ACOs place
So they can sneak in the kitchen to shove food down their face
I see nobodys thinking they're someones in here
I hear "I love you sister" but nothing's sincere
I feel sick to my stomach and drop down to my knees
And scream "if this is my future, then God, kill me please!"
I can't take this no more and I'm tired of trying
The more time I spend here, the more brain cells are dying.
I'm not trying to be mean, I don't wanna be rude—
But everything's filthy and I don't trust the food
Coz the meat comes in boxes labeled "for inmates only"
And the butchies are toothless, so I'd rather be lonely
And the classes they have are basically "ABC"
This might be for some, but this shit ain't for me

And when I'm done ranting, I hear a voice say
You made your own bed, so quit crying and just lay
Let haters hate and don't give up your peace
Stay strong through the famine, you'll eventually feast.[57]

~ Allyson

2 "HOME"

Trauma and Desire

Home
No gas, no light, no food
And Daddy's in a bad mood
Distinct smell of alcohol
Down the hall with bloody walls
Can anybody hear us at all?

In a dark room of echoes and tears
"Lord help us,
Please appear"
On my knees in despair I ask
Mommy, "are you not scared,
Why are you letting this happen to us?"
She says, "stop making such a fuss"
My little brother and sister are afraid
They say "Oh no, he's drunk and being mean"

"Shhhh, be quiet, don't make a big scene
Let's run out the front door and away from here"

Loud screams of a woman
Another can of beer
We hate this house but there's no where to go
We get on our knees and begin to pray
"Dear Lord please show us the way out
Right now we're in desperate need and doubt
Can you change the heart of our Dad
And take away all of the bad?
We're confused and just want to understand
Why do we have to be on his command?
We don't want to grow up and dwell in our past
We just want a normal home at last"[1]

~ Joanne

Poems about "home," which appear in the publication *Hulihia* (Transformation) by the inside women at the Women's Community Correctional Center (WCCC), serve as a political tool to counter the experience of dispossession in the carceral space to which they have been consigned. Indeed, "home" performs as a challenging archive in Hawai'i: a site of US empire and British intervention since the eighteenth century that bears a fraught political and colonial history. Many of the inside women are direct victims of that history and are located in a genealogy of political trauma, including the overthrow of Queen Lili'uokalani, and the subsequent annexation of Hawai'i as a US territory and later a state. The rise and transformation of prisons in Hawai'i are inextricable from the contemporary militarization of Hawai'i and what the Hawaiian sovereignty movement witnesses as the perennial occupation. RaeDeen Keahiolalo-Karasuda, the director of the Office of Native Hawaiian Partnerships at Chaminade University in Honolulu (2013–16), traces early examples of public shaming and terrorizing of Native Hawaiians, such as the staging of the public execution of King Kalākaua's and Queen Lili'uokalani's grandfather, which persist in the contemporary prison-industrial complex in Hawai'i. Keahiolalo-Karasuda points to the hanging of Chief Kamanawa II on October 20, 1840, as "the start of a codified Western legal system that subjugated Kānaka Maoli through cruel and unusual forms of punishment."[2] The establishment of Kalaupapa, a "leper" colony on the island of Moloka'i in the mid-1800s can be regarded as one of the earliest examples

of a missionary prison and a troubled "home" in Hawai'i, and its historic-
ity hosts complex scripts that enact Western punishment and Indigenous
restoration.[3] In an article in the *Atlantic*, associate editor Alia Wong reports:
"Many of Kalaupapa's patients forged paradoxical bonds with their isolated
world. Many couldn't bear to leave it. It was 'the counterintuitive twinning
of loneliness and community,' wrote *The New York Times* in 2008, 'All that
dying and all of that living.'"[4] This type of connection to a wounded home is
evident in the inside women's writings about home to the extent that prison
often becomes a "home" for women who have been institutionalized. The
home as wound is even more pronounced for some of the Native Hawaiian
women who have been perennially denied a homeland.

The geographic and cultural space of the Pacific serves as a semantic,
linguistic, and cosmetic site of resistance, as well as an apparatus to par-
ticularize the writing in *Hulihia*—the prison's biannual publication—even
when the locus of the Pacific is not overt.[5] In this chapter's opening poem
by Joanne, who is Samoan, home represents an ongoing space of trauma,
which parallels the inherent contradiction between the legal assignation of
civic death and the creative, spiritual, and intellectual agency inherent in
the act of writing within a woman's prison. It is easy to see why legislatures,
penal administrators, and the criminal system at large are invested in disciplining and patrolling the incarcerated voice. Historically, the voices of the
incarcerated, particularly in the radical prison movement of the 1960s, were
voices of dissent against the state that threatened to expose state brutality
and human rights violations. In their collectivity, they were a threatening
presence on the national stage.

In this chapter, I explore the writing that came out of the Tuesday and
Friday creative writing classes taught by Pat Clough at wccc from 2003 to
2014, with a focus on *Hulihia VII: Writings from Prison and Beyond: "Home"
Edition*, generated by Clough's prompts on home and homeland. The writing of the inside women subverts the state-sanctioned imposition of civic
death, as do the poems residing in *Hulihia VII*. Although the stories of home
at times reflect the redemptive narratives that Clough endorses, the multiple
valences of home in the women's representations exceed those limits. Ongoing trauma, from family trauma to the trauma of incarceration, lies at the
root of many of these narratives. In these writings, "home" appears as a site of
trauma as well as a site of fantasy and desire, and occasionally—particularly
within the notion of the Kailua Prison Writing Project (kpwp) itself as
home—as a site of healing. The desire for home and redemption, in spite of
the horrors of home, filters through the words on the page, illustrative of the

proximity between pleasure, desire, and harm. The reader witnesses these fantasies and discomforts in the eccentric grammatical usages, the silences, the ellipses, the chronological play, the memories that are privileged in the drumming up of trauma.

Here, the page is a mnemonic re-collection for the skin. The texts are presented as poems, yet they contradict orthodox expectations of what constitutes a poem in their arhythmic and contrapuntal nature. Despite the institutional and programmatic assertions that writing heals and soothes, the women ultimately are unable to escape the trauma of their own experiences. The writing leaks out on the page, resisting the effort to discipline painful stories. Trauma surfaces within the grammatical intrusions, twists of memory, and aberrant uses of language. Thus, sites of desire and fantasy are inseparable from the marked site of trauma: the collateral damage of colonization on the psyche. The women's writing eludes the redemptive script despite its longing to perform a benevolent American citizenship. Harsh and caustic, it testifies to the difficulty of the healing process. Within *Hulihia VII*, a cacophony of voices reside within the terrain of personal, historical, and familial trauma.

The focus on women's writing, rather than on canonized male carceral writing, invites us to think differently about the genre of prison writing. Male and female carceral writing frequently differ in their representations of home. From narratives around the mythic yard, sexual predation, tattoo culture, and gangs, the male body is inscribed as simultaneously a singular machinelike body, yet one vulnerable to somatic and institutional penetration.[6] Archetypally, women's narratives circulate around community. The surrogate home—prison—is further domesticated in an all-female space, as well as in the embrace by some of the women of traditional notions of the feminine, as we shall see from a close interrogation of the poems themselves. Early American penology reform, managed and executed primarily by white, Christian, middle- to upper-class female reformers, sought to "correct" and "purify" the female body. These vanguard agitators struggled to uncover avenues of reform that diverged from the punitive work regimes implemented in early male prisons. Fin de siècle American penology reform fashioned punishments in harmony with societal, cultural, and contemporaneous ideologies about the normative gendered body. These gendered practices of punishment and reform correlate with the preoccupations, themes, and writerly structures evident in male and female incarcerated writing. The character of trauma—a persistent and introspective anxiety, an internal wound—is ubiquitous in women's writing but not in male carceral writing. Furthermore, the KPWP cultivates heterosexuality and narrow notions of the feminine that coexist with the masculinist national narratives that are reinforced by Clough's elite literary canon.[7]

The opening poem by Joanne appears in the middle part of *Hulihia VII*, "Ki'i 'ōlelo a me ho'omana'o" (Word pictures and memories).[8] This volume is dedicated to female prisoners' recollections of home punctuated by its corresponding malady and rapture. The writers included in this journal are primarily inside women culled from the creative writing classes at WCCC. Inside women from two federal corrections facilities, the Federal Medical Center in Carswell, Texas, and the Federal Detention Center in Honolulu, are also represented in the collection. Clough states that the "inmates" in the federal correction facilities, some of them with origins in Hawai'i, "have maintained their connection to home through their writing."[9] The other writers are members of student groups from Farrington High School and Restore Our Community (ROC), both located in the Kalihi area. A domestic nonprofit corporation, ROC educates the community in Kalihi Valley about safety, health, and environmental issues and works to address drug crime among the youth. The decision to extend the plurality of voices to two high school communities reflects the ideology of the program and the institution, which serves to promote redemptive narratives as pathways to healing, and to extend the limits of family to "local" communities.[10]

The women speak variously about home in ways that resist simplistic interpretation. Some poems mourn home as a paradise lost, while others denounce home as a dystopic space—a site of injury. Some women condemn their mothers as passive enablers of abuse, while others celebrate home as a lover or spiritual abstraction. These complex representations breathe complicity with and resistance to societal and institutional projections of home and live alongside Clough's notion of an idealized home. The KPWP, echoing the valences of the women's voices, departs from the genre of carceral autobiography, and particularly from the revolutionary canon of the 1960s, by refusing to employ the linguistic and thematic resistances utilized by Black revolutionary writers of the 1960s.[11] Linguistically and thematically, the *Hulihia* writings showcase penitence and nostalgia, and these proclamations, seemingly politically sanitized, align themselves with a gendered American citizenship rather than an incendiary critique of the nation-state. However, the women offer a form of rebuttal in that they refuse to conform to linear and chronological narratives, and their frequent use of ellipses signals writerly and psychological omissions, disquiet, and multiple meanings. The poems trace a pathway to hope that bespeaks both disavowal of and complicity with the institution of the prison. The multivalent scripts situate the women as orators of a counterdiscourse while uncovering desires and fantasies that can be aligned with the utopic.[12] In this way the women's writing mirrors the redemptive narrative of a liberal penal reform, which is Clough's own vision of reform. However, within this cosmetic collusion lie songs, screams, shouts, and silences of dissent.

The autobiographical writing at WCCC spans diverse genres of life writing: apologia, testimonio, autoethnography, psychobiography, and performance.[13] Thematically and contextually, the writing echoes the nineteenth-century women's penal reform movement that focused on rehabilitation. Similarly, the pages of *Hulihia VII* frame the poems as miniature diaries as they inhabit the containments of the genre, "shaped by inspiration and habit," and marked by the scars of trauma, displayed concurrently in form and content.[14]

Home

A figment of my imagination somewhere far off
A hopeful place I used to wish to find again someday
But the only home I ever knew was broken, empty and cold
Shattered glass, a drunken mother her face becoming old
An empty stomach, dirty school clothes
Slapping my brother around . . . [15]

~ Jessica C.

Jessica's poem "Home" is rife with dissonance: the desire for home juxtaposed with the hopelessness of home. The poem contains awkward syntactical pairings: shattered glass, a drunken mother, an empty stomach. Estranged subjects and verbs that are invariably misplaced accost the reader. Likewise, the violence perpetrated against her brother is a gesture that Jessica assumes, almost against her will, in a familial transference of abuse.

Slapping my brother around
The tears falling from his face as he'd look up from the ground
I didn't mean to, I was just so angry . . . [16]

~ Jessica C.

The inside women share decided histories of abuse, yet inside the prison's walls they are disproportionately disciplined with psychotropic medication compared with inside men: a systematic pacification of bodies, minds, and mouths in a perverse effort to make women "conform to the norms of a male-imagined and dominated life in these cages."[17] This shutting up of "mad" women has its origins in early America, where women who were considered gossips—a signpost of hysteria—were visually and publicly punished: their mouths held shut with a facial apparatus. The need to silence women's voices, both inside and outside of the carceral landscape, situates women's life writing as an archive of resilience and resistance. Filmmaker Tracy Huling describes the women she visits in a correctional facility in upstate New York as "shadow women" and admonishes a society that treats "bad" women as "mad" women.[18]

The tension between the therapeutic and the punitive is evident in the history of liberal penal reform, with its dominant tropes of disciplining female bodies, as well as in confessional literature and discourses of redemption. The KPWP and its resultant *Hulihia* publication exhibit some of the incongruous impulses of the twentieth-century new penology movement. In *Their Sisters' Keepers* and *Maternal Justice*, feminist historian Estelle Freedman addresses the politics of gender-specific penal reform in the nineteenth and twentieth centuries. According to Freedman, women were imprisoned due to their economic vulnerability in an industrializing society and to a Victorian code that criminalized "fallen women." The new penology, rooted in Christian reform movements, extended benevolence to white women of the lower classes while it marked the bodies of women of color as always already deviant. By the turn of the twentieth century, efforts to control the excesses of the white female body and police its purity were entwined with both the Cult of True Womanhood and the Progressive Era.

The tropes of therapeutic emancipation and Christian redemption, the prison as home, and the discourses of nostalgia and repentance—legacies of the new penology—today infuse women's prison writing. Confessional literature follows the historical trajectory of the new penology in that it confirms, even while resisting, the apparatus of oppression. As explained by Theodore Hamm, confirmation lies in the requirement that those inside repent for their sins, even as they catalog the societal ills that generate crime: "The earliest type of prison writing was the eighteenth-century autobiographical narrative, often provided just before execution day."[19] In the nineteenth century, these gallows confessionals were vanquished by a picaresque swagger by the accused—a showcase for sensational and titillating tales of criminality that were performatively masculine. "But it was nineteenth-century slave narratives and the oral traditions of emancipated African Americans," claims H. Bruce Franklin, "that truly sparked the development of prison literature as an identifiable genre."[20]

The *Hulihia* texts manifest identifications with various redemption narratives—religious, familial, societal, historical—and evince claims to redemption that position women's life writing within a precise genealogy of female prison reform. As discussed earlier, contemporary redemption narratives are potentially harnessed to an institutional voice, including the reformist demands for personal responsibility, hard work, and transformation. Even in Clough's choice to name the poetry publications *Hulihia*—the Hawaiian word for transformation—and in the offering of English and Hawaiian *oli* (chants/oral genealogy) created by Kumu ʻIlima Stern, as a preface to all volumes, there is an assertion of transformation, whether literal, psychic, or writerly.[21]

Prison as Home

Hulihia VII: Writings from Prison and Beyond: "Home" Edition is divided into three parts: "Paʻahao" (Imprisoned), "Kiʻi ʻōlelo a me hoʻomanaʻo" (Word pictures and memories), and "Aia ka home e hana au" (Home is where I make it).[22] This triptych structure is reiterated in most of Clough's published volumes. The triad follows a redemptive trajectory—a prescriptive cartography from imprisonment to freedom (from a state of *paʻahao*, or imprisonment, to *aia ka home e hana au*, or "home is where I make it")— that is replicated in the Prison Monologues performances. A redemption narrative is not necessarily constraining or oppressive, but it suggests a somatic or psychic liberation. The fifteen opening poems bespeak a psychic, spiritual, and physical imprisonment. The sixteen poems in the middle part hint at the idea of a middle ground, a byway between imprisonment and freedom. They allude to the power of imagination, whether it resides in writing, in memory, or in images—as an antidote to oppression. The sixteen poems in the last part proffer a mobile and liberatory home that is not limited to physical walls and structures.

The generic titling of "home" with minor variations—Clough's editorial choice—impresses on the reader that home signifies as both universal and individual. In some ways, the narratives of longing can be read as universal, yet in this volume, we witness the particularity and polyvocality of the revealed homes. The most marked entry in its departure from the collective "home" is the denouement, Clough's poem "Finding Home," which on the contents page is listed as "Finding Home" by Pat Clough, "Teacher." Clough employs a parallel structure, juxtaposing her own school days under the stalwart tutelage of the nuns to the incarceration of the women in her creative writing classes.[23] I choose to place Clough's poem first to present the complexities of her own voice of witness, as well as her desire for a fanciful home.

> *A bell shrills in paneled halls*
> *Gleaming linoleum*
>
> *Cushions the crush of girls in blue jumpers*
> *Summoned from lockers with small hidden mirrors*
> *Blush and brush carelessly stashed*
>
> *Nylons and crew socks with two-inch cuffs*
> *Sturdy brown oxfords buffed blood-red*
> *Hem lengths measured*
> *By vigilant nuns*[24]

The daily accessories of petty vanity are cherished items for the schoolgirls living under the perpetual scrutiny of the austere nuns. The reader wonders at the "blood-red" oxfords, a striking image embedded in the sadistic yet "loving" buffing, a metaphor for benevolent or therapeutic care. The blue jumpers of the Catholic schoolgirls mirror the blue uniforms of the inmates, Clough's students:

> *Now*
> *Worn cement sidewalks*
> *In lush mountain shadow*
> *Too many women in long blue lines*
> *Slippers slapping to block buildings*
> *Shackled, cuffed*
> *Behind barbed wire*
>
> *"For the good of society"*
> *Shoveled from sight*
> *Mothers, daughters*
> *Sisters, grandmothers*
> *Poked and probed behind steel doors*

The opening word of the stanza, "Now," isolated in its singularity, takes the reader on a temporal and shifting chronology. Clough wears the voice of the witness and testifies that the humanity and communal assembly of the women is violated by a disciplinary institution: "Shackled, cuffed";

"Shoveled from sight"; "Poked and probed behind steel doors." The "sh," "s," and "c" sounds, a sardonic alliteration, evokes the body in process or the processed body. The critical tone of the poem leads the reader to wonder if the "care" of the institution is analogous to the "care" of the nuns. However, Clough's nostalgia toward the punitive custody of the nuns troubles the implicit appraisal. Here the "steering of spirit" coexists with the "shaming, scolding," and "stretching [of] mind."

> *"For your own good"*
> *Sisters squelched silliness*
> *Steering my spirit*
> *Shaming, scolding,*
> *Stretching my mind*
> *I loved them for it*
> *But not then*
> *Not then*

The twinning "not then" serves a consonant purpose to the chronological shift of "now," avowing that one's perspective can shift with the passing of time. The older, gracious, and introspective Clough can "now" appreciate the correction of the nuns "for your own good," which reinforces the classroom (perhaps even Clough's classroom, where affects of compassion and respect reside) as a site of colonization in the political landscape of Hawai'i. The last and lingering image that seals this volume is of a monkeypod tree resting in a circle—a dream cloud of sorts—the identical tree that lives on the grounds of WCCC. Thus both the cover—an impressionistic painting of the Ko'olau Mountains—and the concluding black and white monkeypod locate the narratives of the women in the specific landscape of O'ahu.

> *They come to my class*
> *And write*
> *And laugh*
> *Cry with relief*
> *Clutching word treasures*
> *To healing hearts*
>
> *Leaving, I linger*
> *In lacey magic*
> *Gripped in the hug of a monkeypod tree*
> *Suddenly recalling*

The girl in blue jumpers
Sent forth by the nuns so long ago

"Sister," I whisper
"I found my home"

The double entendre/enjambment of "sister" as both staunch nun and the community of women at wccc—Clough's simultaneous "sisters" and "students"—is a troubled imagining of home. Her poem suggests that discipline is for the women's own good, even if they do not yet recognize it. In this sense, Clough offers her "good discipline" as a substitute for the oppressive discipline of imprisonment. Clough collapses writing—"word treasures"—with "lacey magic." Like magic, writing, for Clough, serves as a pathway to healing. This romantic, almost mythical, envisioning prompts Clough to reimagine her own "home" both as a teacher in an incarcerated classroom and as a witness to the inside women's healing. The monkeypod tree that Clough selects as one of the visual texts for *Hulihia VII* performs as an aide-mémoire that summons sublimated memories from Clough's past, "Sent forth by the nuns so long ago" within a scripted, biblical narrative.

Clough is indebted to the notion of authenticity: the idea that through writing and the recording and reordering of memory, truth can be revealed in a process of self-discovery. Clough attributes this self-discovery in the women's journey to believing that they are worthy. In our last conversation in the summer of 2017 at Kailua's Morning Brew, Clough emphasizes that the skills the women gained from the writing classes—the excavation of "something inside themselves [obscured] by poor choices, abuse, and addiction . . . the thinking skills and the opportunity to express themselves"—were instrumental in their constructive transition back to society.

Inevitably, the women's writings about home spill beyond the boundaries established by the writing course, the program, and the experience of incarceration itself. Inside women's poetry and prose posit home in a myriad of ways: as a dystopic space deluged with violence, as a counternarrative to the mythic home, as the traumatic reiteration of injury, Pacific homes as "homespun," home as tethered to landscape, home as a healing/redemptive intergalactic space, and home as dislocation (physically, literally, psychically, and spiritually). In their imagery, the women depict home variously as a wasteland wilderness, as a dysfunctional lover, as savior, and frequently as paradise lost.

Many of the inside women experience home as a place occupied by threatening male bodies—familial members and strangers—who violate their bodily borders. Kelly's poem, from the Federal Medical Center (FMC) in Carswell, Texas, is representative of the overwhelming presence of incest and rape in the women's lives:

> *Fear was the foundation of my home, fear of being ambushed, sexually assaulted or even apprehended by what we call "law enforcement." There was never any stability in the place I called home.*
> *My food and water consisted of a substance, a white crystallized substance that resembled a stone that was always in different shapes And sizes. No matter the size, I was never able to fill my immediate hunger.*
>
> *My primary household was a collection of men with no names and no faces. Any and all interactions were done in darkness. No one could face the actual sin, only the unspeakable pleasure it gave.*
>
> *At the end of the day, there was no comfort of a warm bed, or maybe a book to read. No my nights ended wrapped up in pain, shame, guilt and degradation. I was not happy in this place called home.*[25]
>
> ~ Kelly, FMC

Kelly explains that in her childhood home, the lull of bedtime stories was usurped by "a collection of men with no names and . . . faces," and food swapped for narcotics. Comfort gave way to terror in "nights *wrapped* up in pain . . . and degradation." The conflation of nights with a "wrapping up," which suggests comfort, even in the context of rape, disrupts some of the other writers' adherence to conformist narratives. Resistance and orthodoxy coexist in the compound narratives.

Tiffany presents home as a national narrative of trauma, drug addiction, and disenfranchisement. When I met Tiffany, a brilliant and politically savvy woman, she was in the TJ Mahoney & Associates parole reentry program, Ka Hale Hoʻāla Hou No Nā Wāhine / The Home of Reawakening for Women.[26] Tiffany's poem straddles two geographic spaces—New York City and the island of Oʻahu. The poet portrays Oʻahu as an extended incarcerated space of trauma, and her reference to batu summons the exactitude of the methamphetamine problem in Hawaiʻi: one of the most severe in the nation, with its victims disproportionately Native Hawaiians. Tiffany excavates her home as a miniature: a tableau of transience and deprivation. The spectacle of the "home in situ" is a violent home: *"My transient home, a metal drawer / It screeches beneath me . . ."*

Where Is Home?
Home
My transient home, a metal drawer
It screeches beneath me
A metal lock to guard the safety of the few belongings I still own
Is my home really this place?
The sickness of insanity, a revolving door of recidivism
This is no New York City penthouse
That one over there is a gatekeeper, not your doorman
I see it everywhere, the comfortable the complacent
She'll sing the batu blues without a care
She's been given a bed and three meals
Grandma soothes and rocks her babies to sleep in a lonely
corner of this island . . . [27]

~ Tiffany

Tiffany is critical of her "complacent" neighbors who exploit the system for a free home, resulting in a systemic venality, as generations of grandmothers raise their grandchildren after their parents' disappearance to prison. Here the Lilliputian home is a stand-in for the macro: the American prison-industrial complex. The author impugns both the "inmate" and the institution. The title "Where Is Home?" exemplifies Tiffany's tendency toward the rhetorical: the perpetual wondering of the radical citizen.

This is the land of the lost
Where is home?
I will not always be a wanderer, unsuccessful at my attempts to create a
*   sanctuary*
The place I yearn for, all that home has promised to be, pretty pictures
*   in a magazine*
I am discovering the haven I seek
I am still seeking me
Home will reveal itself
The more I find myself, the more I realize that I'll be home when I am
Being me

~ Tiffany

In "Where Is Home?" Tiffany conflates home with selfhood. Like many of the women, she explores the mythic quality of home and exposes the utopian home as an illusion. She concedes her personal failure to create a sanctuary, yet her refusal to accept the custodial as "home" is a gesture of resistance congruent with her presentation as a radical. Whereas most of the women I interviewed spoke highly of the former warden Mark Kawika Patterson, Tiffany was critical of his administration, asserting that it infringed on her rights. In her view, the leadership discouraged women from having positive, intimate relationships in the facility. At the same time, Tiffany divulged that she had found her love at WCCC, her future wife. Prior to her ultimate release from WCCC, Tiffany was actually returned to the facility from TJ Mahoney for infractions. Though there is no evidence that she purposefully violated that program's rules in order to be sent back to the facility (and back to her lover), a consideration of desire and the tension between self-actualization and the need for the other is instrumental. After her release, Tiffany married a man, her compound mode of self-representation an example of the complexities of auto/biography.[28]

This incongruity between home manifest within the self and the desire for a beloved as home is illustrative of the myriad expectations conjured by the term *home*: the demand for a partner to feel complete, the yearning for an idyllic home in a sanitized context, and the need for normative familial relationships devoid of conflict. All these anticipations rest uneasily beside women's frequent privileging of antinormative American narratives. The fact that the women are inmates immediately inscribes them within the tradition of voices from the margins: "un-American" voices.

Joanne's poem "Home" gazes at the island of O'ahu from the west side where she was raised, and it too transmits memories of violence in a "hall with bloody walls."

We don't want to grow up and dwell in our past
We just want a normal home at last
Down the hall with bloody walls
Can anybody hear us at all?

In a dark room of echoes and tears
"Lord help us,
Please appear"
On my knees in despair I ask . . . [29]

~ Joanne

Here the author posits her home as a wilderness—a violent frontier—estranged from the rectitude of a just God or civilization. Joanne's poem carries a plea for redemption: she does not romanticize the homeland but rather paints her home as a dystopic space where the motherland/mother fails to protect her children from the "bad heart" of their father.[30] Joanne mourns the desire for a "normal" (disciplined) home and posits a "good" and "bad" binary of the heart: "Right now we're in desperate need and doubt / Can you change the heart of our Dad / And take away all of the bad?" In this poem, the normative collapses into a mythic future, divorced from an unspeakable past.[31] Just as many inside women turn to God as savior in their redemption narratives, Joanne posits God as guardian of the home. "Loud screams of a woman / Another can of beer / We hate this house but there's no way where to go / We get on our knees and begin to pray / 'Dear Lord please show us the way out.'" Here, dysfunction resides in the same line as religiosity. Joanne employs direct rhyme, which lends the poem a child-like, fairy-tale tone. Yet the tone is ironic because its corresponding story performs a grotesque fairy tale of neglect, abuse, and fear. Joanne's singsong nursery rhyme couples violence with innocence—a frequent feature of the *Hulihia* poems.

Brooke's "Home," rendered in prose, is also a wasteland:

I never had a real home since I was fourteen years old and before that I was getting molested and beaten. I ran from it so home is not a good thing for me to think about. I hate my last home. I was given dog food. I was whipped and spanked with thick paddles with holes. I was getting my head pounded on the wall and mother saw all this happen and didn't do anything.

I don't have a happy memory of home. I finally had enough guts to leave.[32]

~ Brooke

Home for Brooke represents a traumatic reiteration of injury. She presents the dream of an authentic or "real" home even as the emphatic negative or an estranged grammatical construct connotes the impossibility of an authentic home as refuge ("I *never* had a real home since I was fourteen years old and *before that* I was getting molested and beaten"). Brooke bares/bears an enduring physical and psychological battering that is an indelible pattern in her life. She traces the horrific abuse—the molestations, the paddling of her body, and the forced feeding of dog food—that her mother fails to prevent. Like Joanne's mother, Brooke's mother is a witness to her daughter's devastating physical abuse and neglect. The traditional vessel of nurturance, the mother, becomes a vehicle and enabler of pain. Many of the poems contain the characters of men, father figures who are palpable perpetrators; however, mothers, in their traditional role of passive perpetrators, also haunt the narratives.

Home as Paradise Lost

As if to counterbalance the narratives of terror, the women frequently write about a paradise lost—the nostalgia for their homes/homelands, a domestic space, even one replete with abuse. At times they conceive of the prison as a surrogate home and trace their transformative path toward personal salvation.

The Home I Now Carry

In my youth, I found every reason not to be home
I made broad choices with a small mind
I took for granted that your true home is in your heart
Not just the walls, the chores and curfews I sought to avoid
Home is the family I long for that I forsook with selfish choices
And a lover that took root in a garden of many thorns[33]

~ Pamela

Pamela's poem is an illustration of the paradise-lost theme: home is sacrificed to a dysfunctional lover, and the biblical garden of desire is overgrown with thorns. One can read this poem, among others, as a reflection of the language of therapeutic emancipation and Christian redemption that infiltrates the politics of prison administration. The women often achieve transformation through writerly expressions of regret. Pamela mourns taking her home, even a home filled with drudgery, for granted. In hindsight, the mundane home is reinvented as a paradise lost.

Home Is

Cookouts, weddings and funerals
Snooping around your parents' room
Giving up yours when relatives visit
Being sent to your room when Nana's cigar girls visit
Home is where blessings are not material
Where the family bond is everything
Home fills me with happy memories when life presses down on me

~ Pamela

Pamela, who identifies as Black and Native American, privileges the everyday rituals of family cycles: cookouts, weddings, and funerals that take place alongside the reception of "Nana's cigar girls." She documents the queer sexuality in her family circle. Here, the "normative" is collapsed with the anomalous in this nostalgic recollection of the childhood home. Pamela celebrates nonmaterial blessings, and thereby refuses the American narrative of economic ascension. The holes and silences in this recollection of home and family of origin reverberate with state-sanctioned policing of sexual minorities. In the *Hulihia* women's writing about home, we see an erasure from domestic space. Pamela, who is gay but doesn't overtly articulate her queerness, likewise polices the queerness in her narrative. This erasure from domestic space is a complex enactment in the *Hulihia* women's writing about home and an apt example of a paradise lost as the carceral home replaces the familial home.

The Mythologized Home Rooted in Homeland

Home

A mother so loving, her unconditional love pours out with her deadly
*   hugs*
Her hugs store up happy memories that help me get through anything
Her hands rough and scratched show her hard work but gentle touch
Every scratch and wrinkle shows her experience and suffering
Though she doesn't show her struggles, hidden in her eyes you can see
*   them*[34]

~ Melody, ROC

The women who fill the pages of *Hulihia* and write from a physical and psychic diaspora indict the mother-daughter relationship as a mnemonic device of the colonizer/colonized dialogic, even as they express an idealized desire for their lost mothers.[35] In several of these narratives, mothers who have been subjected to abuse and colonization transpose their bodily and psychic trauma onto their daughters. The daughters' recognition of the familial abuse, even more excruciating at the hands of their own mothers, is one of the arms of resistance the inside women exercise in their poetry. In Melody's "Home," "unconditional love" is collapsed with "deadly hugs." This dual destructive/generative fuel of the mother saturates the women's writing. The relationship with the mother imbues an aura of the incestuous, a relationship that closely mirrors dysfunctional lovers. In this way, the incarcerated writing echoes the writing of Jamaica Kincaid, Saidiya Hartman, and Audre Lorde, women from the African diaspora in the United States and the Caribbean.[36] This duality toward mother and motherland is foregrounded in the inside women's writing about home in which shame and resistance haunt explorations of memory and trauma. Many diasporic writers articulate writing as lifesaving as they work toward alternate presentations of themselves. At times, this takes the form of liberating themselves from overbearing mothers; at others, it finds expression as a romantic adoration of the mother.

I'll Be Home

It's lonely here
I need your touch, your voice

I got lost in a crazy world
I know I hurt you momma
I left you worried, scared and searching for me
Days without one call
I left my children in your care, no goodbye
I had to get high

Just one hit
That's all I needed
Strung out with faded memories
Mesmerized by my own destruction
I had to get high

I couldn't look you in the eyes
I was afraid you'd see the lies
I had to get high

All alone behind these prison walls
Thinking about your pretty brown eyes
And every tear I made you cry
I had to get high

Who would have ever thought you would be the one to understand

It ended so wrong
I didn't belong
Please hold on
I will be home and never again will I leave you alone[37]

~ Brandy, FMC

Brandy's ode to her mother is a tragic tale of love lost. The refrain "I had to get high" is formally and psychologically juxtaposed with her duty to her mother with the "pretty brown eyes," who is left behind to raise her children. The poem's denouement is the poet's promise to be with her mother eternally. Here the mother is symbolic of the jilted lover. The repetition of language, ideas, and themes is characteristic of trauma narratives, and this recording and rerecording is a way of making meaning out of pain. Writing in this sense is like the puckering of skin and surfaces. The *Hulihia* texts borrow from the genre of hagiography, but they resist and expand its borders. If the mother is elevated to the status of saint, in some of the women's poems she is simultaneously vilified. Inside women share with diasporic writers such as Jamaica Kincaid "an interest in self-naming and renaming, and the centrality of the mother-daughter relationship as a site of enigmatic trauma."[38]

The women of *Hulihia* employ a fragmentary and fractured syntax, which serves mnemonically to act out the repetitive musings of trauma: the refusal to forget. The triptych framework employed by Clough allows for an interplay between self-representation and the dialogic as the serial poems link together in a mosaic of crossings, or what Leigh Gilmore names an "intertextual system of meaning."[39]

Some women speak of home as longing, as a lover, as a figment of the imagination, others as talismans that they carry with them. In this way "home" performs as a spiritual abstraction:

Home is never so far away from me
When I'm lost in the middle of the darkest forest
Home is never so far away from me
In trying to find a way out of this labyrinth
Home is never so far away from me
Because home is always in my heart.[40]

This privileging of home and the collapse of a home with godliness reflect Christian missionaries' conceptions of home and domesticity, and echo prison programming that aims at reform and redemption. They stand in stark contrast to Indigenous reimaginings and recollections of home that are rooted in a particularized landscape: the islands that constitute Hawai'i.

Amourelle, a white mainlander in her thirties who frequently wears her hair in French braids, summons the individualized daily trappings of her home as chronicles of memory:

Photo albums bursting with captured memories . . .
My arms wrap around my children
My favorite chain, my favorite T-shirt
The comfort of all the familiarity of life's trinkets collected
    along the way.[41]

The poetry collected in this *Hulihia* volume journeys from domesticated memories that are imprisoned, like the women's bodies, to political odes to the homeland of Hawai'i. Most of the "homes" in the volume are rooted in Hawai'i, despite the fact that some of the women were not raised there. In one exception, Karen pens an ode to her Wisconsin farm home:

A drafty white farmhouse high on the hill
. . . I fuss over a pregnant mare
Belly swollen with life
. . . A simple life
Unadorned and pure
I am that girl at home on a Farm.[42]

The characters in Karen's poem are particular to her Midwest birthplace ("drafty white farmhouse," "pregnant mare") but are not divergent from many of the Indigenous women who were raised in farming communities on the island of Hawai'i. The cover of *Hulihia VII* depicts the politicized and contested Hawaiian homestead of Waimānalo.[43] The handpicked Waimānalo landscape is evocative because the prison itself is situated in the majestic Ko'olau Mountains between Kailua and Waimānalo. The cover works like the *kaona* (hidden meaning) of hula—a double entendre, a form of political resistance.

The poignancy and tragedy of home resonates given the threat of climate disaster—an even more pressing concern now with politicians who are hostile to the Environmental Protection Agency. Small Island Developing States are most vulnerable to the deleterious effects of climate change, including "transnational crime, drug and human trafficking, piracy and wildlife exploitation, illicit abuse of resources, rising sea levels, dying coral reefs and the increasing frequency and severity of natural disasters that exacerbate the potential predicament of community displacement and migration."[44] Islands are facing literal extinction: a permanent erasure of home. Given the escalating effects of climate change on global and local home(s), incarcerated women's depictions of home in a Pacific women's state prison provide particularly urgent scripts. This exigency is endemic to the women's homelessness—their civic death in a context of global citizenship and a global prison-industrial complex, in concert with the particularized space of the Pacific Islands within contemporary global environmental contentions.

This chapter performs twin interventions and contributes to contemporary debates in feminist theory: it exposes the internally contradictory evocations of home as both wound and desire generated within a women's prison—an embrace and repudiation of a heteronormative domesticity—and it carves out a space in prison writing scholarship for women's prison writing in the Pacific. The cartography gusts from Hawai'i's colonial past to its present, redolent with the unresolved grief wrought by colonization. The *Hulihia* texts position the inside women's life writing within a genealogy of prison reform through their manifest identifications with various redemption narratives: religious, familial, societal, and historical. Ultimately, we are left with the uneasy realization that comfortable scripts never heal trauma, whether familial trauma, the historical trauma inflicted on the homeland of Hawai'i, or the contemporary trauma of imprisonment. The *Hulihia* women undermine institutional, programmatic, and societal directives only as they excavate imagined paths through their historical traumas. This chapter shifts prison writing from the dominant realms—male, autobiographical, exile, political, international—to the spheres of the intimate. It thereby adds simultaneously to growing bodies of scholarship in several fields: critical prison studies, writing studies, feminist studies, and settler/postcolonial studies.

Looking Back

Everyone at home has gotten used to having me away
With 13 years of prison time
There's not much I can say
The reality of my life today I made all on my own
If I could change one thing in life
*   I would've stayed home*[45]

~ Jennifer

3 THE STAGE AWAY FROM THE PAGE

When we started to go out and perform—not just for the children but for adults, doctors, professors, and judges—it was a confirmation that what we do is full impact, not just for the children but for people from all walks of life. And that's when I realized that what I do makes a big difference. That what I say—my stories and the way me and my team gel makes a difference. It works. It definitely works. I feel that it's not even us when we are up there.

When we are up there . . . we are so anointed.
~ Vailea, Prison Monologues, Women's Community Correctional Center

The Prison Monologues is a curious, hybrid body—not quite theater, not quite spoken word. This chapter departs from and extends the mediated space of the classroom and the text-based testimony of the *Hulihia* publications as it turns to the informal readings of the women's published work that they perform for each other in the facility's dorms and cottages, and then to the larger public performances of the Prison Monologues program.[1] It highlights the complex relationships between public performances and audiences of the Prison Monologues—a theater of witness. Loosely modeled after the work that director-writer Eve Ensler conducted at the maximum-security Bedford Hills Correctional Facility for Women, minus the celebrity actors, the Prison Monologues performances have ranged from intimate school presentations with forty people in attendance to an overflow crowd of fifteen hundred in the Roosevelt High School's sprawling auditorium.[2] Performed at high schools and middle schools across the state, as well as at local and international conferences on Oʻahu, including the annual conference of the Office of Youth Services, the Hawaiʻi State Coalition against Domestic Violence conference at the state capitol, the Pacific Rim International Conference on Disability and Diversity, and the ʻAha Wahine Conference, and in the latter years of the program in the outer islands of the Island of Hawaiʻi and Maui, the Prison Monologues was heralded by Linda Lingle, the former governor of Hawaiʻi, as a "must see."[3]

Nevertheless, the director of the Prison Monologues, Pat Clough, seeks to circumvent the commodification of the women's words and simultaneously permits and harnesses resistance in conjunction with reform. As the reader becomes a vicarious bystander to the Prison Monologues performances, she registers the quandary of a state-sponsored redemption as both censoring and productive. Indeed, in some instances, the performances shore up the legitimacy of the state. Utilizing the lens of performance studies, I analyze the slippage between performativity and life writing, exploring the model of reform behind the Prison Monologues project and the tensions between the "sacredness of testimony" and the "commodification and consumption of testimonial discourse."[4] Within theaters of testimony, individual narratives of trauma are frequently "escalated to the universal narratives of abandoned childhoods."[5] This universal narrative of the fall (suffering) and its corresponding ascent (overcoming suffering) is an indelible character in the Prison Monologues, explicitly designed as a *puʻuhonua*, or a transformative site of refuge and forgiveness.

In an interview at the facility, Vailea, one of the original stars of the Prison Monologues, describes the Monologues as a ritualistic, sacred theater. Vailea speaks for the group in her insistence that the women feel "so anointed up there"—on the stage or in the classroom. All the Monologues participants I spoke to conveyed their belief that the presentations "saved lives"—their own and those of the high school students, whom the women lovingly call "the children." Vailea, a Samoan woman with an avalanche of waist-length black hair, reiterates my observation that even after my twenty-odd viewings of the presentations, the Prison Monologues never become boring.[6] As she intimates, "I felt so misunderstood growing up. We have performed for thousands and thousands of kids. I am at the point that if we save even one I feel good. So you would think that with every single experience, it would become boring. But it's not. Every single time something happens. And every single time I shed a tear for a kid that is going through some hurt. If they are misunderstood, I feel as if I am there with them. Reliving their experiences with them."[7]

Given the ephemerality inherent in performance, the Prison Monologues, unlike a written text, is inconstant. The dramatic utterance houses a transformative essence more vibrant and alive than the words on the page. In this sense, the Prison Monologues program is an extension of the creative writing classes. The Prison Monologues performances resemble community theater in that they blend "theater" with the staging of human rights—in this case, the rights of the women inside, as well as of the school communities that share similar cultural, familial, ethnic, and political locations with the women.[8] The Prison Monologues project straddles the divide between performance and pedagogy, between performance and the sharing of life narratives, and between performance and spoken word. The Monologuers' complex scripts draw on familiar scripts of redemption even as they subvert national narratives that disavow the realities of domestic abuse, poverty, and disenfranchisement. They counter the tragic narratives by performing them alongside hopeful narratives and utilize the power of writing and performance to attract and compel audiences.

Nevertheless, transformation is constrained within gendered cultural scripts and punitive institutional structures. Indigenous healing practices embedded in prisons at once offer avenues for healing and serve as an arm of the carceral system, which mirrors the tribulations in the loss of sovereignty. Indigenous cultural practices are frequently appropriated and staged by carceral institutions and the state to garner funding, while at times not authentically or appropriately benefiting the women inside. In 2015, I visited Grand Valley Institution for Women (GVI), a federal prison in Kitchener, Ontario, as part of the Walls to Bridges prison facilitator training. At that time, the inside women expressed to the women in the training—First Nations activists and Canadian academics—that they frequently felt like objects of "study" or specimens, despite the program's ideology of dismantling the borders between the "inside" and "outside." One woman spoke impassionedly about the power of prison tours to dehumanize those inside. Despite the history of genocide and the contemporary violation of First Nations' rights in Canada, at the time of my visit there were Indigenous smudging practices and a sweat lodge in place at GVI. The incorporation of Indigenous healing practices at GVI, as at WCCC—to "service" the overrepresented Indigenous populations in confinement by the state—thus presents knotty ethical issues.

The Prison Monologues project falls within the genre of community theater, given its penchant for pedagogical lessons and transformative advocacy of both the performer and the spectator. The performances serve as aide-mémoire or cautionary tales about the perils of making "bad" choices not only for the teenagers but also for the adult audience. Lacing its script with prophecy, the Prison Monologues traces the spine of twelve-step programs and redemptive narratives: "If you avoid temptation, you can have a life worth living." Mark Kawika Patterson, the former warden, envisions the project as a political missile to dismantle intergenerational incarceration. In an interview with Dr. Eiko Kosasa at the facility in 2013, Patterson explains that "sixty-five percent of the children of the [inside] women go to jail. They [the youth] are keeping the Criminal Justice system in business."[9] Wryly confirming that the Hawaiian cycle of incarceration mirrors national statistics, Patterson imagines the Prison Monologues as an antidote to recidivism and an opportunity for the women to give back to a community that they have "wronged." The Center for Hegemony Studies, which produced and archived "Journey to Justice: A Conversation with Warden Kawika Patterson and Eiko Kosasa: Part One," describes the Prison Monologues as follows:

> One of the Center's more public programs . . . where women write about their past experiences and perform their written work at schools and other venues, as a means of giving back to the community. . . . Soon after his appointment as warden, he [Patterson] realized that female inmates were imprisoned for non-violent crimes and thus began to implement ways to transition the Women's Community Correctional Center from an institution of incarceration to a place of healing or sanctuary (puʻuhonua). In this initiative, he welcomed a variety of community-based organizations to offer their programs to female prisoners, because he realized that his institution had been dealing with larger societal issues than just individuals who had committed crimes. Moreover, Patterson concludes that it will take the efforts of both the public and private sectors of society to create this sanctuary for incarcerated women.[10]

Evident here is Patterson's belief that the Prison Monologues program, a form of restorative justice, is a reciprocal venture. Not only is it an avenue for the women to give back to the community, but equally important, it fulfills the community's *kuleana* (responsibility) to restore the sanctuary for the women. This reciprocity is in alignment with a Hawaiian epistemology. The warden's insight that the personal narratives of the women deepen in accordance with their longevity in the program points to the therapeutic and restorative nature of the programming.[11] At the same time, the Prison Monologues program has ushered in some renown for the Kailua Prison Writing Project, the facility, and the warden himself. In this sense, the program legitimizes the institution.[12]

The auto/biographical excerpts encased in the Prison Monologues "showcase" are performed as part of a scripted trilogy, which adheres to a chronological trajectory: "Who We Were," "Prison Life," and "Reflections." This trilogy is faithful to the arc of a conversion narrative, duplicated in Clough's structuring of most of the *Hulihia* volumes. The conversion narrative is one of the most common narratives in the Prison Monologues program. A contemporary form of conversion, it draws upon canonical and historical conversions such as enforced prisoner confessions and conversions as public spectacle, deathbed conversions, and ritualistic conversions performed in religious institutions, all of which aimed to deter apostasy.[13] Contemporary audiences acclimated to conversion narratives through experiences in the church readily receive the Monologuers' public renditions of their private transformations. Ultimately, the Prison Monologuers showcase their preconversion tortured identities in "Who We Were" vis-à-vis their triumphant postconversion identities in "Reflections."[14] The writing and performance of the inside women's life stories travel across time and are showcased as a "performing self . . . negotiated between one's past and present."[15]

In *Performing Exile, Performing Self*, Yana Meerzon claims that a tripartite schema structures Western and Greek theaters of exile. This structure also resonates with Clough's tripartite mapping of the Prison Monologues: leaving home ("Who We Were"), living in a new country ("Prison Life"), and passage home ("Reflections"). Following this pattern, the prison is the "new country," a floating island with its exacting customs, idiosyncrasies, and habitual ways of life. In the Greek "democracy," exile was envisioned as both a punishment and an existential journey, a psychological process.[16] All of the twenty Prison Monologues performances I have witnessed addressed exile as both a physical and a psychological location. Meerzon argues that though exile results in displacement, dislocation, and depression, it is also artistically regenerative, and this quality of reawakening is apparent in the Monologues as well.

The Prison Monologues presentations are theatrical. The space of the Monologues, like the *puʻuhonua* itself, is imagined as a sanctuary: a site of transformation. As in other theatrical venues, to cross the stage—whether a bare classroom floor or a raised proscenium—is to passage across a delineated border into another world. Clough contests the reception of the Prison Monologues presentations as "performance," instead envisioning them as "presentations." The students, by contrast, refer to them as "lectures," inserting them directly into a familiar pedagogical framework. As these "presentations" at times occur on a proscenium stage with lighting and props, their proximity to performance is nonetheless palpable. Rehearsals convene every Saturday and sometimes on Sunday; women must "audition" for the Monologues, followed by "tryouts"—all ingredients that inscribe the process as theater.

This rest of this chapter, mirroring the structural three-part conversion narrative, is composed of three sections. The first draws on the warden's, Clough's, and the women's testimony to trace the creation of the Prison Monologues. It is informed by the one-on-one interviews I conducted with the women at the facility and interviews on the outside with women who have been paroled. The second section of the chapter moves to my own creative re-creation of a performance, staged within its corresponding tripartite structure: "Who We Were," "Prison Life," and "Reflections." It is important to note that this performative rendition is not a singular re-creation of a performance but an amalgamation of various performances in different venues.[17] Women assume the formula and texts of prior iterations of the performance, for example, when a woman leaves the facility and gifts her poem or letter to another woman to enact. In the renarration and repetition, the performers and the performances are in a sense transposable. Finally, in the third section, I chronicle the ways in which various interested parties—Clough, the warden, the inside women, the guards, the media, the audience, and myself—read the meanings of these performances. In this way, I conclude with layered reactions to the Prison Monologues presentations.

The Audition

It's Saturday, February 6, 2013. I attend the Prison Monologues audition, which is held in one of the larger education classrooms at the facility. Twelve inside women are present: Liezel, Ivelisse, Vailea, and nine women who have come to audition for them, along with Pat Clough. With the imminent departure of the core members, all of whom will be facing parole in 2014, Clough needs to find new members. She initiates her Prison Monologues Lab—a training ground for new women who wish to participate in her successful outreach program. Clough is adamant about not identifying the group as "performers."

The selection process into the Prison Monologues is particularly rigorous: a process that both Clough and Warden Patterson oversee. The prerequisites to becoming a Monologuer include positive performance in the creative writing classes; "good behavior," which requires compliance with administrative and institutional rules; and having "good" institutional standing, which usually means a minimum-custody status that allows the women to exit the facility.[18] There are also amorphous requirements at play in the selection process, including each woman's appeal and ability to relate to students, as well as Clough's desire for a representative selection of women based on age, ethnicity, and sexual preference. Many of the inside women vie for membership in this elite group due to the obvious privileges it bestows, particularly the opportunity to engage with school-age students, to impact students' lives, and to participate as citizens on the outside. The fact that the postpresentation reception includes a spread of nonprison food is quite a draw as well.

In a nearly two-hour interview at the facility, Vailea confirms the rigorous emphasis that Clough places on the role of writing in the Prison Monologues program: "You know Ms. Pat—the Prison Monologues is her baby. She put me through this whole interview. She encourages us to write—now Ivelisse, Liezel, and I journal every day. I never thought I was a journaling type of gal. And it doesn't have to be a poem. She wants us to be reflective, to be able to express our feelings. To give a voice to anger. To pain. To disappointment."[19]

At this Saturday audition, Clough will evaluate potential Monologuers' authenticity, commitment, and talent. With the support of Liezel, Ivelisse, and Vailea, Clough firmly lays out her rules and expectations of what it means to be a Prison Monologuer. She takes the mic in her role as impresario. Clough elucidates:

> We are not changing the so-called "script." But we are changing the representations of these stories. We are looking for all these stories and voices to not be the same. "Who I Was" is the introduction for the audience. "Prison Life" is for those who don't know [what life is like inside]—even the children, *especially the children.* The "Reflection," including the letters home and kids' day, is part of the enriching experience while here. All of this stays the same. So don't go out and just *wing* it. We work from the core, foundational pieces of writing. Writing is very important to them [the Prison Monologues women] and to me. That's why taking the writing

class is extremely beneficial. It is about *integrity*. And it starts here. Reiko and Liezel were both part of my first creative writing class ten years ago. We have won so much praise: it is the *courage to repeatedly tell the story*.[20]

Clough inserts herself as a character and community member of the Prison Monologues—as part of the collective "we." According to groundbreaking performance studies theorist and director Richard Schechner, if "rituals are performative . . . and performances are ritualized," then Clough's insertion of her own testimony as a "codified, repeatable action" is among the ritualistic practices of the "beloved community."[21] Clough's insistence on the integrity of writing echoes her commitment to the transformative power of the Kailua Prison Writing Project, as well as to her belief in the grueling work of writing as craft. One of the prerequisites for membership in the Prison Monologues program is attendance in at least one term of Clough's creative writing classes. Most of the women selected for the program are already students in her intermediate/advanced class, unless they have exceptional writing and dynamic performance skills. An example of such a student, whom we met in chapter 1, is twenty-three-year-old Lahela, institutionalized as a juvenile in the Hawai'i Youth Correctional Facility. Clough admires Lahela's poetry, her articulate comments, her desire for change, and her youth, all of which forge Lahela's connection with the mostly teenage audience. However, her minimum-custody status at the facility is often in jeopardy due to administrative infractions. Her sister, who was arrested with Lahela for the same crime and sentenced to the facility, cycles in and out of the segregated housing unit, which has a deleterious effect on Lahela's moods. Despite Clough's aspiration to recruit Lahela to the Monologues, the maintenance of a minimum-custody status is not negotiable.

As an introduction to the Prison Monologues program, Clough positions the three-part structure as pedagogical lessons for the audience: lessons that are byways from the outside to the inside. Another instructional lesson that Clough wants to impart is the necessity for discipline and courage "to repeatedly tell the story." The fact that the Prison Monologues presentations ritualistically perform a narrative for an audience that is at once communal and markedly individual—a tale that performs destruction and resurrection—positions them as a theater of witness.

Clough passes the mic to the more reticent Liezel. Clough and Liezel are close, and in some ways Liezel is Clough's second pair of eyes. Clough trusts Liezel implicitly and is instrumental in her commutation. In fact, when Clough departs after the summer term, she invites Liezel to teach her class to the inside women with mild and moderate disabilities.[22] Clough expressed to me that she would prefer that all her students arrive at the classes with at least a high school diploma, but due to the lack of support from the educational liaison, this is not the case. Liezel gently and deliberately instructs the auditioners:

> The Prison Monologues is not about vanity. It's about looking at a bigger world. Getting out of the small world in here. When we started the Monologues, two kids were invited with us to the state capitol. They were included in a professional community as part of the domestic violence conference. We were the keynote speakers. Adults are the *new* audience for the Monologues. Why are they drawn to us? We teach them how to reach the kids. *So* what did we learn from the adult audience that we didn't expect? They have their PhDs, their therapist licenses, but they don't know anything about the kids—*our* kids. It is not about reading or writing a paper. *This is not acting—we are not acting.* This is real life. The hurt we've been through is real.

The inside women claim the teenagers as their own kin, forging affective ties across generations. It is their veritable suffering—"the hurt we've been through is real"—that enables the inside women to reach their teenage audience: a bond that eludes the teenagers' teachers and community members. Liezel highlights one of the tenets of Clough's program: the Prison Monologues is not theater—an ideology that Vailea and Ivelisse resist. Vailea jumps on the mic:

> Attitude is important. The consideration for others on the team. People are hustling for us. Ask Melinda when she messed up, we addressed her on the spot. It's not about her—it is beyond the gate. Don't waste our time—we don't want to waste their time. Some people have come out with us and they are not in sync with what we believe in. You guys will have the paparazzi chasing you soon and I ain't lying. We break down thousands of kids and bring them to one place. They see the bond and affection we have for each other on stage. [And in turn] they open their minds and hearts to each other.
>
> Now the chairs have personalities. The kids want to sit on them—*they do*! They participate as if it's a place we have returned to. They face each other . . . they pay attention to each other. In this sense it is theater. It becomes dramatic—a *dramatic* gift of each other's lives. Please know how

important the Prison Monologues has become to us. We have no problem telling someone to step back.[23] If you come on, *humility* plays the biggest part. Never forget where we come from. If we decide that you are toxic to our group, we have no problem telling you so. *Just food for thought.*[24]

Clough elegantly sidesteps Vailea's callout—itself tinged with a sniff of drama:

Think about your delivery. Not about being dramatic right now but *feeling* your message. Like in class when we all feel it. They [educators, prison staff, politicians] want to be more effective. They want to have your sensitivity and credibility without having had your life experience. It's hard to do. That's why they are forming partnerships. You have been through the system: you know what works. The women who developed the Monologues didn't have a professional community as a goal—but now the community is asking *us!* They have never done this before. The professionals are boxed in by the system, by a lack of initiative, a lack of thinking outside of the box. Who would have thought that you were the ones to be their teachers? It is enormously exciting to see what type of potential comes out of here.

A host of competing themes punctuate the audition, which is a template for what Clough and the Prison Monologues women expect from the incoming members. Vailea passionately argues for "drama"—the "paparazzi"—a position antithetical to Clough's core beliefs, and in opposition to the humility that Vailea herself demands. Ivelisse, who matches Vailea's penchant for drama, is markedly and uncharacteristically silent for the entire audition. I later uncover that Ivelisse and Clough have been struggling around Ivelisse's "stepping out of line." Liezel claims the teenagers as her own children, while Clough exhorts the Prison Monologues cohort as community leaders. Vailea ends her edgy speech with Clough's favorite expression: "Food for thought." Her swift ability to code-switch between cultures and languages, such as "People are hustling for us. . . . You guys will have the paparazzi chasing you soon and I ain't lying. We break down thousands of kids and bring them to one place" and Clough's pedagogical phrase "Food for thought," illustrates Vailea's brilliance at working an audience. Vailea employs Hawaiian Creole English when talking to the inside women and uses it hyperbolically in performances, but in the same breath she utilizes standard English and duplicates Clough's language.

At the onset of the audition, Clough distributes a rating sheet that serves as an introduction to the Prison Monologues with a numeric rating scale. She asks the women to rate themselves numerically in accordance with the ten categories on the sheet: Why are they at the audition today? What is the purpose of the Monologues? How would they rate their own relationships with motivation, initiative, curiosity, leadership, teamwork, honesty, credibility, and timing?[25] She emphasizes her philosophy of the Prison Monologues, which requires a "serving," rather than a "helping," temperament. According to Clough and the Monologues team, Melinda was "let go" from the Monologues because she exhibited codependent behavior with the other members on the team. Clough says: "Serving is knowing yourself—developing skills, insights, and self-knowledge. You offer your message because you know who you are—you are humble. Helping creates a dependency—your dependency on being recognized, seen, admired, and needed. Here the image is more important than the message. This is *not* what I'm seeking!" There is a whiff of discipline in the auditioning process.

In this Saturday's Prison Monologues Lab audition, participants share (audition) their own traumas for the core Monologues women. One of the women recounts that despite meticulous documentation of abuse in her home as a child, child protection services (cps) returned her to her father, who raped her repeatedly beginning when she was a middle-schooler. In halting prose, she reassembles her memories of sitting on a long bench in the drab cps office, her short legs scuffling before her and seeing the shadow of her father's shoulders loom in the glass reflection. He had come to collect her, to take her "home." She recounts how beaten and ashamed she feels because she is pregnant at the time with her own father's child. There is a hush in the audition room, but there are also nods of recognition. Each woman auditions her own traumatic and personal remembrances that translate pain into performance. In performances of pain and atrocity, as Richard Schechner argues, the "real" transforms into representation and catastrophe risks losing its purchase in its multiple replays.[26] In today's highly mediatized world, there is a strong desire for the "real." Yet catastrophe does not relinquish its "purchase," despite its reiteration, when testimonies of shared suffering and identification are bound by collective experience. As the auditioning women share their histories of incest with the core Prison Monologues group, a currency of pain lingers in the room.

The Performance

We are in the cavernous President Theodore Roosevelt High School auditorium on windy Nehoa Street, which sits on a hill a stone's throw from downtown Honolulu. The school's website attests that it is the highest-achieving high school in the state, but with financial investment in the private schools, such as President Obama's alma mater—Punahou—and the recent gang activity at Roosevelt, this claim seems dubious. Over one thousand bodies pack the auditorium. It seems that the entire school is here on this sunny Wednesday afternoon.

Six women—Vailea, Ivelisse, Liezel, Melinda, Barbara, and Reiko—sit on six wooden stools elevated on a proscenium stage before the teenage audience, teachers, and administrators. Their prison numbers are inscribed prominently on their navy carceral tops—their last names, an afterthought. The inside women shift their legs and torsos on those wooden stools. A moment of measured silence follows, redolent of a prayer. Vailea's robust voice booms as she rises from her stool and strides across the stage.

"Good afternoon, y'all! " The "y'all" is out of place against Vailea's Hawaiian Creole English. "We are here so much—I feel as if I am a student here with you." Reserved giggles rupture the tension that hangs over the scene.

Vailea is on fire today. "If we have a chance to touch a life, it is beautiful. One day you will be professionals, leaders in our community. We are just like you—except behind bars. Close your eyes. Are you there with us? Open your eyes and receive every single hurt. Prison is the devil's playground. So which of you are Samoan in here?" Her direct performative command transports the students to their own injured spaces. It summons powerful identifications with the audience and collapses the women inside with the students outside—a gesture that serves to dismantle the walls between those in the "free" world and those inside. This enjambment can be construed as a cautionary parable for the witnesses.

Vailea's employment of a childhood game, connected with dreaming and magic, is a theatrical sleight of hand. A teenager with gargantuan blue earrings, hemmed by a pink flower decorating her ear, shyly lifts her hand in response to Vailea's question. This cultural exchange is a frequent element in the presentations and their dialogic response. After a presentation for criminology students at Chaminade University in the Kaimukī neighborhood of Honolulu, I speak to a Samoan student, who confides that she wanted to ask Vailea a host of questions, "but I shame. Vai made me think of my 'ohana."[27] Frequently, the Samoan students are drawn to Vailea because she performs her Samoanness as a cultural entrée into a familial connection that is often troubled for the students. The Samoan students gravitate toward Vailea, either publicly through specific questions addressed to her or by their crowding of her after the performance. This identification across cultural and national boundaries is complicated. Many of the Samoan students are first-generation Americans. Their parents, predominantly born in the unincorporated territory of American Samoa, are US nationals who are denied citizenship. Thus the teenagers are located within the trauma of a colonized relationship with the nation-state—not unlike Kānaka ʻŌiwi (Native Hawaiians). The alliances the Samoan students form with Vailea are polyvocal ones that stretch across familial, national, cultural, and generational divides. Vailea shares the experience of familial abuse with the students, as she does during our interview—"we all got lickins"—a discipline that Vailea frames as a cultural tradition. Samoan parents, she explains, value discipline, and respect for the elders is paramount. Many second-generation Samoan teenagers live in a world culturally detached from their parents.

A four-minute video, directed by Kimberlee Bassford of Making Waves Films, is projected on a wide screen above the women perched on the stools, accompanied by a soundscape.[28] "The camera follows the Monologues presenters through the process of coming into prison, scenes in the dorms, and brief interviews."[29] The opening video is poignant and powerful. Haunting music plays as a backdrop. The close-up frame of the inhospitable barbed wire fence, juxtaposed with a wide-angle pan of the magnificent Koʻolau Mountains, maps a tone of discordance as the viewer witnesses Ivelisse encased in belly chains, being processed by an invisible guard. The scene abruptly closes with a visceral shudder of the clanging doors behind Ivelisse's retreating back. Like performance, visual narratives proffer an alternative, and perhaps more charged, experience than the written word.

Part 1: "Who We Were"

After the video, in real time, perched on stools in a classroom or auditorium, the presenters begin their readings.

Ivelisse grabs the mic. She inhales and exhales, then waits until a reverent hush saturates the tense atmosphere: "I want to take you on a journey through a life that started out normal but somewhere in time turned chaotic, worthless, and desperate. I was trapped in a powerless, unmanageable addiction that has wasted two-thirds of my life."

Different casts of Prison Monologues women recite the opening lines on different occasions. Clough confides that the group experiments during the rehearsals until they discover what "works." This refrain of "what works," by both Clough and the women, reinforces the magic of theater that relies on a present-centric moment. The script that ensues is culled from many previous performances and from the *Hulihia XIII* journal itself. Individually authored poems, prose pieces, and declarations are adopted, adapted, and ultimately performed by a number of women and are therefore not always the speakers' own writing. In this way, the Prison Monologues becomes a communal tapestry in which narratives of trauma and hope are shared.

Ivelisse walks to the center of the proscenium stage at Roosevelt High School. She is enshrined in an unnerving blue light. Her typically boundless energy is subdued as she solemnly reaches for the mic and begins:

Time stands still as I near the gates of the prison
Shackles, handcuffs, chains around my waist
As I step off the bus, I look at the razors all around me
They represent the clean cut of this place—I will bleed here
As I walk through the gates,
The stopwatch of the next 10 years suddenly begins
Memories of my life shoot through my imagination in still shots
The pain, the tears, the laughter, the people

All slowly fade away

I took life for granted—numb to cause and effect
This time, will I learn from the rules or will I learn the lesson?
It's the system I could never beat
Over and over I've been locked away, or on the streets
I run for my freedom but never knowing what for
And that life becomes a part of me
The streets will always be a part of me

But now I step forward, take a deep breath
The doors slam shut
I'm in prison

Ivelisse's commanding performance of her "Who I Was" poem provides moral instruction about the consequences of poor choices, while testifying to a desire for the streets that is etched into her skin: "The streets will always be a part of me." This tension lends a rawness to the presentations, the slice of "real life" that mirrors that of the students themselves. Ivelisse's arresting line "the clean cut of this place—I will bleed here" is a double entendre: the razor wire, unlike the streets, is clean-*cut*—both redemptive and punitive. The space of the prison, as Ivelisse attests, is violent for its inhabitants, yet here Ivelisse acknowledges her new home as a potentially transformative one.[30]

Liezel, who has the lithe body of a child but a weathered face marked by pain, speaks in a heavy accent: "Look at us as your textbook, not as inmates." She offers up a pedagogical framework, a smorgasbord of lessons gone awry. The premise of the inside women as teachers and also as "textbooks" positions the inside women as consummate educators.

Ivelisse hands Liezel the mic, and Liezel wistfully begins to read "Who I Was," a poem that mourns her thwarted dreams:

A black and white portrait captures my innocence as a little girl.
My gaze is fixed on a balloon.
A string is tied to my wrist and I have no other cares in the world,
just the safety of my balloon.
During high school, I stood on a stage at an award ceremony:
first honors in academics, quiz bee champion, outstanding medal
      award.
I was a girl scout.
Oh how I've outgrown hopscotch and jump rope.
Sanrios, Hello Kitty and pajama parties,
The "I've got a crush on him" emotions.
I had big dreams,
I had lots of
"when I grow up, I want to be" ideas in my head.
Some came true, most did not.[31]

Liezel's poem, published in *Hulihia VIII* and showcased as the opening performance piece in the "Who We Were" part, echoes the *Hulihia VII* theme in its mourning of a paradise lost. It demonstrates a classical "descent into perdition" leitmotif that presupposes an ascent or a conversion narrative. Liezel speaks with a restraint that contrasts with Vailea's vivacity and Ivelisse's angst.

From the sonorous auditorium emerges a strong but slightly quavering voice that belongs to Reiko, a reserved forty-something woman with long hair and a stern beauty: *"I was raped and molested as a child."* One young man in the far reaches of the auditorium in a simple white and blue T-shirt is rocking back and forth, his hands like fisted steel over his eyes. In a conversation with Warden Patterson after the women return from their first performance in Maui, he confides:

Reiko is now in Hina Mauka. She resisted it [at first]. I think the Prison Monologues will be good for her. You see it with the women and men who are the most institutionalized. With Reiko—she was scared to come to me and I said you are going home and she said, "What's home?" Reiko doesn't know her parents. She was adopted into a family as a kid and they were the ones who molested her. She has been in prison her whole life and *this* is her home. She's scared to go on the outside. She said, "I'm an addict because of what I've gone through," and she doesn't want to give up her addiction. In the first three months of Hina Mauka, women get all sorts of reasons to leave . . . but Reiko has turned around and I am sure she will be successful there [at Hina Mauka].[32] I just want to tell you this so you know what's going on. It's good for Reiko to tell her story out there. One thing I notice is that the stories get deeper, the longer the women are in the Prison Monologues. For example, Ivelisse and Vailea. Vailea has probably changed the most through the Prison Monologues.[33]

Everyone has their own idea about who has changed the most—a "rehabilitation rivalry"—because of the Prison Monologues. Vailea tells me it is without a doubt Reiko: "Reiko has done the longest time—thirteen years. I remember when she first came out with us, her face just lit up. It made me so happy. Reiko had a really hard time talking about her kids. But now she does it all the time. The children are so supportive of her. They rush her after the performance, all crying 'Ms. Reiko, it's going to be OK!' Reiko had a really hard attitude—she has spent much of her time in closed custody."[34]

Warden Patterson confides:

Reiko was the most radical one. She escaped from occc [Oʻahu Community Correctional Center] through the fence.[35] Someone from the outside clipped the fence and it brought her much notoriety. I have known her through that—not really known her a long time—but known *of* her. She had a thirty-year sentence, reduced for good behavior. When we go deep into a community—Nānākuli, Bobby Benson, or Waipahu—I usually send only three of the ladies, Ivelisse, Vailea, and Liezel, the ones who are seasoned and who I know can improvise, can change things up if they need to. Bobby Benson asked us to come back in January and then I will take all the ladies. I would like to set the tone—to teach the other ladies.

Liezel, Vailea, and Ivelisse could run the Prison Monologues themselves. We sometimes go out without Ms. Pat—but not too much this year.[36]

The warden emphasizes the importance of a seasoned theatrical cast (a corpus)—one with improvisational aptitude. Vailea concedes that the warden has *some* power in deciding who will join the Monologues, but she also jokes about women who *claim* to have the warden's permission. Through my interviews, observations, and participation in rehearsals, I have gleaned that the opinions of the core Prison Monologues group— Vailea, Ivelisse, Liezel, and now Reiko—trump the warden and even Ms. Pat in who is allowed to enter, and ultimately remain, in the tight-knit team. This unwritten pact subverts a top-down decision-making process. In our lengthy interview, Vailea mischievously endorses the group's intuition about which new woman will work out or not: "Sometimes we just say, 'No Ms. Pat, NO!'"[37]

Conversion and redemption assume complex roles in the Prison Monologues presentations. Vailea divulges that the "children need" her and the Monologues women, yet in her own testimony about Reiko's pain and pathway to change, Vailea insinuates that it is the inside women who need the "children." In speaking about her future once she is released from WCCC— Vailea is the first of the core group to be granted parole—she explains: "It is Ivelisse's and Reiko's and my dream to form our own group when we get out."[38] Vailea describes her personal conversion narrative, which was reinforced by her experience on the Monologues team: "I always wanted to be a pastry chef because I love baking. But he [God] has been tugging at my heart and telling me that I am on the wrong path. I finally woke up a few weeks ago and decided I was going to go back to school at Kapiʻolani Community College for a degree in social work. The children need me. And I am just a servant in all of this [*laughs*]."[39]

Part 2: "Prison Life"

The presentation moves on to the second part of the triptych, "Prison Life." Liezel frequently introduces this part, as her calm demeanor conveys a sense of presence that the students call "leadership." She begins: "This section is about what we do in prison and what prison feels like. It's much easier to talk about what we do daily. What it feels like is much harder. We intend for you to have an experience of both." She solemnly passes the mic to Reiko, who reads Daniella's poem as if it were her own. Reiko, who is Native Hawaiian and Filipina, shares a similar cultural genealogy with Daniella, which allows her to more easily approximate the narrator.

> I wonder how many before me have sat in this cell
> Listening each night to the door slam shut like it's the gate to hell
> If only I didn't do this, if only I hadn't said that
> If only . . . if only, I can't take them back
> I'm not going to lay here and be sad and depressed
> I'd rather think of my kids and happier times—minus the mess
> The baby's laughter and smiles, small hands reaching to me
> My sister in a princess prom dress, magical and pretty
> Hula skirts twirling in unison, a beautiful lady in red

> "Ipo Lei Momi" playing in my ears, wearing a paper haku on my head
> I lay on this metal bed tonight
> And tell myself—the future is promising
> Soon—no more headcounts, no belly chains
> No more scratched mirrors
> No more panties hanging from bunks
> I will be free

Daniella's poem, "Prison Life," is rooted in the everyday life of the prison ("panties hanging from bunks")—and juxtaposed with an idyllic American dream of femininity ("My sister in a princess prom dress, magical and pretty"). These two oppositional offerings of the feminine—one mundane, the other idealized—are representative of the duality encased in the Prison Monologues: the allegiance with and resistance to narratives of redemption and authorization of the nation-state. Daniella's poem reaches for direct rhyme, which lends itself more effectively to performance rather than to the words on the page, and it simultaneously houses off-rhyme—"me"/"pretty." She references her part-Hawaiian heritage—"Hula skirts," "paper haku," and "'Ipo Lei Momi'"—as memory markers that rescue her from the monotony of prison life.[40]

The "real" labors as a commodity in our increasingly disembodied and disassociative world. The performance or celebration of an authentic self is what lends power to the Prison Monologues.[41] Like the poems in *Hulihia*, the Monologues leak out of their tidy borders, resonating with their teenage audiences' lives, whether familial incarceration or the teenagers' own array of the incarcerated: friends' suicides, parental abuse, drugs, alcohol, incest, immense alienation. Loneliness. Even though each performance follows this triptych spine—"Who We Were," "Prison Life," and "Reflections"—no two presentations are exactly alike. The setting, characters, and narrative arc are informed and altered by the venue, the audience, and the questions that arise, as well as by intangibles like the moods of the "actors" and their synergy on the "stage." The Roosevelt High School proscenium is an anomaly, as most presentations occur in bare classrooms on level floors; however, the props, such as the chairs and the women's letters, transform even the everyday classroom space into a theatrical one.

After a few melancholic poems that depict the depressing landscape of prison life, Vailea grabs the mic and playfully bellows: "So if you think that all we do in prison is sit around and boo-hoo all day." She wipes her eyes dramatically and continues:[42]

> We have jobs in prison that contribute to the running of the facility. Called worklines, we take turns cooking and delivering our meals to the dorms, doing the laundry for 260 women, maintaining the grounds and buildings, and the lucky ones go out into the community as the landscape crew helping to keep Kailua beautiful. We also take classes—parenting classes, anger management, life-skills, culinary arts, creative writing, and we can earn our GED if we came to prison without it.
>
> But back in our dorms at the end of our day, we are left with thoughts of home, family, what we miss—our kids, their birthdays, the moments we took for granted. Memories haunt us, letters from home make us happy or make us cry. Sometimes we create our own entertainment. In many ways, the evening is our time to be who we really are.[43]

Countering the cliché of doing hard (a slow and monotonous) time, Vailea offers up the evening dorms as a liminal space, where the women can be their authentic selves. The improvisational scene is perhaps the most theatrically complicit ingredient in the entire performance. This humorous departure from the mournful script usually elicits guffaws and chuckles from a spirited audience, grateful to be saved from the anguish of the earlier scenes. However, Vailea confides that at an appearance at Hawai'i Pacific University, which included many international students, the audience was mostly silent in response to the raucous skit. The skit is peppered with local references and is written in the local dialect—Hawaiian Creole English—so despite its universal themes of power, privilege, and humiliation, it targets a local audience. The scene, usually a crowd-pleaser, was created by Vailea's sister-in-law Teresa, a member of one of the first Prison Monologues troupes, for Vailea and Ivelisse. As the women write their own pieces not only for themselves but also for each other, the texts are enshrined as a repertory of sorts, which aligns the Prison Monologues with both theatrical and improvisational praxes.

Ivelisse and Vailea move to the front of the proscenium stage as the other three women drift to the back, congregating as a heckling chorus and ancillary audience. Ivelisse sashays audaciously into the make-believe intake room at WCCC. Vailea, with wire frames perched high on her nose and a smirk on her face, stretches to her full height and girth, assuming the institutional silhouette of an adult correction officer (ACO). She commands in a brash voice, bereft of empathy:

Step up here, come on, I don't have all day
3 blue uniforms, 2 white bras, 3 white panties (*Ivelisse disgustedly holds them up*)
6 pair white socks, 1 pair black slippahs
1 white bath towel, 1 white wash cloth
1 white pillow case, 1 white sheet
1 white blanket, 1 raincoat, 1 hygiene bag

IVELISSE: Um, exCUse me, *don't you know who I am?* I thought you already knew. I can't use that in my hair cause only brand names is what I wear. You want me to put on what? That doesn't even match my complexion. I shop more in the Clinique, the Lancome, you know, the MAC section.

You must be crazy if you think I'm gonna put on that. *Don't you know who I am?* I only sport ECHO or Baby Phat, Apple Bottom jeans, Ed Hardy gear, a pair of Guess boots and a set of Victoria's Secret sexy underwear!

VAILEA: That's right, keep it a secret—keep ALL that a secret!

IVELISSE: Come on, I mean don't get it twisted, don't you know how I roll—manicured fingers and pedicure toes, hair done up tight, outfit crisp and clean. Don't you know who I am? That's right, I'm a QUEEN!

Coach bag in my hand—Gucci or Louis Vuitton. Nikes on my feet or K-SWISS is what I got on.

I mean you really don't expect me to wear any of those? It doesn't even go with any of my clothes let alone coordinate with any of my accessories.

And of course my IPOD and my cell phone are a daily necessity . . . *I mean don't you know who I am? UH!* (The chorus chimes in chanting: "Don't you know who I am?")

VAILEA: Are you done? Cause if you are, let me *tell* you where you are, in case you got—AMNESIA.

You are no longer at the Hilton. From now on you sportin' not a damn thing cause now you in prison.

NO more shopping at Macy's Pearlridge or Ala Moana. You shoppin' at Correctional Industries in Hālawa cause that's where we get our store.

And if you want some matching accessories—I know *exactly* who can hook you up. I got a nice selection of ankle bracelets and one-of-a-kind steel handcuffs.

You pick—your choice, makes no difference to us, cause in a few minutes you gonna be sittin' in the lockdown hole cause that's how WE roll.

From now on you're inmate—number #A101270. And that's who you are. Now GIT!

And take your new clothes with you.

Ivelisse takes the bag and walks toward the audience. "That's how it is. We were each someone else before we became a number."[44]

The skit, although humorous, poignantly conveys the shattering transition from the free world to an enclosed one—an entry into a civil death. The women, stripped of the material signifiers of selfhood and the rituals of the familiar, are shocked at the erasure of self that accompanies incarceration. The written rendition is unable to capture Vailea's and Ivelisse's facial expressions, the large plastic garbage bag that stores the *inmate's* new "closet," the humongous white briefs that the ACO mockingly holds up before the snooty diva Ivelisse, or the stained white sheets sporting a massive hole. The skit functions within a familiar theatrical vernacular—the requisite humorous rupture from pain.

Part 3: "Reflections"

The arc of the presentation then turns to the most distressing aspects in the lives of incarcerated women: the loss of and displacement from their children. The final part, "Reflections," begins with a brief video depicting Family Day—one of the most powerful and emotive parts of the Prison Monologues program. The video clip comprises a loop of still images of mothers with their kids. In the prison, Family Day is a rare occurrence, and the still images showcased on a large screen attest to this deprivation. The parade of faces, unaccompanied by text, is commanding in its minimalism. The familial resemblances between mothers and children are at once uplifting and depressing, as the viewer contemplates the impact of incarceration. I have watched this video over twenty times, and every time I cry. Vailea sings—an accompaniment to the Family Day video, her honeyed soprano incongruous with her brazen persona. The revisionist Luther Vandross lyric "If I could dance with my father again" is reinscribed as "If I could dance with my daughter again." Artfully preceding "Letters from Home," this intertextual backdrop is deeply nostalgic. On the basis of this popular portion of the performance, Vailea has been baptized the "songbird."

The Family Day video leaves the audience emotionally shaken—teenagers sheltering their tears behind hair, caps pushed down on foreheads—and is followed by the equally plaintive "Letter from Home." Vailea—now transformed from prison guard to mother—sits subdued on her stool. She pulls an envelope from her work pants, opens it, and reads with slow deliberation the letter from "her" daughter:

Dear Mom,

I was sitting here reflecting on different parts of my life and trying to picture you being here. The funny thing is I can't remember any times you were here. The time I skinned my knee, you never put the band-aid on. When I was sick with the flu, you never made me chicken soup. When I got my period, you never explained what to do. I have a beautiful voice. I have won many singing competitions. You've never heard me sing. The first time I fell in love, I needed you to share my excitement. When my heart was broken, and I thought I'd never be the same, I longed to cry in your arms.

Mothers and daughters are supposed to share times and memories together. I should be able to look back on my life and have a lot of mommy-daughter moments . . . I have none. I'm not telling you this to hurt you; I just want you in my life. It seems that only when you get busted and go to prison, you feel guilty, and then you want to have contact with me. Your bad choices have affected my life.

I want a mom, full-time. I want hugs and kisses. I want a reason to love you. I need you here in my life. Don't you get it? I love you and I'm begging you to please think about me the next time you get out of prison. Think before you break the law, use drugs, and go back to prison with the same "I'm sorry."

Mom, please can we make some mommy-daughter moments—or is it too late? [45]

The deliberate trope that Clough orchestrates in "Reflections"—a recycling of Prison Monologues women parked on a stool reading a letter from their daughter or son, which they received "yesterday"—is an apt example of the transubstantiation of the "real" into re-presentation. The women carry the stools with them to the high schools in the white prison van, and they frequently invite the teenagers to occupy a stool in the postperformance dialogue. The chairs are mobile and persistent characters in the presentations and hold much significance because, as Vailea explains, the students love sitting on them and occupying the women's places. Other than the homemade letters the women bring to each presentation, tucked into their uniforms, the chairs are the only physical props utilized in the Prison Monologues.

Daniella, one of the original Prison Monologuers, who is now working at Honolulu Community College while on parole, discusses the performative gesture that collapses the powerful "letter home" with a perennial present. Daniella is an authentic witness to narratives of desertion, as she abandoned her biological family of four children for an imagined community: the world of *batu* (crystal methamphetamine) and alcohol. In a recent solo performance at Nānākuli High School, many of the students relate to Daniella's desire for an imagined community because of its promise to eradicate, even temporarily, the reality of their bleak present.

The compelling visual narrative of mothers and children in the Family Day video, followed by the letters, is heart-wrenching. The audience witnesses the collateral effects of incarceration—an injured family and community. During one of our long talks at Whole Foods in Kailua, Clough tells me that it is not always the reader's bona fide letter: it could be a letter written by another Monologuer who has been released and has given permission to one of the remaining Prison Monologues women to read the letter as her own. An archive of painful memories is thus built into the Prison Monologues repertory, which functions as a site of collective trauma and collective mourning.

"Letters from Home" is the most troubled segment of the scripted monologues, and perhaps the most theatrical because handmade cards or letters are used as props. The letters are indeed verifiably from the women's daughters; however, the women frequently inject into the script "I *just* received this letter from my daughter last week." This collapse of temporality—past performed as present—recurs in each performance: a repetition of the traumatic moment. In addition, the performance of "Letters from Home" allows the teenagers, some of whom were abandoned by their biological mothers, to cherry-pick their fantasy mother from among the Prison Monologuers. Ivelisse, for instance, is a young mother herself, which appeals to the teenagers, and her "Letter from My Daughter" is an audience favorite. Ivelisse is singled out by the teenagers, who frequently encircle her after the performance. She is the youngest and the loudest—the one residing on the margins. Her long Medusa hair, neck tattoos, thick mole, and pouting mouth are all features of desire that reel the teenagers in. I wonder at the length of Ivelisse's and Vailea's hair. "We don't get haircuts too frequently here," laughs Ivelisse, always the *kolohe* (rascal).[46] Ivelisse is twenty-six years old and has been in prison since she was eighteen. She is bejeweled in tattoos.

Vailea's letter from her daughter is a public confessional of shame that fits within the historical genre of prison autography.[47] Nineteenth-century prison memoirs aroused the public's thirst for spectacular memoirs of transgression, crime, and conversion. Contemporary audiences, too, are compelled by modern memoirs of transgression and rebirth. Life-writing theorists Sidonie Smith and Julia Watson argue that in our "contemporary culture of self-help . . . personal narratives of debasement and recovery as models for conversion, survival, and self transformation" carry considerable currency. Furthermore, "there is a growing audience for life writing focused on grief and mourning."[48] Noted life-writing scholar Paul John Eakin suggests that American national mythology rooted in individual triumph over adversity feeds the obsession in contemporary Western culture for confessional and personal storytelling. Smith and Watson contend that while narratives of loss are common historically, "in several recent memoirs . . . narration acts ambivalently as memorialization of mourning and its melancholic refusal."[49] After witnessing the Prison Monologues on multiple occasions in a variety of venues, from the intimate classroom presentations to the swanky Ala Moana Ballroom, I speculate whether the overwhelming audience response is about the passive pursuit of pain as *spectacle*. Clearly as a culture we are attracted to the horrors of the body, as is evident in the redundant spectacles of torture saturating every media conduit in America.

Yet the teenage audiences of the Prison Monologues are less implicated in this desire for *passive* pain, for they are frequently the active receptacle of real-life pain. Student audiences worship the Prison Monologuers for their representations of pain that echo their own genuine suffering. Teachers at middle schools and high schools across the state of Hawaiʻi confess that the women reach their students in ways that they cannot. Judges and lawyers, too, admire the women. In fact, the inside women's involvement in the Prison Monologues has literally saved some of them from an extended incarceration.[50] Anuhea, through her public performances with the Prison Monologues, was released early from WCCC and is now a community leader in her hometown of Hilo on Big Island. In the Prison Monologues made-for-television video, Anuhea is featured as a model of reform. In that video, an elated Anuhea stands in the Maunawili courtyard at one of the *Hulihia* dedications in civilian clothes, a dress hugging her pregnant belly. As she speaks to the incarcerated women about her past transgressions and current life, she rubs the large circle of her belly, gesturing toward a restorative healing and a continuity of life.[51]

Evolution

The multifarious responses to the Prison Monologues signal the power in suffering and collective witnessing to challenge a carceral structure that impinges disproportionately on Native Hawaiian and other Pacific Islander communities. As many theater practitioners have shown, prison theater functions as a restorative circle of reconciliation that ushers in an evolution for both the performers and the audience.[52] Yet performance also lends itself to the potential for voyeurism, or what Yana Meerzon refers to as "estrangement." She aligns this estrangement with exilic children's "borderline" existence, or what scholar Homi Bhabha characterizes as a "stillness of time and a strangeness of framing."[53] This estrangement is more likely in the prison: an exilic space that etches a violent border between public and private. It is this precise barricade that makes the study of theater in prisons that much more compelling.

The Prison Monologues, like Augusto Boal's Forum Theatre, is a form of participatory theater called "Simultaneous Dramaturgy," in which "the audience has the right to intervene and correct the actions or the words of the actors."[54] Even though the Prison Monologues women do not literally summon the audience to inform the script, they do rely on their audience's feedback via the question-and-answer period at the culmination of the program, as well as through direct audience address within the seemingly improvisational moments in the script. In fact, in a Prison Monologues Lab presentation at Nānākuli High School, Clough and the women enacted a form of participatory theater by inviting the students to read some of the writings of "inmates" who were not present. In this instance, the specter of a larger community of incarcerated women inflected the presentations; the individual performances of trauma opened up to incorporate a communal, national narrative of trauma.

Boal named his audience as spect-actor, to challenge traditional theater's oppressive use of the stage. "During a [Forum Theatre] performance, participants' voices are heard; its main aim is to change the people—who are 'spectators' and passive beings in the theatrical phenomenon—into subjects, actors and transformers of the dramatic action."[55] Boal's theory is "underpinned by a democratic aesthetic: in other words, it seeks to rekindle the capacity of all participants to perceive themselves and the world through art."[56] The democratization of the "stage," in which the audience occupies the place of both spectator and actor, is a key element of the Prison Monologues. The women frequently invite students to occupy their wooden stools (on the stage or in their classrooms) following the performance, which simultaneously aligns with Boal's approach of activating viewers and refutes his idea that actors are interpreters confined by their own subjective experience.[57] As the Prison Monologues perform as a space of atonement, the invitation for the students to sit in the places of the women "prisoners" and read their scripts works as an act of "witnessing beyond recognition" and reinforces the reciprocal process of performance.[58] Thus the actors too can be affected by the exchange, rather than confined. After "Who We Were"—the part that presents the women in their previous lives of "crime"—"Reflections" allows the students to share vicariously in the loss that the women encounter inside. Sitting in place of the women and reading their scripts incorporates the students into the performance as empathic witnesses, while encouraging the teenagers to make different choices in their own lives. The exchange is simultaneously moral, pedagogical, and emotional. In our last meeting at Morning Brew in Kailua, Clough explains that the initiation of the stools occurred in a performance by the closed-custody women at La Pietra High School. This was before a minimum-custody status was required for the women to go out to the schools. "It was kind of dramatic," Clough reminisces, "seeing the women in their orange jumpsuits, handcuffed, and the exchange with the stools."[59]

Daphne, one of the original participants, offers a lens into the reciprocity of the Prison Monologues, as well as its authority to intervene in national discourse. Daphne's script, "Giving Back," testifies to the social justice activism that the Prison Monologues inspires, and her tribute is used for the program's promotional materials:

Shortly after my release in 2010, I joined Warden Patterson's Trauma In-formed Care Initiative Team at WCCC and participated in a conference sponsored by the National Center for Trauma Informed Care (NCTIC) in Baltimore, Maryland. I have also been organizing Alumni events for TJ Mahoney and the Bridge furlough programs, as well as an apprecia-tion luncheon for employers that hire women from prison. As a student at Leeward Community College studying for my Substance Abuse Cer-tificate, I also work part-time at United Cerebral Palsy foundation. My goal is to go to UH Manoa in Spring of 2014 and begin the Social Work program while attending Leeward Community College—and completing my practicum for CSAC. I would like to receive my MSW in Social Work. I live by the words of Gandhi: "Become the change you would like to see."[60]

I have noted that most of the Prison Monologuers and alumnae decide to work in the arena of social work after their release, primarily with "lost" teenagers. The Prison Monologues thus functions as a manifold conver-sion tableau—personal, professional, and institutional—for the women inside and the audience outside. At times, the categories of "inside" and "outside" are inverted as the outside audience, afflicted by failed jobs and relationships, often share narratives that the inside women consider a more profound imprisonment than their own. This type of respect for the inside women is evident at some of the larger public events. On May 20, 2014, at the Pacific Rim International Conference on Disability and Diversity, the Prison Monologues showcase was advertised as a personal meeting with "amazing women for an afternoon of inspiration and transformation. [Women] who rock with their poetry, who write with their soul and who spread the word to thousands of people."[61] The fact that transformation was promised in a single afternoon speaks to the utopian impulse of the program. The verity that the inside women drew a standing-room-only crowd of human rights and disability rights activists illustrates the Monologuers' ability to impact local, state, and even national discourses on criminal justice.

Despite the popularity of this particular program, critics have taken prison arts programming to task for its propensity to exact confessions and compel repentance from "inmates." How, they ask, do we recognize if an "inmate" is genuinely sorry for her transgressions against society? Vailea speaks to the difficult issue of authenticity, as she reveals that her initial impetus to join the Monologues was merely to get out of the facility and eat nonprison food. The catalyst for her transformation was the appearance after a performance of a sobbing "little girl" who uttered through a waterfall of tears: "You and my mother are the same. The only difference is that she's not in prison." The middle schooler's words work as a powerful refrain that haunts Vailea, who confides that she revisits that scene at every school she performed at in the last four years: *We have reached thousands of children.* This experience transfigured Vailea into such a staunch believer that when she had the opportunity to select her reentry program, she chose to remain at WCCC's Bridge program over Ka Hale Hoʻāla Hou No Nā Wāhine (the Home of Reawakening for Women). Vailea could no longer imagine her life without the Prison Monologues.

The nature of performance occludes, as well as confirms, performances of "authenticity" by the Prison Monologues women. The women perform a veritable suffering that resonates with their audiences. Vailea confirms that principals, teachers, and social workers come to the Monologuers for advice, confiding, "We have known the students for years and they never tell us all the things they share with you." Teachers express the need for an authentic perpetrator and victim within the framework of the redemptive narrative in order to reach their students. In this instance, the women are perpetrators and the community is the victim, although the audience frequently gleans that the women are victims of traumatic pasts and abuse. The demand for what I refer to as the "exceptional survivor" is evident in the demand for the Prison Monologues showcase within local communities. The Monologuers are a mise-en-scène of authenticity (tangible trajectories of suffering), and many of the teachers herald them as pedagogical successes.

The Prison Monologues women perform as templates of success for the women in the larger facility. When they return from performances and presentations, the other women back in the dorm are often hungry for the details. Vailea says: "Some of them want to know what we ate, but most of them want to know about the children. The most important thing we do is teach forgiveness—you can only heal when you can forgive." For the inside women, forgiveness is a private and public endeavor that allows them to see themselves as both perpetrator and victim of personal and systemic injury.

When the Monologuers stride across the stage, the conventions of performance make their identities legible as "authentic" inmates.[62] The fact that the body of the ACO who always accompanies them is never far away marks the performance as a potential site of danger. Everyday garb—blue and white prison uniforms with white T-shirts peeking beneath the collars—transforms into costumes under the glare of stage lights. When these performances occur in convention rooms, the performances mirror academic presentations. Occasionally, the audience shifts from public school groups and university students to carceral and legal workers and politicians. The audience and the performative space, from the clinical space of the classroom to cavernous auditoriums, shape the performance. On one occasion—the Office of Youth Services annual conference at the Ala Moana Hotel—the Monologuers perform behind podiums and conference desks for a standing-room-only crowd. The inside women distribute small "business" cards that sport a miniature simulacrum of the cover of *Hulihia VIII*—a pencil portrait by an inside artist of a Hawaiian woman with a lei of flowers adorning her hair against an undeniably feminine pink background.[63] The *Hulihia* cover doubles as a business card, and the Prison Monologuers are now celebrities on the human rights/rehabilitation circuit. A long line of professionals waits to speak to the inside women. Surrounded by their groupies, the Prison Monologues women resemble rock stars.

As repetition or iterability informs performativity, there is both repetition and a departure from the script within the historical life of the Prison Monologues.[64] In 2014, the program entered its sixth year, during which time the fundamental concept and structure of the script remained largely unchanged.[65] However, some things were in flux, like the recycling of inside participants upon their release from the prison. Initially, the Prison Monologues troupe was composed of middle-aged and older women to whom Clough gravitated for their maturity and depth.[66] With the escalating demand for the Prison Monologues in high schools across the state, Clough incorporated younger women to appeal to the youthful audiences. After Clough's "stars" exited the facility, the skit could no longer be performed. "The skit was written for Ivelisse and Vailea by Teresa, Vailea's sister-in-law. No one else could perform the skit and anyways it was time to come up with something new," Clough confides. After numerous conversations, I glean that due to her commitment to the "truth" in the narrative, she rejected the escalating drama in the Prison Monologues toward the end of 2013. However, by then she was flooded with invitations from community organizations and panels requesting the Prison Monologuers as keynote speakers, and it was difficult for her to replace her "stars." The Prison Monologues was now an affective body of energy, traveling in a direction incompatible with Clough's tenets of humility, integrity, and community.

I AM INVITED to travel with the Prison Monologues to one of its repeat presentations at the Bobby Benson Residential Treatment Center, a drug treatment program for teenagers in far-flung Kahuku on the windward side.

The trip takes two hours, in part because the only way to reach Kahuku is to drive twenty-five miles west on the old, windy Kamehameha Highway that stretches across the island, hugging the sea. The night is stormy, and rain obscures the windshield as the ACO—the driver—forges ahead. In the prison van, Liezel sits in the back, reading unobtrusively, while the other women trade stories about past transgressions.

At the Bobby Benson Center, "celebrity" Prison Monologuer Ivelisse is a live witness to a teen's mother's death from cancer. Ivelisse grew up in Kahuku, where she committed crimes that she chronicles nostalgically on the two-hour ride in the prison van. Both Ivelisse's reminiscences en route, as well as the performances themselves, elicit a site of desire that is connected to nostalgia for a fictive Hawaiian "paradise lost." Kahuku is one of the few places on Oʻahu largely untouched by tourism. I remember catching the bus from Ala Moana to Kahuku, a four-hour round trip, to supervise special education teachers at Kahuku's middle school. The bus drops you off right on the highway next to the beach park, and the walk to the middle school is about fifteen minutes past the high school down a dusty road filled with squawking chickens. I was shocked by the dire situation of the special education teacher, who had little institutional support and few resources. Ivelisse's affection for Kahuku is attached to a desire for a lost home and homeland, which forges an immediate intimacy between the women and the teenagers. Indigeneity plays a role in this expressive framework and is simultaneously highlighted and sidelined within the structure of the Prison Monologues program.

MANY THEORISTS ARGUE that theater and prison are ideal bedmates in that theater grants the "inmate" the power to gaze back at the spectator/captor—prison guards, administrators, visitors who are present at performances. Furthermore, those inside and outside are attracted to theater due to the performative nature of punishment and the tension between the hidden and the public that prisons depend on.[67] Prison theater practitioner Paul Heritage argues that the regenerative power of performance, particularly as it connects to carceral theater, is that it allows for the fashioning of alternate selves. It comes as no surprise, then, that theater and arts programming have faced persecution from penal administrators. The WCCC is an anomaly among penal institutions due to the warden's full support for and endorsement of the Kailua Prison Writing Project. Heritage chronicles his experience as a theater arts practitioner in a male prison in urban São Paulo, where theater as a vehicle for creative expression is scapegoated by the institution for inciting a prison riot, which eventuated in the banning of theater arts programming in Brazil's prison system for over two decades.[68] Heritage points to a global crisis in the prisons in which prison administrators are hostile toward arts initiatives, in their rigid view of arts practitioners as "reformers." In this sense, arts programming can become an enemy of the state even while sustainable programming relies on institutional support. Heritage laments that the carceral space is a corrosive one for all its inhabitants: "The anger that is vented is about a system in collapse and about men and women who are constantly endangered by the work they do in conditions that dehumanize both captives and captors."[69]

Similarly, the Prison Monologues is more threatening to the WCCC prison guards than the *Hulihia* publications and the creative writing program precisely because the Prison Monologues "cast" is able to leave the prison. Exit from the facility is considered a privilege, which challenges the carceral workers' notions of "value" and "worth." This distrust of prison theater programming, as well as of the "inmates," results from a cynicism based on moralism and class. The ACOs are frequently poorly compensated for their long hours of service. Some arrive at the facility with an aggressive stance toward their "charges," as well as resentment toward educational prison programming, since they do not have the "luxury" of furthering their own education. I too have experienced the distrust of the guards on a few occasions on entering the facility.[70] Vailea corroborated that some of the other inmates and ACOs are jealous of the Monologuers; however, in her view, this envy is not pervasive: "The ACO Lisa, who goes with us most of the time, is firm but very supportive." Due to the minimum-custody status of the Monologuers, they are never handcuffed, and the ACOs June Sula and Lisa Kaululaau in particular are more like "tough-love" guides for the women than punitive despots. At one performance at Chaminade University, I notice Kaululaau wiping a tear from the corner of her eye, her substantial frame leaning against the wall as the Prison Monologues women share their pasts of abuse and drugs with the criminology students.

Clough and Warden Patterson have generated publicity designed to quell the concerns of carceral workers and the public about the freedom exercised by the inside women in the Prison Monologues. For instance, the Prison Monologues brochure claims that the women understand their teenage audience because they have experienced their traumas and repent their "bad decisions":

Under the leadership of Pat Clough and with the support of Warden Patterson, inmate writers are making their voices heard in Hawai'i communities, striving to interrupt the cycle of self-destruction that leads so many women and young people to prison. With "Prison Monologues," the outreach program of the Prison Writing Project, the women visit high schools, treatment programs, shelters, and conferences. They offer their audiences a first-hand perspective on prison life and the consequences of bad decisions. Each inmate participant has lived the traumas of the students they meet. Each carries a message of hope reminding students that they are still free, they are not alone, prison is not a home.

The brochures highlight testimonials from the students, who idolize the inside women. As one witness attests: "The difference between these women and me is that they have turned a bad situation into great lessons to teach teenagers like me to not make the mistakes that they made. They are identified by an inmate number but to me, they are my heroes." In the publicity materials, Clough and Patterson portray the Prison Monologues as an arm of community outreach, and thus an educational program—a communal intervention that interrupts cycles of destruction. One wonders whether this frame exonerates the social, economic, and carceral systems from culpability.

The Prison Monologues as community theater blends theater and the staging of human rights reinforced in Paul Heritage's example of the restoration of prison arts programming in Brazil. Here, Heritage aligns the promise of performance with that of human rights: "What emerged from the pollution-fueled smog of a São Paulo summer's day, was a confluence of theatre and human rights. The same promise that we find in performance is the deferred victory implicit in declarations of human rights. Like theatre, these declarations are always brought into the present by their enunciation and are based on the experiences of the past. But they point to a future that can be different, can be changed. In 'Theatre of the Oppressed,' Boal provoked us to consider that theatre is perhaps not revolutionary in itself, but rather a rehearsal of revolution."[71]

Daniella ends the day's performance at Kalākaua Middle School. She grabs the mic and proclaims:

First, we'd like to say that we're not here to tell you that you have to, you need to, or you'd better—do anything. Our childhoods were rained on by stoppers, words that were defeating. That's not what we're here to do to you. What we are here to say is each of you has the power to change, to hope, to rise above the things, situations, and yes, people that hold you down. The same power that holds the stars in the sky lives in you. Hope is not lost even if it feels that way. If you feel weighed down by expectations, shake it off. If you have shame in your life, fight it by speaking about it and doing what the voice in your mind says you can't do. If you think you're insignificant and not valued by anyone, know this. We believe in you. Each and every one of you are why we are here. You don't have to hide and you don't have to pretend. You don't have to carry the weight of the world on your shoulders. It's OK to be simply who you are—not who everyone around you thinks you should be. It's OK to be perfectly imperfect. We learned that the hard way. Thank you for having us today.[72]

Daniella's denouement to the presentation is published in *Hulihia VIII*, and beneath it appears a photo of three of the Monologue women, Ivelisse, Vailea, and Liezel, wearing multicolored lei. Vailea is wearing hers like a sling. The women are encircled by what appear to be middle schoolers—all small and wearing backpacks. Even though the image is still, the shy smiles exchanged between the women and the three boys are ineffable.

4 LOVE LETTERS

Dear Unbreakable Survivors,

There are many things I'd like to say to you, but I can't quite figure out the words to say. It's ironic because Mrs. Wilcox, our amazing English teacher has taught us how to incorporate our emotions and feelings through writing. . . . Yet here I am . . . staring blankly at this page, with nothing but scattered thoughts.

Scattered thought #1: Have you ever befriended someone so beautiful? And over the course of time, they started telling you about all the horrible people who've hurt them in their lives, like friends and family, and the only thing running through your mind is "who would ever want to hurt someone like you?" I wanted to scream out to *you* all, "you're beautiful," "you're wonderful," "You're magnificent," "look at you, you made it, you're here!," "*I love you.*" It seems so surreal to me—that yes, people do actually go through these things. They are not just a few made up stories merely written for entertainment. I'll never understand why it always rains hardest on those who deserve the sun.

Scattered thought # 4: (On the day of your speeches) I haven't cried like that since my best friend committed suicide 3 years ago. I miss her terribly of course, but I think suicidal people are just angels wanting to go home. But, how I wish she could've been here. How I wish she could've heard your speeches too.[1] How I wish she'd known.

I met a girl once,
Who sighed and told me she was not lovely.
And it confused me that she could not see
The sunlight shining through her scars.
Oh how I wish she'd seen what I'd seen.

Thank you all so much, for allowing me to feel again. Even if it was expressed through tears, thank you for allowing me to feel something because something is definitely better than nothing.

Love always,
Giselle[2]

Giselle's fractured and redeeming passages, "Scattered Thoughts," speak back to the three inside women from the Prison Monologues Lab who share their testimonial narratives during her English period at Nānākuli High School—a Title I school on Oʻahu's leeward side. The stories that Giselle and the other students witness that day are of three women from wccc's Prison Monologues program: Liezel, incarcerated for her involvement in a death of a child; Kailani, whose repeated rape by her grandfather paved her pathway into drugs and alcohol; and Mahina, implicated in a driving accident while "high on Ice," resulting in the death of a minor.[3] As these testimonies of incest, drugs, and murder spill out, the students accompany the inside women on an intergenerational pilgrimage to their own pained and sutured memories.[4] I frame the high school students' reactions to female "prisoners'" monologues as "Love Letters." The students' responses, drawn from two high schools in Hawaiʻi, represent native Hawaiian epistemologies.[5] The women and the high school students represent a range of Hawaiian and Pacific intersections, and the Kailua Prison Writing Project is rooted in Hawaiian practices of hoʻoponopono (reconciliation and forgiveness) that resist state-sanctioned inscriptions on Indigenous bodies. In this chapter, I analyze the written responses of students at Nānākuli and Kapolei High Schools to the Prison Monologues "presentations" to their classes.[6]

Giselle's "Scattered Thoughts" is an aperture into a performative dialogic: a showcase of participatory life-writing interchanges between high school students from two Title I schools on Honolulu's leeward side and the inside women.[7] These life-writing texts—mini-memoirs—transcend the genre of enforced confessionals and its corresponding retraumatization. Despite the horrors of adult traumas that visit the students, the students utilize the inside women's performances as projections into a future that they do not have to inhabit: an imaginary space, separate from their lives impacted by colonization. Through both identification and *disidentification*—a term I borrow from queer performance studies theorist José Esteban Muñoz—the students inscribe and imagine futures liberated from the frontiers of incarceration.[8] The students resist the prescriptive pathways of both their biological and surrogate families—the inside women—through gestures of love and defiance. Ultimately, the Love Letters and their dialogic interchange are a register of healing, not retraumatization, in which the students subvert national and prescriptive discourses of redemption and reform.

Giselle's remarkable confession, poetry intruding on prose, positions her as a secondary and participatory witness to the inside women's pain as she shares the agony of witnessing the suicide of her best friend, whom she doesn't name. Giselle expresses a perpetual longing for the family she never really had, which mirrors at times the elusive binary patterning of the loved and beloved. The women's performances, as both "poems" and "speeches," passage her to a place she has evacuated: a space of affect and hurt. The Prison Monologues performances release her from anesthetization and transport her back to a place of feeling. In this letter, Giselle suggests that her friend, who "could not see the sunlight shining through her scars," could possibly have been "saved," as is she, by witnessing the women's "speeches." Giselle experiences both the women's writing and her own as transformative and redemptive. Giselle's address of her "Scattered Thoughts" performs a simultaneous identification and disidentification. Separated from a larger and more condemnatory community that may not witness the women as survivors, Giselle sees the women within a discourse of societal suffering. She memorializes them as "unbreakable," even though their *breaks* and ruptures are performed so overtly.[9] Her writing, poetic and bare, serves as testimony for her reader. In this sense, she is a secondhand witness to an audience comprising the other students in her eleventh-grade English class, her teacher (Mrs. Wilcox), myself as intermediary, and you—the imagined audience reading this chapter.

"Love Letters" is the appellation I have ascribed to the letters and index cards the students offer to the women in the Prison Monologues and the Prison Monologues Lab after their school visits.[10] The sixty homemade cards and sixty indexes written by the students function as mirrors to the Prison Monologuers' confessionals. They are created as talismans for the six performers and the three women in the Prison Monologues Lab at WCCC. The narratives of trauma represent odes of longing to parents disappeared from their lives; they construct surrogate families and resurrect disappeared mothers, liberated from the complications of blood and kin. Just as the teenagers are witness to the inside women's transformation, the women in turn become witnesses to the teens' transformation, via the epistolary. Ironically, the women in the Prison Monologues who are vanquished mothers to their biological children are surrogate or performative mothers for the teenagers at the high schools, as the Love Letters reveal. The teenagers return the gesture of trauma in their elegies to the women: a calligraphic liberation.

I foreground the written testimony of the inside women and the students as a political apparatus to counteract the disciplinary regime at work in any carceral space, particularly one located in the larger colonized landscape of Hawai'i. The privileging of the inside women's and students' voices and the making sacred of personal testimony borrow from Native Hawaiian and Pacific Islander scholarship, such as Ty P. Kāwika Tengan's *Native Men Remade: Gender and Nation in Contemporary Hawai'i* and Katherine Irwin and Karen Umemoto's *Jacked Up and Unjust: Pacific Islander Teens Confront Violent Legacies*.[11] The inside women and the students at Nānākuli and Kapolei High Schools, the majority of whom are Native Hawaiian or part Native Hawaiian, are direct victims of Hawai'i's ongoing colonial history and are located in a particular genealogy of political trauma. Unlike the well-funded private Kamehameha schools in Hawai'i that are overtly politically identified with Native Hawaiian history, Kapolei and Nānākuli suffer from paltry resources, and many of the students are disidentified from a political framework. As Meda Chesney-Lind and Brian Bilsky state in "Native Hawaiian Youth in Hawai'i Detention Center: Colonialism and Carceral Control," "The carceral system has long been implicated in the colonization process, as exemplified by the imprisonment of Queen Lili'uokalani in Hawai'i. The overpolicing of Hawaiians continues to the present."[12] Similarly to the overrepresentation of Native Hawaiian women at WCCC, the authors posit that Native Hawaiian youth, who account for 30 percent of Hawai'i's youth population, account for nearly half (46 percent) of detention home admissions. That racial overrepresentation is also a gendered problem: "The racial disparity is particularly notable for Native Hawaiian girls, who account for 52 percent of those detained and are being held for the noncriminal status offense of running away from home."[13]

The bonds that the inside women form with students via epistolary and oral testimony are cultural productions that highlight political trauma, familial trauma, vulnerability, and marginality. The language employed both in the students' Love Letters and in the women's performances represents a mixture of Hawaiian, English, and Hawaiian Creole English—all inflected with exilic words that represent various Pacific locations including Samoa, the Philippines, the Marshall Islands, Palau (Belau), Guam, and the Federated States of Micronesia.[14]

This language speaks against the powers of colonization that inflicted cultural genocide through the demand for standardized English and the shaming of Hawaiian and Hawaiian Creole English.[15] The ban on the Hawaiian language was preserved until 1986, and today, according to census data, those who identify as at least part Native Hawaiian constitute only a fifth of Hawai'i's population.[16] The students who come from Hawaiian Creole English-speaking families on the west side of O'ahu seamlessly transit between Hawaiian Creole English and standard English in their Love Letters to the women. This fluid speaking between tongues can be read as a dissonance with, and a resistance to, the institution and the state.

This unique archive showcases a participatory life-writing exchange and the avenues in which trauma itself performs as the dialogic. The students' life-writing texts, which are direct responses to life—the narratives of memory, pain, and abuse of the inside women—house an assortment of witnesses and a cacophony of testimonies. In this sense, unlike in the "Home" narratives presented in chapter 2, pain is sutured and restorative because of its corroborating live audience.

Philip Auslander's *Theory for Performance Studies: A Student's Guide* reads: "Every theory frames and focuses our attention on some things while leaving other things outside the frame or out of focus. Thus, Performance Studies is always in search of new theories that might open up new ways of seeing and interpreting performance. Performance Studies is theory: it is the myriad conceptual tools used to 'see' performance."[17]

The methodological interdisciplinarity of my research reverberates with the theoretical frames of performance studies and queer studies, which collide in ways that trouble our notions of gender.[18] I draw on these performance theorists to engage the performative nature of the Monologues presentations and the analogous student reactions. Utilizing queer performance theorists' frameworks of disidentification as well as Judith Butler's formative theory on the performativity of gender, we can see the Love Letters as weapons of disidentification in their resistance to a majoritarian citizenship.[19] Race, gender, and indigeneity shape the violence faced by women at WCCC and the teenagers, who come from similar racial, cultural, and economic locations. Both are "queered" by witnessing and experiencing tragedy, violence, and generational trauma.

The students' auto/biographies are created and performed in response to the inside women's re-presentations of pain, which in turn elicit a dialogic response in the sense that the inside women subsequently write back to the students. These micro "truth and reconciliation circles" that puncture the prison walls, and which I articulate as performances of *pu'uhonua*, are generative and enduring. The performances described in chapter 3 are the seeds of what becomes an extended chorus of performances that unfold once the women leave the high schools to return to the facility and the high school students reluctantly return to their classrooms. This extended dialogue appears at times as poems, published as epistolary interchanges between the pages of the prison publication, *Hulihia*; at other times as unaltered student responses to the performances in the form of index cards, letters, questionnaires—frequently generated by the students themselves; and then, most enigmatically, as lingering afterthoughts that impact the students indelibly. These afterthoughts—the concrete changes that the students frequently actualize and record—are revisited when the women return to the school the following semester or year.

I argue in this chapter that the performances by the inside women in the Prison Monologues program and the students at Nānākuli and Kapolei High Schools suggest novel ways of embodying grief and trauma that move beyond the confession as a tool of redemption. As we follow the exchange between inside women and students, we see the emergence of coherent narratives of self—a wholeness that arises from finding one's voice in the wake of trauma. The primary archive of this chapter—the letters and indexes themselves—is a "call-and-response" to the women's performances/instruction/moral lessons/lectures, and the nuances of these exchanges are illuminated by a particular trauma scholarship.[20] The chapter is organized around the following themes: love letters and circles of intimacy; confessionals and autoethnographies; prison monologues/dialogues as expressive *pu'uhonua*; indexing speechlessness; and hearing and healing. These themes trace a journey through intimacy—its dangers and pleasures, its utterances and omissions.

Love Letters and Circles of Intimacy

After making my way gingerly around a crowing threesome of roosters and passing the oversize truck in the reserved space labeled "Warden," I ascend the three stairs to the administration office. Inside, I ring the bell at the desk, and Josie, the warden's secretary, comes out to greet me. She is dressed in a blue and yellow muʻumuʻu, local kine.[21] I have come to read the correspondence between Kapolei High School and six women in the Prison Monologues program: Vailea, Ivelisse, Liezel, Melinda, Brenda, and Reiko. Vailea, Ivelisse, and Liezel are all pioneers of the program; Melinda, Brenda, and Reiko are recent additions. I give Liezel, who works in the warden's office, a quick hug. Liezel walks quietly like a cat. She is efficient, effective, a natural administrator.

Josie delivers the Kapolei correspondence in a colorful package. As I open the manila envelope, the dissonant shapes and colors of the letters, penned in the students' handwriting, spill over the warden's koa desk. Pastel pink, baby blue, verdant green contours linger and loiter. Tortoise scripts, elongated vowels in pen, pencil, and high school marker, stumble over the edges of school papers. Many of the students underline their physical space in the classroom during the performance, showcasing a *lived* presence: "I was also in the last class in front wearing white converses and a blue tank top with long hair in a bun" (Makelina). These concrete self-descriptions connote an anxious attempt to be recognized, as if the teenagers are attempting to write themselves into the scripts of the women's lives; "I don't know if you remember me but I was one of the girls that said goodbye to you and Liezel." Subsequent to these guiltless and precise physical descriptions, the students frequently write hesitatingly: "I don't know if you remember me . . . ," reinforcing the vulnerability of their position as lover/beloved. This particular elegy is addressed to Vailea. Makelina concludes her love letter to Vailea with: "You have an awesome voice. I almost cried. I hope to see you again before I graduate. Love and god bless." Makelina reinscribes Vailea as an imperative witness to a milestone in her own life: her graduation from high school. It is bittersweet: Will Vailea still be in prison when Makelina graduates?[22] Will Makelina indeed graduate? The future of many of the teenagers is tenuous as they are injured by drug addiction and abuse.

The silhouettes on the oval koa desk recall the Valentines of our youthful and idealized imaginaries. Teenage boys and girls single out desired mothers: the beloved, love, and lover. They resurrect their own vanquished and abusive mothers and adopt the inside women as surrogate, stolen mothers. The women in turn select beloved daughters and sons to take the place of children they abandoned to drugs and the streets—all in a performative reimagining of family. *An invention.*

Scribed testimony (writing) speaks back to performed testimony (performance). As the women frequently articulate a fantasy relationship with their children outside the prison, the substance of a "home/homeland" represents a nostalgic site of desire, one painted in the hues of a nostalgic misremembering—a paradise lost. For many of the inside women and the teenagers, desire traces a pathway not only to a lost (domestic) home but also to a homeland: a longing for national and cultural belonging as well as for intimacy. The performances are staged within a testimonial theater of witness that blurs the boundaries between speaker and witness. The varied audience response, including the teachers' confessionals, confirms the authenticity of the Prison Monologuers and thereby reveals the ways in which the act of performance can erode barriers between prisoners and "free" persons, constructing complicated relationships of affiliation, family, and similitude. The acts of witness elicit a testimony of trauma, alongside the imagined alternative homes and families.

Confessionals and Autoethnographies

The students' letters to the women function as both confessionals and autoethnographies. They evince the fluidity of boundaries between the prisoners inside and the girls and boys outside, as well as the transformative imaginable of that interaction. Thulani, for instance, chronicles a life of abuse—her parents wanted for drug crimes, her attempts at suicide, the taunting at school because she is "fat, short, and unloved." A litany of trauma fills her paper, a somatic and psychological re-membering:

> *I am 15 years old with a storie to be told. When I was 2 years old my father passed away, I've been living life without him for 13 years. Throughout my 13 years without him I experienced what life really was. I was sexually touched at the age of 9, by my 45 year-old uncle. He touched me in places I never wanted to be touched.*

For Thulani, real life is about pain. In giving voice to her memory, Thulani asserts her agency: a verbal counter to her uncle's violations: *He touched me in places I never wanted to be touched.*

But I was young. I didn't know better. I was always bullied around
    because I
Was Fat, short, slow at everything and stupid.
I've always felt unwanted and unloved by my family
I would try to kill myself . . . stack 2 pillows on my face
And 5 telephone books on top of the pillows
Just for the weight

Life got harder.
Moved from Town to Nanakuli.
From Nanakuli to Pearl City

We moved in with my mom boyfriend's family.
My younger brother and I barely ate because their
Was only little food.

I did weed during my 9th grade year . . . I was just so stressed.
I did so much weed (spice) that it ended me in the hospital
For a whole week. I laid in that hospital bed thinking "what the hell
    Thulani."
When I got out of the hospital I felt thankful that god gave me another
chance
To live.

Thulani's poetry traces an unstable and impermanent home environment, uprooted yearly between neighborhoods. Yet her catalog of exile, displacement, and rejection culminates in a climax of redemption. The willingness to share these narratives, juxtaposed with the denouement of hope, is remarkable and is characteristic of the testimony of Thulani and her peers. Thulani, like many of the teenagers, faces a crisis that eventuates in transformation: a decided script of redemption and regeneration. As her writing divulges, Thulani has been hospitalized due to a drug overdose. At this turning point, she thanks God for giving her a second chance. Many of the Love Letters culminate with the teenagers gifting love, wishes, and hope for the women and, most important, bestowing their own confirmation in the act of forgiveness. The letters excavate personal trajectories and genealogies, but ultimately they perform as a community tapestry that comprehends cultural grief. The sophistication and capacity of the students to self-reflect is arresting and unexpected: a justly selfless performance. The Love Letters function as a circle of healing: a way of giving back. *Pu'uhonua.*

Warden Mark Kawika Patterson worships community. As we gather around the oval table in his office in the administration building, he speaks of the "circles of intimacy" created between the women in the Prison Monologues and their "benevolent community."[23] Patterson explains, "When I see the audience rush the women at the end of their performance, I always keep my distance, because this circle of intimacy is sacred. It should not be interrupted." As he recounts: "I come from a matriarchal family. The women were the glue . . . they held our family together. What we are missing in our lives today is the valuing of people's gifts. We have forgotten our people's gifts." The warden's positing of the postperformance encounter between audience and "inmate" as a "circle of intimacy" inserts the Prison Monologues within the Indigenous framework of *puʻuhonua*. The "circle of intimacy" that he names as "sacred" prescribes a compassionate hearing. His words offer a particular avenue in which to *see* the postperformance encounter—testament to the emotional assembly generated by the performances. The first school that employed the epistolary with the women at wccc was La Pietra Hawaiʻi School for Girls, a predominantly haole (white) and economically privileged all-girls community. "They were the first school that invited us," says the warden wryly. "It was not the first school we thought of. We wanted to return to the communities that the women come from . . . the west side."[24]

The Love Letters perform discourses of pain and abuse with the goal of the re-formation of the self, understood as "reform"—a disciplining of the body—as well as the re-formation of the wounded body.[25] Frequently, the students conclude their letters with gestures of *puʻuhonua*: "Mahalo nui loa," intone the students, positing the women as redeemers.[26] One student writes: "Thank you all so much, for allowing me to feel again. Even [if] it was expressed through tears, thank you for allowing me to feel something because something is definitely better than nothing." Despite the potential for reinjury, many of the letters express an unexpected process of rebirth: a journey back into living.

The theater of testimony, as discussed earlier, utilizes Native Hawaiian tropes: an extended healing circle and the concept of *puʻuhonua*—sanctuary and reconciliation. The precepts of *puʻuhonua* are performed within the presentations themselves, as well as being embedded in the text and subtext of the Love Letters. Despite their liberatory and resistant content, these Indigenous practices of testimony are also disciplined by codes and expressions—master narratives—that conform to contemporary cultural, political, ethical, and moral expectations.[27] Within the therapeutic gesture reside transformational expectations on the part of the "transgressor" and "victim." Within the pedagogical context, in particular, there is an anticipation of an intellectual, moral lesson; yet within the framework of the twelve-step program, from which the Prison Monologues subliminally borrows, there is also the assumption of a higher power. The act of retelling traumatic narratives works on two levels. First, the traumatic narrative loses its potential to *terrorize* through the reiteration of traumatic details, thus releasing its orator. Second, it aims to facilitate a communal healing, with its *mana* (spiritual power) to release its audience. Despite the aspiration to restore, healing is always incomplete: the students return to school, their biological families, child protection services, or the beaches, and the "inmates" depart to the prison.[28]

The Prison Monologues women's performances and their corresponding rejoinders can be viewed in conversation with the crisis of our national gulag: the warehousing of America's "surplus" populations—women, the poor, people of color. The performances that occur in Hawai'i's schools constitute an indictment of the terror and dispossession propagated by the nation-state. Prison activist and scholar Simone Weil Davis condemns the violence implicit in the forced, cultural expectations of the confessional, principally for the incarcerated.[29] Although the Prison Monologues adhere to a redemptive narrative, contrary to the aforementioned examples, the teenagers resonate with those scripted confessionals. One wonders if the Prison Monologues testimonials would be considered as authentic or effective if redemption was absented.

Feminist prison arts practitioners caution against encouraging sensational testimony from the women inside due to its potential to reinjure already traumatized women, and in this case a traumatized youthful audience. However, most students' letters express a sense of relief and comfort in hearing testimony that resonates with their own lives. Moreover, many function as gestures of empathy, as the high school students, despite their own lives pockmarked by pain, encourage the women on their difficult pathways, at times absolving them of their crimes. Many of the letters express the tone of a sympathetic magistrate—an inversion of the women's experience in the carceral and legal setting—most particularly for Liezel, whom the teenagers decry has been wrongly accused. Just as the Prison Monologuers are "teachers" for their audiences, the teens—in a pedagogical reversal—assume a parental posture toward the inside women. Generally, however, the students play the roles of daughters and sons.

The teenagers' writing frequently assumes a breathy tone, partly due to their inexperience as writers and their erratic and aurally influenced grammar and syntax. They proclaim their roles as undying witnesses for the women—whether metaphorically, spiritually, or concretely.

The compelling voices within the carceral institution reinforce exacting cultural scripts and forms of redemption. In the Nānākuli teenagers' written responses to the Prison Monologues Lab women—Kailani, Liezel, and Mahina—we encounter the performance of the genuine, empathic witness. The teenagers identify with Kailani and Mahina as fledgling performers, encouraging them in their retellings. "Mahina," one student emotes, "we are so proud of you even though this was your first time, we made you part of our family in our heart because of your courage and heart touching stories." However, some admonitions sneak in: "You are not *bad* women but have been influenced by *bad* people." Some of the teenagers hold simplistic ideas about "good" and "bad," although they rarely condemn the women. They witness the inside women's actions as "bad choices," sporting "bad consequences," yet they claim the inside women as their "role models" who provide pathways to "good choices."

The Prison Monologues function as an extension of the making of public memory, in which the teenagers transform into secondhand precarious witnesses, straddling the divide between empathic listener and victim—and even at times perpetrator—of traumatic histories.[30] As discussed previously, the circles of student witnesses are more like the women—culturally, demographically, narratively—than different. The precarity arises because of the performed testimony's potential for emotional reinjury, as the inmates' life stories may closely resemble those of the teenagers. Thus the psychoanalytic trope of transference is a potential character within the staging. Yet the students' letters and the women's testimony suggest that, more often than not, the relationship that emerges from the reciprocal performances is one based on hope rather than retraumatization.

The extended community of witnesses—the high school students and their teachers—forms an embodied community via the power of performance. Performance proffers a dialogic, multilayered, permeable exchange between the students and the women inside; between students and teachers; teachers and the inside women; students and their extended families; and the inside women and their extended families. The performative exchange elicits stories of bodies as well as spirits: a repertoire of corporeality. The injured body is enacted by the inside women and is in turn written and performed back by the teenagers.

Acts of reciprocal witnessing may also occur at the performances themselves. In the spring of 2013, I joined the inside women in the white facility van on a journey to the Bobby Benson Residential Treatment Center in Kahuku, where a fourteen-year-old teenager read aloud her own poem about rape and losing her mother to drugs and cancer.[31] Ivelisse serves as a living and concrete link to the teenager's mother, while the teenager represents Ivelisse's own daughter, who has been denied the opportunity of mourning. Besides being surrogate parents, the women, like the letters themselves, are conduits of information—an informal network of exchange, bridging present and past lives. At times, the women at WCCC know the disappeared biological mothers of the teenagers, who imploringly demand material evidence of this. Frequently the teenagers ask the women to send love to their mothers who are incarcerated at WCCC. After the performance, the teen and Ivelisse hold each other in an embrace that mnemonically summons the dead mother, with Ivelisse transubstantiated as the vanquished mother in absentia. "You know my ma," whispers the teenager into Ivelisse's hair. The inability to mark the passing of a loved one is one of the voluminous mournings that the inside women at WCCC share with their teenage audiences. Refusal of the right to mark ritual corrodes community, which aligns with the anguish of the civically dead. The inability to say goodbye to parents who die while the women are incarcerated haunts the women's writing and their disclosures in class. The location of Ivelisse's personal genealogy in the geographic space of Kahuku fortifies her as a secondhand witness for the teen to whom she is testifying, rehabilitating, "re-forming."

Literary critic Shoshana Felman argues that the secondhand witness typically disrupts the shape of the narrative, but as the Love Letters disclose, the students—secondhand witnesses—facilitate testimony.[32] The staging of inside women's testimony appears to offer both the women and the students a mirror of their own life experience, an affirmation of their human worth, and hope for a different future. After witnessing the Prison Monologues on more than twenty occasions in a variety of venues, I have come to understand the ability of oral testimony to join the lives of the inside women with those of the students, in a complex referencing of individual narratives with communal ones.[33] The Love Letters reside unapologetically in the genre of testimonio due to their collective testimony of and for the beleaguered: both the inside women and the students.

Nico, a student at Kapolei High School, draws an incandescent yellow sun on a mint green paper: "because you rarely get to see the sun in *there.*" This visual souvenir that the women can carry as an amulet—a signifier of healing—into the prison is a gift that many of the teenagers create. The smorgasbord of childish symbols can work like portable graphic texts, mnemonic devices that stand in for hope and solidarity. Nico concludes: "I love the fact that you treated our class like family. I wanted to cry my heart out yesterday. For the time you shared your stories, I think everyone in the room felt human for a while." The concept of *'ohana* (family) is a distinct and tenacious feature in the letters, in which teenagers generously inscribe the women into a familial union in an emendation of the many disunions in their lives. Through the act of invention, the students and inmates project desire onto each other, and their compassion is performed in the present, while simultaneously easing past hurts. Yana Meerzon argues that exilic writer Josef Brodsky situates exile as a liminal space—one in which the "past becomes the place where you are not anymore and the future is a place where you cannot yet be."[34]

The teachers give the students prompts: "What surprised you the most about the performance? What touched you the most?" Some of the students answer the prompts directly, while others abandon this prescriptive writing exercise, privileging creative expression that itself performs as a *pu'uhonua.* A dusky pink paper embellished with a light blue and purple border postulates the women's life stories as a "miracle": "There was so much raw emotion tied into it that I couldn't help but cry." This kind of public display and crying against one's will are present in many of the school performances. I frequently see large, seemingly tough young men hugging their caps tight around their eyes as they wipe away their tears.

The Love Letters are surprising in what they convey about gender. Unexpectedly, the teenage boys' Love Letters are more intricately and flamboyantly decorated, professing more emotion than those of the girls. There is something simple and wrenching about these homemade cards, reminiscent of childhood cards concocted for secret Valentines. Kawika, who signs his elaborately decorated card in curvaceous handwriting, confides: "I also had a father that I lost to prison. He got Life. I couldn't forgive him. Today, you showed me that he loved me. That he really wants to be there in my life just like how you guys are doing for your kids. I know I just met you guys but I love each and every one of you."

This acquired intimacy is intimacy in a rush, not unlike the intimacy of lovers. And the love defies the transitory circumstances of the encounter. Brandon documents his transformation in his ability to witness the women's humanity: "When I first saw you guys I was like 'Damn these ladies look hard core and could probably whoop all of us!' . . . But I come to find out you guys aren't that mean, you guys are actually pretty cool. I am also surprised that you guys did little things and is serving all these years."

Some of the boys are introspective and reflective, showcasing a vulnerable intimacy with the women, which surprised me: "I know it must have been difficult for you to share your experiences in the facility. To be honest, for the longest time, I thought all prisoners were a blight upon the world. For some reason, I didn't view them as fellow human beings. I never gave them respect because I was a fool." Brandon charts his transformation from societal stereotyping to the compassionate embrace of a morally judged citizen: "Hearing your stories changed my opinion. I don't mean to say that I am better than you—because I am not—but your skit about life inside the correctional facility made me realize how luxurious my life is. You all changed my view on life."

"Thanks a million," Akoni proffers on a card resplendent with comic characters, "you guys were brilliant." Akoni attests that the women made him a stronger "drug *healer*" and provided him the opportunity to understand why his parents do the things they do. Many students see the women as redeemers even as—in a rhetorical inversion of the biological household—the teenagers wear the voice, eyes, and heart of a moral guide.

Tadashi reinforces a Christian framework that is familiar to the "inmates," many of whom are required to graduate from the Total Life Recovery's faith-based program: "You are strong women of God. My brother is like you. He drank alcohol and did drugs. He stole from our family. He is now rehabilitated in California and studying to be a pastor." The teens tender narratives of shame, abandonment, and parental transgression; however, beneath the surface there is a melodious forgiveness—the pedagogical recipe the Prison Monologues women emphasize in their one-on-one interviews.

Many of the teenagers confess to multiple viewings of the Prison Monologues. "It was just as touching as the first time," exudes one student, attesting to both the regenerative power and the ephemerality of performance.

Freed from Sin

Her heart is filled with so much pain
She's at the border of going insane
Laying on her rocky bed
Just letting fear take over her head

Feeling trapped like there's no way out
Trying to clear her head of every doubt
A pen and paper is all she needs
To free her mind so she can succeed

She's cleaning up for a better life
Like slowly pulling out a knife
Don't ever give up, don't ever give in
For a day will come when you can say
"I'm released of my sins!"

> ~ Ahulani[35]

Ahulani's opening line, "Her heart is filled with so much pain," exemplifies one of the personal testimonials that constitute a composite/communal autobiography of pain. Like the women's writing on home in *Hulihia VII*, the teenagers' offerings frequently resist simplistic receptions. Ahulani's poem makes references to fear and pain as destructive forces that are simultaneously desired. She testifies to the power of the word to liberate the protagonist in her poem: "A pen and paper is all she needs / To free her mind so she can succeed."

Indexing Speechlessness

The testimony in this section indexes a speechlessness that occurs after wounded life narratives are shared with the teenagers. I do not read the Nānākuli correspondence at WCCC; instead, Pat Clough arranges a meeting and interview for me with Christine Wilcox, the Nānākuli English teacher and at that time the chair of the department. Clough had an enduring collaboration with Wilcox and was devastated by her untimely death. Wilcox arrives to our interview in Mānoa with her hands overflowing with the correspondence.[36] She informs me that the index cards are a student-generated idea. The students suggest that they write their postperformance notes to the Prison Monologuers, who would then digest their confessionals back in the prison and in turn correspond with the students. The index card is a departure from standard practices and eventuates in a *Hulihia* publication that features some of the students' and women's correspondence through poetry. The index cards, less formal than the Love Letters, more naked and less decorative, are nevertheless love letters to the women.

Wilcox grew up in the Kalihi projects. While teaching at Nānākuli High School, she was pursuing her second master's degree in curriculum studies at the University of Hawai'i at Mānoa. Although she does not readily share her background, she confides: "I grew up poor but surrounded by love. Five of us have advanced degrees." She comes to our interview armed with a letter printed on a steel green paper that she wrote to her eleventh- and twelfth-grade students after the Monologuers visited for the first time. Her vulnerability suggests the power of the Monologues and the students' letters. She tells me, "There were times that I felt as if I couldn't handle all the pain that entered our class after the women visited. There was a time when I wanted to quit." Her letter begins:

To Our Beautiful Students of NHIS

Each year, for the last three years, when the Prison Monologue Presenters return, I am excited! When the events take place, I am reminded about the raw emotions their stories evoke within you. You are later assigned to construct a letter/poem/picture—your choice as long as your approach comes from your heart. . . . I later find a quiet spot at home and read. The depth in which you share, the "soul searching" of dark pasts exposed, the existing struggles—standing strong as a tree to not get knocked down, the creative creations expressed through your poetry, the connections, the sympathy and empathy, ALL displayed in black and white . . . WOW! To be honest, I sometimes have a difficult time hearing (some) of your stories. Why? This is because it fills me with melancholic emotions as I gain insight into your past and (sometimes current) conflicts. It makes me wish I could've been there to hug you when you felt like you were worthless . . . to the point you didn't even want to exist. I wanted to be there to take the place of an absent parent due to CPS, drugs, incarceration, or even the sad ultimate reality—death. I cry a river of tears leaving my eyes puffy and my nose looking like Rudolph the Red-Nose Reindeer. Ask my husband, Mr. Wilcox; he respectfully gives me my space but checks in from time-to-time just to make sure I'm okay. I later share with the inmate's teacher, Pat Clough, and we compare notes about both our students' receptions. We are left speechless! It's a wonder why we continue to do what we do—we have developed a love for our students.

Endless Aloha,
Mrs. Wilcox (11 years and counting . . . damn right!)[37]

Like Wilcox, many students share that they find themselves without words after hearing the Prison Monologues life stories—a temporary state followed by an outpouring of words. Shoshana Felman addresses the moment of speechlessness implicit in witnessing.[38] The recounting of trauma for the secondhand witness, explains Felman, is mediated by a remembering, or rather a misremembering, since full knowledge of what actually happened is unattainable. As Wilcox articulates during our lengthy interview, it is arduous to straddle the divide between teacher and confidante, the keeper of secrets. It is only after the Prison Monologues visit and the testimonial sharing as a "debriefing" that the students are inspired to disclose their narratives. When I ask Wilcox what makes her so effective with the students, she responds, "Although my home was not broken, I grew up knowing what it was like to be hungry, to not have any food to eat. Many teachers have never experienced this." While Wilcox escaped the plight of drugs and abuse, she has cousins who have been in and out of prison.

The comments on the index cards move from simple declarative sentences, to questions, to encouragement, to consolation often framed in a religious context, and often, to heartbreaking gratitude:

You guys are never alone. We may be young but we're always here to listen. I sometimes feel the same way sitting alone with no one to listen [to me]. No one to express my feelings [to].

You have inspirational stories. My dad always's tells me "your not judged on how you fall its how you get back up." You truly got back up a dusted yourselves off. You made a difference. Mistake can be fixed. You showed me that anyone can get back up from the deepest fall.

I have preserved all grammatical transgressions as a way to preserve the integrity of the students' words. As Wilcox confirms, grammatical intrusions into pain are acts of violence: "Who am I to violate their thoughts?" In her letter to the students, Wilcox sanctions the students' writing as acts of liberation: "As your English teacher, grammar goes out the window. Why? This is TO NOT restrict your flow, your emotions and your truth. I slightly cringe seeing those errors. But I know this, your freedom of expression during that moment, supersedes any rule."

Resonant in the students' indexes is the display of the geographic, familial, and intimate devastations that the Nānākuli teenagers undergo and what some social theory critics like Michael P. Johnson and Kathleen Ferraro call "intimate terrorism."[39] As Ferraro articulates, "Women who survive intimate terrorism often describe ways in which abusers manipulate their perceptions of events ranging from routine, everyday occurrences to entire biographies."[40]

The teenagers' recollections and recording of their lives are strategies of resistance: counterrecords to the master narratives of their perpetrators.

Mom did drugs
Dad was her dealer
She went jail while he re-married into whole new life
I was born with drugs (why I look different)
All this happened when I was a baby (2 lbs 2 oz)
Mom got out
changed and on right path (14 years old me)
Moved to Alaska to stay away from bad
influences
Nothing changed I still can't see her
Adopted into a good family

~ Anonymous

This particular student's confession crams the space like an exploding poem with parenthetical expository explications that seem to tumble over the borders of the index card. Due to the limited space and the fractured nature of the poem, it appears to be hijacked midsentence. The perpetual trajectory of loss is evident, despite the insistence that the narrator was adopted into a "good" family. However, the reader is left questioning what constitutes "goodness" in this particular familial setting. Does "good" simply imply a space in which one's body remains unviolated? The speaker exposes a common narrative in which women more frequently than men suffer sexual assaults: rape, incest, and being pimped by men. The narrator, who chooses anonymity, nevertheless inserts identifying features of the physical self into parenthesis—*(why I look different) (2 lbs 2 oz)* and *(14 years old me)*—as a curious afterthought to convey the trajectory of a child who arrives in the world marked by drugs. The mother's exilic displacement to Alaska chronicles a desperate need to distance herself from temptation, even at the expense of abandoning her child.

Another disturbing student testimony assumes the role of perpetrator:

I hate drugs and I ~~when~~ went to Juvi for biting up a kid.

Beneath this violent sentence, the student has scribed two versions of *hate* and *hat's*, as if the auteur is auditioning words for their grammatical appropriateness.

As the letters and the index cards demonstrate, the Nānākuli and Kapolei high school students frequently respond by serving up their own or their family's transgressions as a way of connecting with the inside women. Occasionally, the students ask the women to comment on their own regrets: "How were you able to last that long? If there was one thing you could change what would that be?" Some students have questions about the everyday life of prison, such as, "What is the best kind of food?" collapsed with a pensive "I regret not listening to my parents." This indication of the everyday rituals in life is a feature of ethnography, which inscribes the students as anthropologists of sorts. The testimonials perform as various types of personal regret for the students—regret at disappeared parents, regret about failing societal expectations, regret at not belonging: "The lack of a relationship with my mom starting down the wrong path, hard to get back on the good one."

In a longer letter, Malia writes: "I miss you guys and I want you guys to come back. You guys are like family to me now. Even though I only saw you once, I really like you guys and I became close." The display of similitude and "intimacy in a rush" is evident here. Malia both identifies and disidentifies with the women. In response to Kailani's disclosure of serial rape by her grandfather, she scribes: "I don't know what I would do if the same thing happened to me." She tenders insanity as the sole outcome she envisions for herself. In this sense, she is morally "weaker" than the women who maintain their sanity, yet she assumes a moral superiority by scolding Mahina for being "angry at God for keeping her alive" after her driving accident that kills an underage passenger.

One writer of an anonymous index card confesses an unspeakable or unsayable narrative:

> When I thought people could understand me they really couldn't. When I was young I used to hate life, I lost my father when I was 2 years old. I am 15 years old now! With a storie that's scared to be told. Life to me now is worthless, I'm done and over it . . . I hat[e] Life, being used, unwanted and scared! I'm thankful for having you guys around to open me up and Realize a lot of things can happen just don't give up!
> Mahalo

On the far right-hand corner of the index is perhaps the auteur's name scratched out with an almost emphatic vengeance, an act of ferocity. The intentional erasure of identity sits on the card, its inky body a moniker of defiance. However, it simultaneously signals a prior transitory resolve when the auteur desired to be breathed into recognition. Alison Bechdel employs a similar erasure within the pages of her visual autobiography, *Fun Home*: an erasure that is simultaneously generative and destructive.[41] Ann Cvetkovich argues that "the act of witnessing" disintegrates as the teenager Bechdel is unable to "document the everyday events that are so frequently the subject of adolescent journals."[42] She posits that "the graphic act of striking out words with a mark that is a cross between word and image . . . provides its own eloquent testimony to the impossibility of documenting truthfully what she is seeing or experiencing [and that it] suggests the potential ordinariness of the unrepresentability that is the hallmark of some theories of trauma."[43]

The Nānākuli teenagers' effacements are not about global genocide, however; they speak to a localized, familial annihilation in a world in which one anonymous teenager desires death as an escape from overwhelming torture, neglect, and abuse in her life. Nevertheless, the student testifies that the Prison Monologuers are her *redeemers:* they resuscitate her from the pain of her life, the invisibility of it, by extending an alternate pathway to recognition. She marks life as without value: "Life to me is worthless, I'm done and over it . . . I can't wait for it! I hate it. I hate life, being used, unwanted and scared!" This breathless, run-on sentence marked by erratic punctuation, spelling, and ellipses is followed by the contradictory impulse of gratitude for the women and for the ability to "open up"—to testify—to excavate hope. Many of the teenagers' retorts authorize the women as *prophets* in their sovereignty to see them, *know* them without *knowing.* In these interchanges, knowing and love are abridged: an act that collapses the Hawaiian concept of *mana* with a Christian framework, characteristic of colonized places. The indexes mirror Bechdel's everyday utterances of teenage angst, only here the angst is life-threatening and obliterating. They transport a similar character as the diary.

Aisha pens a letter on Friday, March 28, 2014, that begins, "I don't even know what to say." Speechlessness gives way to a flood of words, as Aisha seeks to be forgiven for her mother's incarceration. She gives voice to her complicity, but most stridently to her guilt:

Dear prison monologue presenters: (Liezel, Kailani, Mahina & Ms. Pat)

I don't even know what to say. I'm pretty much speechless right now. You all have touched my heart with your personal history, poems, and letters. As I sat among the audience and listened to all that you had to say, I could literally feel tears forming in my eyes. I tried to raise my head and not let them fall. Suddenly a little puddle formed on my index card. All that you've shared honestly meant something to me. I could relate to them in many ways especially when those two strong words were mentioned "C-R-Y-S-T-A-L M-E-T-H!" That alone made that little puddle on my index card twice as big as it was before. Crystal meth was the drug that made a once unbreakable bond between me and my mother shatter to billions of pieces. She was an addict, always gone late at night, missing from my bedside, pupils larger than ever, and always on her feet and occupying her hands with something.

Sometimes she'd bring me along with her to her friend's house where they all looked and acted just like my mom, as if they were playing follow the leader. Until one day the secret slipped from my mouth when I was watching TV with my aunty. Some kind of ICE intervention was on and I seen a clear glass looking object and said "Mommy has that too." My aunty questioned me and I answered truthfully not knowing I was getting my mom in trouble.

I was only a little girl. I didn't know things I said would cause me to loose my mom for a lifetime. CPS got involved because my aunty told my grandparents who then called the cops who stole my mom away from me.

For Aisha, the life stories in the Prison Monologues are historical documents invested with the power both to silence and to usher in speech. Evident in Aisha's letter is the perpetual desire for her mother, despite her mother's addiction. Within the semantic slippage of asserting it was the police "who *stole* my mom away from me" is the buried and perpetual hurt of a never-ending loss that persists in Aisha's present as a teenager. Embedded in this script of longing is perhaps the desire to be "mothered." Here the confessional of brutality—Kailani's daily rape by her grandfather and her flight to crystal meth—renders the witness, teenager Aisha, temporarily mute. However, this inescapable identification with pain ultimately ushers in release, followed by speech. Aisha testifies to the tears that fall unwillingly, whether blighting or enhancing the index card.

Hearing and Healing

Hearing and healing are essential components of the dialogic interchange. Once back at WCCC, Mahina gifts a written testimonial to the English class at Nānākuli. Mahina's written story, more intricate and detailed than her oral performance, loosely follows the spine of the students' direct questions inspired by the "presentation." In her letter, Mahina inscribes the students' writing as a weapon that sustains her:

First of all, I want to thank you for my folder. It really means a great deal to me. You may think "Why? It's just paper!" Well, for the days I sit alone, I can open the folder and be reminded that I do not stand alone. I stand strong with an army full of beautiful children. I am 25 years old and am from the island of Maui.

The reason for my being in prison was choosing to drive recklessly with 4 minors in my car high on Ice. It was the accident that nearly took my life. It took place on an old dump road called Oma'opio. This dump road was very windy and dark at night because there are no street lights. The passengers in my vehicle were 14, 15, and 17 years of age. I was driving with no license. In a split second I took my eyes off the road . . . my front right tire went off the road a little. I looked up, pulled back on the road entered a dip and drove around a turn about 50 mph. My car completely lifted off the ground and slid straight into a telephone pole. My tire on the driver's front side hit the pole head on and my car instantly wrapped around the pole leaving me crushed. They had to cut me out of the car and medivac me over here to Queens.

My body instantly bloated from the impact of the car hitting the pole. I stayed in a coma for about 3 ½ weeks and when I awoke, the one who was there with me was the wicked stepmother . . . I had no idea what happened. I made the front page of the Maui news. I had tubes running out of me everywhere. I couldn't eat solid food or talk. I couldn't sit up. My stomach was cut open 4 inches wide. An open wound with a hose was attached to a wound vac. They left a black sponge in the open wound.

The most terrifying feeling was when I couldn't move a single limb in my body. I had many internal surgeries. I broke ribs, both lungs collapsed. I damaged my intestines, bladder and broke both pelvic bones. I have pins in them. That's why I had to learn how to walk all over again through physical therapy. My right arm shattered. I have a bar in my arm. I fractured my right knee along with my ankle. The swelling never went away. I had no voice—completely no sound.

I was hella mad at God for keeping me alive. I was bed ridden for 7 months and in a wheel chair. That was too long for me. The doctors said I may never walk again.

I went straight back to drugs pushing myself to walk, numbing the pain with drugs. I kept driving without a license—getting pulled over until I ended up in a program. I cleaned up but kept on dealing drugs while in the program. My son's father wanted to get back together but I didn't want to be with him. Unknown to me, he was working for the cops and bought drugs from me. He wore a wire and recorded our phone conversation. Crazy, yeah!? Now that I look back on it—it was my choices, wrong choices that have cost me 10 years of my life. I knew right from wrong but because I did not love myself, I just didn't care. I have done a total of 4 years in prison going on 5 and let me tell you, I really miss my freedom.

I hope I have answered your questions—well some. But mostly, I would like you to see how easy it is to lose everything, including yourself, if you give up hope and dedicate your time to making choices you know are unhealthy. Try to make it a habit to always think things through especially when it could be a life-changing event. For me to open up and be honest with myself gives me confidence. Because the more I share and people relate, I don't feel alone or singled out. I don't beat myself up and treat myself bad. Instead, I search for solutions that strengthen loving myself. What I also found out about myself is I give great advice to friends but never walk it myself. All of you sharing your secrets with me has motivated me to walk my advice. Doing that makes me feel better about what happened and gives me courage to be the role model for someone in their life. I don't know what it is with you kids but when I am here . . . I don't wanna leave.

One more thing, thank you so much for the program you presented to us. I have endless appreciation for you all. And I gotta say that you are all my heroes 'cause I never made it to high school.

In this written testimonial, Mahina works through a personal history of trauma as she recounts the day of the accident in excruciating detail. Mahina has a large scar running down the center of her face—a visual and permanent marking of her trauma. Many of the students honestly confide in letters to her that they are initially frightened by her appearance until they realize that she is "sweet" and "serious." The students identify with the narrative of her abandoned son, encouraging her to "heal" for her son's sake. As Mahina cobbles together agonizing details of abandonment, betrayal, loss, and unimaginable physical pain to re-form traumatic memories, she is ushered into the community of ʻohana (family). She relinquishes both her body and her voice, which symbolize the forfeiture of self, and it is within the precise recounting of tragedy and her audience's capacity to hold her that the restorative circle of justice repairs.

As Aisha demonstrates in her written response to Mahina's detailed scripted testimony, the restoration continues long after the Prison Monologuers' school visit. Although Aisha herself does not engage in drugs, Mahina's narrative is a stand-in for Aisha's biological family's relationship with drugs. Hearing Mahina's oral testimony, followed by its written reiteration, allows Aisha to heal Mahina and herself. This witnessing—both aural and scripted—delivers Mahina back into the community of 'ohana from which she has been excommunicated.

Dear Prison Monologues presenters

Mahina, I really enjoyed listening to your stories I can relate to your stories. I don't do drugs or sell it but my mom and dad does I live with a foster family and I love them alot. My biological mother is finally getting help but my dad still does drugs his been doing drugs for as long as I lived Ive disowned my biological mom I told her I want nothing to do with her but my dad is a different story for some reason I still want my dad in my life. My dad has been in & out of prison a lot of times. You only have a little time left in WCCC don't let ANYONE bring you down. YOU GOT THIS! KEEP YOUR HEAD UP!

LOVE ALWAYS, Aisha

Aisha's letter, lacking traditional punctuation, which is strikingly in short supply when the trauma escalates, is characteristic in the encouragement it bestows on the women. Aisha does not explain her willingness to forgive her father, even as she disowns her mother. This asymmetrical affection for one parent over another is typical of complex familial encounters. In another letter from Aisha, she professes that she connects with Kailani because she doesn't "trust boys/guys . . . and that's why I have a girlfriend." Her words demonstrate queer desire, where sexuality presents as a layer of an apprehensive "disidentification" and identification. Kailani comes out to the students in her performance/testimony, sharing her struggle to accept her homosexuality, which surfaces within her writings in Clough's creative writing classes that I observe at the facility. Aisha identifies with Kailani as a queer part Native Hawaiian woman, while Kailani both identifies and disidentifies with her queer sexuality growing up in a traditional family on the island of Hawai'i. These dialogic relationships, which Kamuela, a high school student, refers to as "healing from the inside and out" and what feminist theorist Julia Watson articulates as a chiasmic "network of transversals," bespeak the unique power of the Love Letters.[44]

Depression is a state of being that saturates many of the Love Letters. In the accounts of far too many teenagers' parents disastrously disappeared to incarceration, and the inside women's lives behind bars, depression haunts the narrators and protagonists. In *Depression: A Public Feeling*, Ann Cvetkovich interprets Saidiya Hartman's *Lose Your Mother* as a narrative about the gaps, holes, and silences in the historical record. Cvetkovich reflects on these abysses as pertinent to her own inability to connect the gaps between "depression and the histories of slavery, genocide, and colonialism that lie at the heart of the founding of U.S. culture."[45] She desires to write depression into Hartman's catalog of the "afterlife of slavery," as well as excavate it as a text of political depression. The Love Letters likewise redeem trauma from posterior spaces—the prison and the schools—and reinscribe suffering within a public, communal landscape. The students' consolation, their whispers of intimacy and identification, are all gestures of compassion toward the women inside and the boys and girls on the outside. The Love Letters are acts of imagination, desire, and empathy that rewrite traumatic historical records: a hearing and healing.

> *Thank you prison monologues for coming to our school*
> *I think you are all really cool*
> *Your stories were touching and heavy for the heart*
> *I felt a little sad when we had to part*
>
> *I hope in the future we will make all the right choices*
> *No matter what others will say with their voices*
> *Because the power one can have over the mind*
> *Won't usually be too kind*
>
> *Drugs could easily mess us up*
> *Even if our dealers greet us with "sup"*
> *They will have us by the throat with their evil claw*
> *Not to mention, it's illegal by law*
>
> *We are all capable of seeing wrong from right*
> *Though, it may take more for others to see the light*
> *You should always try to stick to the right path*
> *So we all should stay in school, learning english, science, and math*
>
> ~ Kai

I can tell it wasn't easy for you ladies sharing your stories with us
And seeing you ladies fighting through the pain
Because of everything that you ladies kept inside for years.
But now you ladies had the courage to tell somebody
Tell us about your life
And how it finally healed you from the inside out.

~ Kamuela

5 POSTRELEASE AND AFFECTIVE WRITERS

[As a critical race theory method,] counterstory serves as a means for marginalized people to intervene in research methods that would form "master narratives."
~Aja Y. Martinez, "A Plea for Critical Race Theory Counterstory"

To be clear, we do not submit such writing to offer accounts of how college-in-prison helps people become "better" or "new." Nor do we position our narratives as explicit efforts to change social institutions. Our ultimate goal is, instead, to shift academics' and instructors' perceptions of incarcerated populations from people who are changed by education to complex individuals who are thinking about writing just like others on the inside and outside. This intended outcome, we believe, is not the same as transformation. And so, we use counterstory to generate "[n]arratives counter to [those] majoritarian or stock stories" to avoid flattening the experiences of and harming people in prison.
~ Larry Barrett, Pablo Mendoza, Logan Middleton, Mario Rubio, and Thomas Stromblad, "More Than Transformative"

I return to Hawaiʻi in November 2019 after a two-year hiatus. I come to present a paper at the 2019 Annual Meeting of the American Studies Association and to conduct final interviews with women who were inside and are now on the outside: Nicole Fernandez, a prison administrator; Judge Karen Radius, who started the Girls Court in Hawaiʻi; Kat Brady, a longtime prison abolitionist and activist; Lorenn Walker, a restorative justice attorney; and Noriko Namiki, CEO of YWCA Oʻahu and director of Fernhurst, one of the parole reentry locales that services released women from WCCC. In an interview with Namiki in downtown Honolulu, she critiques the lack of tracking of the women's progress once they are released from WCCC. Namiki works with transitioning women on storytelling and its role in the "rehabilitation" process: she asks some pointed questions about the ethics of inside women presenting their stories publicly.

Clearly, the Prison Monologues is not a panacea for all the women, as some of the women circle back inside. Namiki tells me that TJ Mahoney, WCCC's work furlough program, lost the state contract in 2015: the state contract was given to Fernhust, but TJ Mahoney retained the federal contract. Located in Makiki, the Fernhurst facility is home to the only community-based work furlough program in the state of Hawaiʻi, called Ka Hale Hoʻāla Hou No Nā Wāhine, or the Home of Reawakening for Women.

Namiki states: "Through this program, female inmates are released from the Women's Community Correctional Center (WCCC) to Fernhurst. They can work and live in the community, with time to transition to life outside of prison. The women living at Fernhurst gain access to practical resources to help them secure jobs and maintain them, as well as the social-emotional support to build healthy relationships and successfully transition to their new lives." Namiki mentions the persistent surveillance that inside women are subjected to when they leave prison to work—they are strip-searched upon their return to prison. I don't recall that the Prison Monologues women I interviewed ever spoke to me about this degradation, and rather focused on the rewards of the program: testament to the routine brutality in prisons.

Chaminade University

Reiko calls my name from the parking lot of Chaminade University. I am standing in the shade, in a weak attempt to avoid profuse sweating. After a few years on the East Coast, my body is no longer acclimated to the sweltering sun that is omnipresent in Honolulu's neighborhood—Kaimukī.

Reiko runs up the stairs. There is no other way to describe her other than as glowing—and not from the heat as in my case, but glowing and shining from within. Her Mauna Kea Kiaʻi earrings are glistening. I have returned to Hawaiʻi at a critical juncture. Native Hawaiians resist state violence as they protect Maunakea—sacred mountain—from the construction of the Thirty Meter Telescope. This is prior to the COVID-19 lockdown. I am privileged to be invited up to the Mauna by the Hilo-based members of ʻOhana Hoʻopakele—Ronald Fujiyoshi and Kaleihau Kamauu, a formerly incarcerated activist. ʻOhana Hoʻopakele is a community organization that envisions the building of *puʻuhonua(s)* as an alternative to prison. As activists and academics Marilyn Brown and Sarah Marusek articulate in their article "'Ohana Hoʻopakele: The Politics of Place in Corrective Environments":

> Through wellness centers (puʻuhonua) and the practice of traditional hoʻoponopono (indigenous conflict resolution), this group [ʻOhana Hoʻopakele] advocates for a spatially-oriented rehabilitative approach to restorative justice. A central feature is the land upon which the program will be situated and its organization as a self-supported ahupuaʻa. This indigenous land division contains diverse and sustainable resources where the participants will be connected to Hawaiian culture and practices central to the concept of wellness for the person and the community. The group's vision for this program is far-reaching as it will serve as a model for justice in the Restored Hawaiian Kingdom.[1]

I travel up to the Mauna with Kamauu, who has spent over thirty years inside in both Hawaiian and mainland prisons and was instrumental in spearheading Native Hawaiian cultural and spiritual practices (ceremony) inside prisons—puʻuhonua—to address the overincarceration of Native Hawaiians.

Reiko introduces me to one of the deans and pastors at Chaminade, whom she embraces warmly. Her hair is swept up, and she is wearing a Hawaiian print sleeveless shirt. Reiko is close to fifty years old and has spent over twenty years inside. It is bittersweet to be returning to Chaminade University. I remember that the last time I saw Reiko perform with the Prison Monologues was in 2012 in one of the classrooms for the criminology students. Reiko is now enrolled in Chaminade as a dual-degree student pursuing her bachelor's degree, with her education fully funded by a scholarship. Her wide smile replaces, actually erases, her once masked and impenetrable visage. Her testimony was always among the most powerful in its potential to shatter (both her violent past and the present audience)—a testimony that gave voice to the betrayal of family. Reiko was the victim of incest as a child.

When she spoke there was always a pregnant silence in the room: her narrative inked in brutality. Today, in the sweltering sun, Reiko fills in the holes of her story. Reiko is Kanaka Maoli. Her mother was sixteen years old when Reiko was born and gave her up for adoption. Reiko's adoptive family—who are Japanese Hawaiian—provided a house that she describes as lacking love, intimacy, and hugs. Her adoptive mother's boyfriend began intruding on the sanctity of her room nightly. A terrified seven-year-old Reiko would hold her body stiffly in her attempts to protect herself, stifling her breaths. Her "father" was not deterred, and so began the frequent rapes. Reiko told her adoptive mother about her partner's nightly "intrusions," but her mother did not believe her. The devastating pain of betrayal was Reiko's pathway to the streets: to her hardness—to the closing of her heart. "The hardest thing I have ever done is forgive my mother. But I knew until I could forgive—I would never heal." Reiko is now on a pathway of glorious healing. She has a loving, supportive partner—a woman whom she calls her "rock"—and she has reconciled with her biological family: her biological aunty, whom she physically resembles, and her own sons. Reiko passionately articulates: "Warden Patterson saved my life. I remember messing up: while in the hole and all the fights I got into in the prison. I was so angry. I don't know why the warden singled me out but his notes that I found in little balls gifted a message of promise: 'Reiko I see you. I believe in you.' Those notes kept me alive."

The fact that the leader of a prison facility could be an agent in saving the life of one of his "charges," as Reiko's words suggest, complicates the abolitionist critique that all work inside of the carceral is complicit with state violence.

Reiko centers part of her own healing process on her ability to forgive her adoptive mother for abandoning her and abusing her as a child. There are many stories to breathe in on this visit. The following is a composite of Reiko's story that she shared with Lorenn Walker, a restorative justice practitioner and former attorney. I thank Reiko and my colleague and friend Lorenn Walker for granting me permission to reprint Reiko's testimony.

In March 2016, Reiko, of Hawaiian, Japanese and Caucasian ancestry, is 46 years old. Her biological mother was 16 and her biological father was 21 years old when she was born and gave her up for adoption through Hawai'i's state child protective services. This is Reiko's story of victimization, to offending, to desistance and community service, in her own words, which she has reviewed and granted permission to publish:[2]

When I was seven, my adoptive mom's boyfriend started standing outside my room at night and looking at me. Eventually he came in and sat on my bed. He touched me. I would pack on extra clothes, like wear five shirts and shorts, but he would find my private parts. He made me do things to him. I told my mother innocently, "Oh, Uncle was in my room last night." She didn't believe me. She said I was a liar. I think she was afraid of being alone and wanted him more than me. I think she was abused herself and was angry I wasn't her real daughter. She beat me with anything she could grab. Once she beat me for being sick. I was coughing in bed with a fever. She came in and hit me in the head with her fists. A lot of times she locked me in a closet. My imagination saved me from that. I would go in my mind and imagine a life where I was loved. She yelled all the time I was stupid and not worth nothin'. I believed her and felt unworthy for years.

When I was eleven, I started sniffing paint and doin' drugs. I ran away. I met horrible people on the street. Guns were held at my head. The first time when I was raped; the second time when I was raped after I ripped off a drug dealer; and the third time when my boyfriend played Russian roulette with me. I was put into foster care and lived in every group home on Oʻahu. I ran away from all of 'em. I went mute when I was twelve and was put into the Hawaiʻi state mental hospital. I was locked up alone in a room. I did whatever I could to make 'em think I was crazy. I said I heard voices. Got so depressed I started believin' I really was crazy. Somehow I snapped out of it. After I got out of the mental hospital, I assaulted someone. I was 13 and put into Koʻolau [Hawaiʻi's youth prison]. I was there until I turned 18 because I escaped twice and got more time.

I had my first baby when I was 18 and three more after that. The last one was born when I was in prison. I was shackled to the bed when I gave birth. He was taken from me and put into foster care. I haven't seen him since he was adopted around five months old in 2000. I held him in the judge's chambers and said goodbye. He is 16 years old today. I abused my other three kids I had. Not as bad as my mom, but I was not good. I did a lot of crystal methamphetamine. I would fall asleep after being up for days. We lived in a house by the beach. I'd wake up and the kids would be playing by the ocean. They were little, like 12 months to 4 years old. I'd snap, and go off screaming and hitting 'em. When I was 29, I got sentenced to prison—mostly for theft charges, but I also got into a lot of fights and assaulted dozens of women I had relationships with. I was a very angry person. It was my escaping from O triple C (Oʻahu Community Correctional

Center) that got me a sentence of 40 years.[3] I got out of prison when I was 44 years old, two years ago. I always had a hard time learning in school. I was in special ed since elementary. I got motivated in prison to get my GED because my friends all were. The prison also paid us about 34 cents an hour to go to school for it. I passed the test after my third try. Prison was a place of healing for me. I got treatment. It helped me see my worth. I wasn't just a broken unworthy child. Today I value integrity and being responsible for myself. I work for a non-profit, helping women in prison come out and succeed. I want them to see if I could do it, they can too.

My biggest goal in life right now is to have a relationship with my kids. In 2012 when I was in prison, I had a restorative reentry circle. The circle helped me plan for how I could work on repairing things with my kids. Their paternal grandmother who raised them since I went to prison didn't come to the circle, but she gave information that was read. She asked me not to contact the kids until they were 18. I respected that. After they turned 18, I found 'em through Facebook. We stay in touch now with that. I'm careful respecting their boundaries. I don't push myself on them. They still have anger and resentment to me. I understand their disappointment. I made a lot of promises I broke. I do what I say I am gonna do now. My hope is that someday they see I can be trusted and know how much I love them.

Since being released from prison in 2014, Reiko has remained law abiding and works helping women transition from prison. She maintains her relationship with her children through social media, hoping for more involvement in the future.

Reiko tells me that in the two years since this was published, she has established a relationship with her children.

In the summer of 2022, Reiko earned her bachelor of science degree in environmental studies and a minor in psychology from Chaminade University. In the Hawai'i Friends of Restorative Justice newsletter, Reiko appears next to the former warden Mark Kawika Patterson richly adorned with lei.

Interview with Nicole Fernandez, Offender Services
Administrator at Women's Community Correctional
Center, November 14, 2019

I return to the administrative office at the Women's Community Correctional Center, where I had spent so much time. Things look pretty much the same except there are now plastic postings on the walls displaying the items that visitors are not allowed to bring into the prison. I take the bus—a ritual and mnemonic reminder of the many times I traveled along the Pali Highway. The bus deposits me in front of the Youth Correctional Facility, where I read the many signatures of depleted hope among the graffiti on the side facing the highway. I think of Mark Kawika Patterson, who is now the warden there. Nicole Fernandez, who is tall and in her forties, comes out to greet me.

"I would always joke with Ms. Pat that I was her little fan club," Fernandez laughs. "I remember going out with Ms. Pat and the women to a school. I think it was somewhere on the west side. It was really moving to me, and from that point on, it was something I really believed in."

Nicole Fernandez, who has worked in her current position as offender services administrator since 2013 and prior to that as "just a regular case manager," has been at WCCC for eight years. She is well positioned to speak about the Prison Monologues and the Kailua Prison Writing Project as she was the sole case manager for a number of years and knows the women intimately on both a professional and a personal level. She tells me, "Seeing the women perform and the kids' responses—that dynamic was really moving to me. It was something I really believed in. You could see that the women were healing themselves. Sharing their stories through their writing—whether it be through a poem, a creative story or a song—was *magical* for them. Just knowing the women in here and what brought them to prison and hear them share about it. It was just healing for them—you could tell." Fernandez imparts the salience in the veracity of witnessing—the accounting for healing as well as the reverberation of magic—the magic that Clough articulates in the assemblage of the Prison Monologues program. I wonder if witnessing the Prison Monologues is healing for Fernandez herself, in that it confirms the humanity of the inside women she comes to know. She continues to elaborate on the fact that the Prison Monologues ushers in a "motherliness" for the women, explaining, "You saw the motherly side to the women." Fernandez speculates that the women's desire to perform their life stories for the students is in a sense an effort to ensure that the teenagers know they are not alone, that they can overcome, and that hope resides. Fernandez speaks about hope, investing it with the magic of redemption. Beyond the performances, she witnesses a transformation in the women who participate in the program and go through the journey with "Ms. Pat," as she calls Clough.

The Kailua Prison Writing Project affords the women the opportunity to share secrets they have kept bottled up for years. Fernandez explains: "The women are in a space where they now feel safe and ready to share. We saw women heal in a way that we never knew possible. You know I saw someone for the first time share her story that she kept secret for all of these years. And to see them feel comfortable with the writing process to share their stories. And to see them outside today doing so well . . . it is really clear that this healing process needed to happen for them."

Fernandez reinforces the miraculous character of the KPWP in that it accomplishes an almost impossible, unimaginable healing: a repair.

We discuss one particular woman—a participant in both my and Clough's writing classes—who despite a wealth of support on the outside is ultimately unable to sustain her life on the outside. I recall her words as she slipped back into a destructive path of using: "I have been institutionalized my whole life—it's easier on the inside."

In the essay "More Than Transformative: A New View of Prison Writing Narratives," the collaborative corpus of inside writers argues that writing and education can be life-changing for incarcerated individuals. Yet it is imperative to provide alternatives to these "master narratives about prison literacies. . . . For some in prison, education doesn't facilitate critical consciousness or material success after release."[4] The writers emphasize the need to disrupt the master narrative of prison writing and the need to consider process for inside writers—particularly when it comes to intersections with academic writing. In summation, there is a need to attend to the volition of the inside writer: to shape their "be-coming."[5]

Assessment as Life Stories

Fernandez refers to an assessment process that is akin to an archive of life narratives, albeit via an institutional lens:

> As case managers we sit down with the women when they first arrive; we do their assessment—kind of like their whole life stories—and come up with programming. We help them with family issues. We try to get them to use their coping skills. Hina Mauka's therapeutic community models what residential treatment would look like in the community, but it is in here—the facility. Hina Mauka is considered the highest level of treatment. The women who went through the program and who were also part of the creative writing program—who participated in both Ms. Pat's writing classes and the Monologues—were extremely willing and open to

their journey. The women who have the internal motivation for change and are willing to take the slow road to stay out are the most successful. The process in the Kailua Prison Writing Project allows the women to address the things that brought them here to prison.

I ask Fernandez if she thinks that the retelling of the women's stories, particularly for the teenagers, can potentially be retraumatizing. "I think if someone is willing to share their story, they are beyond retraumatization. If a woman is not open or willing to talk about it, then we leave it." Fernandez was involved in the process of selecting which women should go out to the community. I ask about the qualities that the women needed to possess in order to be selected for the Prison Monologues: "The biggest thing for us was 'walk the talk.' The Prison Monologuers are role models for the youth: so they need to be well behaved. It's OK if you got into trouble in the past—but now the selected women must display good behavior, have no write-ups, and should be doing their programs." Within this display of "good behavior" there resides a disciplining of the body to cohere with carceral logics.

I think about the dynamic Lahela—the young and talented writer who, despite Clough's desire and support, was never allowed to exit the facility and join the core Monologuers. When I ask about the facility rules and what constitutes an administrative infraction, Fernandez explains, "They can range from if an officer tells you not to do something and you do it to fighting to stealing from the kitchen. You don't get written up for not doing your programs . . . you can refuse treatment but the parole board might look at that. We do assessment when an individual comes in and we make a recommendation which goes to the paroling authority. We don't force the women to partake in programs—but they may not get paroled if they don't do any programs."

I ask Fernandez if she thought the women's involvement with the Prison Monologues influenced sentencing and eventuated in shorter sentences. She responds, "The paroling authorities are their own entity. The essential component for shorter sentences is 'walking the talk.' Liezel and Reiko both stayed misconduct free and became model inmates for the facility. Reiko did a complete turnaround—she showed that she was a model citizen out in the community. Most importantly, she gave back to the community." Fernandez explains that Reiko and the other Prison Monologues women form "families" with each other, as well as with the extended community.

This giving back to the community that one has harmed is at the center of restorative justice discourse—it appears in most restorative justice work I have witnessed in prisons. Yet, it is imperative that this harm is witnessed in concert with the racial, legal, societal, and cultural injury that has been inflicted on the most impacted communities.

At the end of the interview, I ask: "So what made Ms. Pat so important as a leader for the KPWP?"

> For Ms. Pat—it's her authenticity: her calm, soft-spoken manner. Yet you know she's really genuine. She didn't come into this thinking that it would result in the Prison Monologues. That's the beauty of it. It kind of developed on its own without an agenda. It was something that just started with the creative writing. Pat really cared about the women. She helped them find their voice. So did Warden Patterson across the street. The women performed in front of the governor, the legislature, which was really quite amazing. Going out to the community reminded people that the women are just like us. What I loved about the Monologues is that it reminded people that the women are still women: someone's aunty, mother, daughter, sister, cousin—and that brought their humanity back to them.

In "I'm Not Your Carceral Other," Vicki Chartrand critiques restoration as a colonial project, likening the carceral other to the subaltern:

> Common parlance today focuses on the prison's disciplinary and repressive character. . . . [H]owever, disciplinary power is not only punitive and restrictive, but attempts to limit and habituate us to narrow understandings of incarcerated persons, ourselves, and our sense of justice. These forming activities and strategies become even craftier when the grand narrative is built on the idea of "reforming" people—as if this is somehow a laudable or achievable goal. One cannot help but think of modern colonialism's assimilation, segregation and elimination policies that continue to haunt our nations when "reform" is on the agenda—logics and techniques that are found throughout our social world and intensified in the punitive microsites of the prison.[6]

Belonging/Unbelonging

There is something about violence and violations in the "household" that begs for silence.
~ Joy James, *Warfare in the American Homeland*

As I arrive at the end of this book, I write from a space of unbelonging. Exiled from my family of origin after my father's death; assigned expatriation as I refuse to don the trappings of a heteronormative existence or aspire to affluence. Exiled in sickness and pain: my fragile body wears the accumulation of trauma. The COVID-19 pandemic ushered in the agony of not seeing my father, the denial of goodbye. I attended his Zoom funeral and witnessed the shoveling of sand (what sounded like stones) across my father's grave. Submitted to eternal exile for writing my truth. Told that I am unforgivable/unforgiven. I can only imagine the collective punishment of the women I have come to love.

I depart with a letter from one of the inside writers—Summer Mayo—to Ms. Pat in response to her receipt of *Hulihia* and the transformative generativity in seeing her writing in print.

3/22/14

Dear Ms. Pat,

I received the Hulihia book and can't begin to tell you what joy it brought to my heart. It's ironic that I'm valuing the book like a treasure. That even now with my freedom regained, it seems to be my only refuge. There is a profound pulling that's created in the book along with all the work you do with the women. I've thought deeply on your presence as a teacher in my own life and the inmates. I asked myself "What is it that Ms. Pat has done?" My conclusion was that you were the sculptor and I was the mold. The consistency, the content, is already there. You just helped me find it and improve. It was my story all along and you inspired me.

Some of the women I met at WCCC are living miracles and there is a realness to their lives. It makes you want to listen and learn more. The poetry makes me look at my life. The writers, despite their pasts, made me a better person. When I'm ungrateful, or I start to forget that I'm one bad decision away from being back in prison, I open the book and read one of the girl's poems. They have become a part of me and I thank you for giving me that precious gift.

The notion of a circle of writers that extends beyond the borders of the prison—that stretches between the inside and out—is commanding. The individual blame that this particular writer assumes, rather than allocating culpability on societal failings, is something I have noted is significantly more prevalent in women's prisons rather than in men's prisons. Summer frames *Hulihia* as a treasure: as her only refuge even though she has "regained her freedom." *Hulihia* itself performs as a *puʻuhonua*.

> I loved my piece that you chose and edited, it really came together. Seeing my name in a bound book is one of my biggest accomplishments and I shed a few tears when I sat and read [it] for the very first time. What we did in those classrooms changed me and the life I once lived along with the one I lead today.

I am arrested by the tension between the solitary artist/writer and the one who is fashioned by the collaborative process. The tenet of being born into life or fashioned into living by writing—confirmed by the published word—is recognizable/palpable to me. I touch it like an onion.

Summer proceeds to engage with the written pieces of her peers—the "girls" at wccc—the circle of writers in Ms. Pat's classes.

> A few of the pieces I really enjoyed were Cheryl's pg. 48, Leia's pg. 39, Davida's pg. 35, Sai's pg. 19 and Pam's pg. 18.[7]

Summer inserts herself in the extended circle of writers—now both inside and outside. The borders between bodies and pens are muddied. As she responds to her editor, mentor, perhaps friend, Summer speaks back to the other women at wccc. Temporal crossings.

> I took your advice and have begun a writing group here with the girls. I've sat with a select few of them and shared my writing and testimony individually. Our group name is "Hopena" which translates to "hope and destiny." I had eight girls that attended and I had them do a "Dear John" assignment by saying goodbye to something, saying something you've never said to someone, or letting go of something they had been holding onto, such as their shame. The moral of the prompt was for them to find their voice and express it through their writing.

The vernacular of redemption appears in Summer's letter, perhaps something she emulates from Ms. Pat.

> Then we closely read Davida's poem on pg. 35. This poem hit me so hard with emotion when I read it. I saw myself as her looking in the mirror as I did many times at wccc. Abused, tired, and hopeless, having felt like I aged from my past. The girls liked it and we all had an

open discussion with various perspectives. I pushed them a bit wanting them to voice themselves and [I] have begun to establish that our group is not based on me, that it's them that make the class.

The afterlife of a community that persists beyond a singular dynamic leader is the spine of abolition feminism in action within radical communities of love, such as Black Lives Matter.[8]

I plan to hopefully keep in touch. Have you started a new Creative Writing group at wccc yet? And how has the prison monologues developed? I want to continue to be involved as much as possible and possibly when I move back to Hawaii I can help. In so many ways I wish I could still be there to meet on Saturdays. Thank you miss Pat for helping me change my life and find my voice, I'll never forget [you].

Mahalo, Summer Mayo

The imprint of the Kailua Prison Writing Project and the act of writing on the women's lives is ineradicable. Even when the women are "freed" (here and in many of the testimonies), there is a desire or longing to be back in the Saturday rehearsals or what Summer refers to as the refuge of the journal. All of this speaks to the program as a home for the women.

I will close with Leia's poem that Summer now teaches in her own circle of writers—no longer in the Pacific—but inextricably linked.

Locked up, locked down
from the inside out.
Shut up, shut down
from head to heart.
Lookin' at the light, eyes shut tight.
No one there, peering into the dark,
shadows and thoughts grasped and lost.
Time spinning, no need for a clock.
Floating above the seconds,
the start of the new day
waiting patiently in the palm of my still gentle hand.
Safely tucked away in the passages of my bible,
I am surrounded by the greatest odds.
Captured in these thick brick walls,

The cold concrete floor rolls out my field of dreams.
I believe in what I've never been taught.
I see what I have never been shown.
I know what I've never been told.
I have what no one can take away.[9]

~Leia

EPILOGUE

Palliative Praxis or Pathways to Transformation?

Oblivious to the trees and the long quiet street, my inside was searching for a word. A milk-near word. Something rising through all the remnants of past hearings. How was one to break through all these dividing borders? "Suture," I think. Perhaps "suture" is the word that can wash this world. Carefully, to stitch, to weave, this side to that side, so that border becomes a heart-hammered seam.

~ Antjie Krog, *Begging to Be Black*

To suture takes on a pressured imperative as the United States confronts a dispiriting political rupture and the ruin of a worldwide pandemic. The current ethos of vengeance and the continued expansion of the prison-industrial complex raise ever more urgently the question with which I began my inquiry: How can healing take place in a carceral setting? Here, I revisit this question as it explores the opportunities and limitations of a prison writing program in the Pacific. I approach the epilogue as a tapestry of anecdotes—a stitching together of autoethnography and analysis.

Since I began my work on the book, the conversation around mass incarceration has changed drastically. Criminal justice is now interrogated as the criminal legal system—a distinction that many critical prison theorists and educators insist on in our classrooms. This linguistic reframing is not utilized everywhere. One weekend in 2020, I attend a prison reform conference at John Jay College, a departure from the abolitionist circles in Philadelphia. Two wardens are participants on the panel, and *inmate* is the term du jour. I am arrested by the assertion of the only female warden on the panel who brazenly states: "We have always known that prisons are sexy—so glad that you are now hopping on board." This discourse about the fetishization of the prison-industrial complex signals that communities from both the left and the right are advocating for change (and in some circles for abolition), yet there is also a danger in this commodification. The perils of commodification infiltrate the transformative National Conference on Higher Education in Prison I attend in Denver in November 2021. Yet, I am buoyed to witness the focal lead that inside folks assume at the conference—as well as the critique of prison programming for its limits, particularly as we face the reinstatement of Pell Grants for inside students after three decades.

In a telephone interview in 2016, playwright and novelist Sarah Shotland confides: "Sadly, I feel pessimistic about the role of creative writing and arts programming and their impact on recidivism in the prisons."[1] Shotland, who teaches in the MFA program at Chatham University in Pittsburgh and founded the Words without Walls Program, has taught in carceral settings for a decade. She tells me:

> People are not invested in reducing recidivism rates in prisons because it is a huge for-profit business. In testimonials by administrators about our program, they attest that they like our program because it keeps people *occupied*, which infers docility. I don't want to think that I am only doing palliative work, keeping people quiet and docile. I wonder if they would endorse me if, say, I wanted to teach a class on Marxism or a cultural studies seminar that interrogates the system. We are reading Malcolm X next week. So the next time you speak to me, maybe I won't be doing this anymore! [*laughs*]

Words without Walls operated from 2009 to 2022, offering eighteen creative writing classes per year taught by Chatham University MFA students in the following venues: a men's medium-security facility, several jails, a psychiatric hospital, a drug rehabilitation program, and transitional housing projects. Shotland articulates her anxiety about transporting the "dysfunction of the academy," which she sees as largely antidemocratic, into the dysfunctional prison system. She struggles with ethical dilemmas such as whether and when a workshop model is right for an incarcerated classroom, and whether a student actually desires criticism. Writing workshops house ethical strategies and pedagogical structures that are different from other academic seminars. This is particularly true when the writing workshop entails some form of life writing, and these moral dilemmas are magnified within an incarcerated classroom.

In writing this book, I, too, confront the ethical dilemma of how to do "justice" to the women's words and life stories.

There have been decided moments of seduction when I have fallen in love with the women's words. I find it curious that many creative writing prison programs revert to cliché and euphemism when selecting their title or brand: Words without Walls, Walls to Bridges. These names signal hope, a projection into a future where there are no impenetrable walls blocking people out, which is particularly caustic at a time when a recent occupier of the White House advocated not for the destruction of walls but rather for their resurrection. According to Shotland, there isn't a single system in place in Pennsylvania that tracks recidivism rates. I am left perplexed. Despite the rhetoric of the Left, the proliferation of prison/university initiatives, and the prison abolition movement, are people really invested in dismantling the prison system, or is big business at play?

Gillian Harkins and Erica R. Meiners, both of whom come from queer, feminist, antiracist, and economic justice backgrounds, articulate that they are "struck by the hetero-gendered, economic and racial dynamics of volunteerism in most U.S. prison education programs." They argue that shifts in the prison-nation offer opportunities to engage abolition frameworks in new ways.[2] "An abolition-democracy, to use the term of Angela Davis and W. E. B. DuBois, requires reconstructing the structures and traditions that safeguard power and privilege, just as much as taking down those that visibly punish and oppress. Challenging the prison-nation therefore means fighting to close prisons, but it also means doing the perhaps more difficult work of opening up and reconfiguring other institutions that have shut their doors to those who have been abandoned by our punishing democracy."[3]

Daniel Bergner's God of the Rodeo exposes the marketing of prison life at the hugely popular Louisiana State Penitentiary annual rodeo or "The Farm."[4] "Inmates," many of them lifers, are exhibited on dangerous bulls in a competition for the prized rodeo belt—at times at the expense of their lives. Gladiatorial in nature, the rodeo show is a spectacle of masculinity and consumption. Tourists flock to The Farm to have their photos taken alongside the competitors, and rodeo belts are sold by the thousands. In "Discipline and the Performance of Punishment: Welcome to 'The Wildest Show in the South,'" Mary Rachel Gould analyzes the collapse of the carceral with consumption:

> Once described as the bloodiest and most dangerous prison in the United States, the Louisiana State Penitentiary at Angola hosts one of the only remaining prison rodeo and crafts fair in the United States. The event, more commonly known as "The Wildest Show in the South" is open to visitors every Sunday in October and for one weekend in April. Advertisements for the day-long event promise "untrained convicts roping and wrangling livestock" and the opportunity to browse among "authentic" prison crafts and concessions . . . [which] transforms the prison into a space of tourism, the incarcerated men into objects of surveillance, and returns punishment to that of a spectacle by offering the bodies of the incarcerated as a form of public entertainment.[5]

If the prison-industrial complex is indeed a capitalist venture, then is the reduction of recidivism really the aim? Many creative writing prison workshops in the United States claim a direct correlation between their classes and a reduction in recidivism, and studies point to statistical evidence that with education those inside do not return as frequently to prison. Yet there have been drastic cuts to prison education programs, despite the studies' affirmative statistics. If prison writing programs assist in reducing recidivism, as the testimonials of the women at WCCC certainly confirm, why do these programs remain undocumented and largely unsupported? Lack of funding, the programs' dependency on their teachers and administrators, and the turnover of inside women themselves who, like Liezel, occasionally exit the facility earlier than scheduled, leave the programs fragile and vulnerable to attrition. In 2016, Pat Clough decided to take a hiatus from the Kailua Prison Writing Project. Although another teacher and I were able to teach creative writing at the facility, there was no one to take over the Prison Monologues program in Clough's absence. Without Clough, and deprived of the support of the prominent former warden Mark Kawika Patterson, who had left WCCC, the Kailua Prison Writing Project faced expiry.

My pedagogical praxis and my attitudes toward the categories of "guilt" and "innocence" of the women inside have also evolved over the years of my association with the program. When I initially began observing the writing classes and interviewing the women inside, I envisioned the women solely as victims of an unjust society. I was a sympathetic audience for the women's traumatic narratives, which leaked into the classroom. Over the years, I came to question my assumption, and accepted that the women could potentially be, and often were, both victims and perpetrators. In my last conversation with Pat Clough at Morning Brew Café in Kailua in May 2017, Clough said: "I never forgot where I was."

Here I turn to my own pedagogical practices within an incarcerated classroom, with a particular focus on the pedagogies and rituals that I implement. In my classroom, I attempt to employ a writing workshop model that encourages the inside women to become effective peer critics. I frequently encourage the women to give feedback to their peers prior to offering my insights and always ask the writer to articulate what she needs from her reader. Having spent many years in creative writing workshops, I attempt to import this circle pedagogy into my Poetry and Performance Lab. Like Shotland, I bring in revolutionary texts to the classroom from time to time through the "back door." Partially due to the laxity at wccc, the guards "manning" the bubble have stopped checking the materials I transport to class, submerged within stacks of unruly papers. From time to time, I show the incendiary HBO program *Def Poetry* hosted by Mos Def uninterrupted.[6] After sitting in on Clough's writing classes for close to two years, I can attest that the selection of a writerly canon influences both the texts generated by the inside women and the types of conversations that circulate in the classroom. In fact, the influence of the canon extends to the oral testimony, discourse, and public and private conversations that I share with the women in class, and at times after class.

I never directly witnessed mention of wives, girlfriends, or lovers during Clough's classes, even though Alana says that 90 percent of women in the facility are gay, or at least "gay for the stay." Alana, who does not identify as gay, has nevertheless met her life partner in the facility while taking my summer Poetry and Performance Lab in 2016 and is excited to join her in life when she is released from the prison. One could argue that Clough has better boundaries than I do, but as in classes in the "free" world, there are all types of educators.

A recurring theme that those inside express in testimonials from creative writing programs in the prisons is that writing gifts them a "voice"—and that prior to the class they were without a voice. This is the emotion that Ivelisse expresses in the promotional Prison Monologues video, which ends with her uncharacteristically shy, halting words: "I found my voice."[7] Although many women testify to the transformative impact of the Kailua Prison Writing Project, it is not a panacea, for it remains located within a disciplinary regime. This is evident even in the unexpected and varied ways that the women themselves occasionally resist the pedagogical praxes. Clough confirms that her classroom at times functions as a disciplinary space:

> The control I maintained though for sure ... it was informed by my own background, had more to do with the place (prison) and the personalities—some on meds, some with chronic disorders that caused fights. I steered toward calm acceptance. Firmness was often essential and I think they came to respect each other more. I'd like to think that carried over into the dorms. I think the women came to value honesty. They were quick to point out when someone wasn't and they learned how to speak to each other, as well as read to each other knowing they were in a safe space and they were valued.[8]

The privilege of sitting in on Pat Clough's class for two years allowed me to witness another writing teacher's pedagogy up close, including the tours, detours, and trajectories of two classes over two terms. Initially I was a bit wary of the white, mostly male canon of writers that Clough implemented. I recall being quite surprised at how passionately the women responded to Robert Frost, particularly after teaching Frost in high schools to unenthusiastic students. I remember thinking, perhaps rather narrowly: What could the women inside have in common with Robert Frost? Thus, when asked to substitute for Clough on a couple of occasions, I arrived at the Tuesday class, armed with Haunani-Kay Trask's series of poems from *Night Is a Sharkskin Drum*. While some women celebrated Trask's righteous anger, as I had expected, others resisted her words rooted in resistance. One Native Hawaiian woman from the island of Hawai'i loudly protested against Trask's anger, insisting to the class that living "off tourism" as a bus driver in Hilo had kept her alive. I felt foolish after the class and took a closer look at my assumptions about pedagogy, race, and culture. In fact, the texts that Clough used resonated more deeply with some of the women than Trask's politically charged poetry. Of course, this can be explained by the collateral afterlives of colonization: an internalized colonial imaginary. Ultimately, what began as a critique of Clough's archive evolved into self-critique. Clough also countered my assessment of her literary canon in her letter to me: "I wish I had had a book list of source material I used over the years I taught at wccc. You would have seen more Pacific Rim anthologies, art work depicting Hawaiian legends that we interpreted in writing, Hawaiian writers and teachers who brought in their own work to share, such as Lee Cataluna."[9]

Along with *Def Poetry*, I like to utilize visual texts in my classroom. On a couple of occasions, I screened excerpts from Eve Ensler's video *What I Want My Words to Do to You*. Alana clearly prefers the racy *Def Poetry* and dismisses Ensler's work for falling into the category of a process group. Ensler has the women in her Bedford Hills writing class revisit their crimes in response to what seems, in the video, to be the initial writing prompt. There is no evidence of building trust as part of the class community—a quality so palpable in Clough's classes. Instead, the film showcases a "damaged community."[10] Ensler asks the women to write letters to their "victims" and share their writing in the next class. This "request"/demand results in scintillating tales of grief, sorrow, and brutality. As a viewer of these heartbreaking confessionals—the forty-year-old woman who kills one of her johns, a man in his seventies, due to her accumulated rage at a lifetime of abuse—one may query where redemption begins and where it ends. Perhaps these are the tales that an outside audience craves. Prison writing can be an act of disidentification, a concurrent harnessed and liberatory praxis that inserts the "prisoner" into a fantastical lens consumed by voyeurs.

From teaching my Friday afternoon class, I have come to know both Nicole and Alana through their writing and intimate conversations, as they are repeat takers in my Poetry and Performance Lab. My encounters with Nicole have been transformative, and in some ways painful. I choose to share some of these compelling interactions as a way to trace my own preconceptions as an educator in an incarcerated classroom, as well as an avenue to demonstrate that personal inflections transform pedagogy.

Nicole arrived in class on March 3, 2016, smelling of the kitchen. I spot her at the edge of the classroom doorway, her eyebrows arched in an atypical huff. With a pen perched in her ponytail, she strides across the linoleum floor, her pants legs stuffed into black rubber boots. Her energy today is decidedly heavy. "I am quitting the kitchen," she erupts, as she chronicles the pettiness and power struggles enacted in the kitchen. "I expected there to be dysfunction between inmates, but not between inmates and the chefs from the outside." Nicole is the veggie chef. She tells the other women, "Don't expect dinner to be anything tonight. It's chowder. I am sure you're going to taste my mood in that soup!" Mama is a large-boned, tattooed, part Native Hawaiian woman—a fixture in the kitchen who informs me that she has lost close to two hundred pounds in the facility due to the food. Apparently, she has decided that she hates Nicole, even though last term they were tight.

Halfway through our class, a petite man with a heavy Filipino accent knocks timidly at the door and anxiously addresses Nicole: "You *are* coming back to the kitchen—aren't you?" The kitchen is not one of the highest-paying jobs in the facility at twenty-five cents per hour. Even so, Nicole likes the job for the easy gossip and lively atmosphere. But that was before the dysfunction set in.

Each week Nicole turns in breathtaking pieces—lengthy poetry, mostly. Her writing is sumptuous: a cascade of words replete with delicious imagery. Each week the rest of the women are amazed, as am I, by her brilliance: her skill with language, her constructive critique of her peers' writing, her sophisticated theories on writing and life. As the context of Nicole's auto/biography seeps into the classroom—multiple rapes, "falling in love" with one's rapist, murder—I realize that she is writing from an exceedingly dark place.

When Nicole hurtles into class on that February day, she blurts out that she has never taken any type of psychotropic medication. "Meds," she insists, "are not my addiction." The only time she acquiesced was as a teenager, based on her lawyer's advice in order to support her insanity plea. Nicole was charged with murder but did not receive a life sentence due to her underage status in the state of Georgia. But Nicole is far from mad. During the term, I encourage the women to submit work for the PEN national writers' competition that the organization holds for "inmates" every year in four genres: poetry, fiction, nonfiction, and playwriting. One Friday, I agree to meet with Nicole about her submission to the competition, as well as to offer advice about a fantasy novel that she wants to publish. Nicole arrives at our meeting in one of the small education rooms, fortified with her portfolio that contains the samples the women have been working on: an experimental creation of each other's bios; her cover letter to the editors of the PEN writing prize; her title page, which lists her poetry; and her selection of poems. Nicole is extremely diligent about her writing, and one day, when she has to miss class due to an illness, she sends her poem to class with Alana. In fact, this particular writing class is the most engaged group of writers I have ever had the privilege of facilitating. During our first one-on-one consultation, Nicole divulges her crime. "I have done bad things," she tells me. "I will be here for a long time." Later I learn that Nicole "has a retainer on her" from the state of Georgia, which keeps her at a medium-security status and in the kitchen. "There are only four jobs I can technically do with a medium-security status—sewing is one of them—and I don't sew."

When Nicole tells me about her crimes, I am shaken, horrified. I grieve, in part, for my naive assumption that all the women are in the facility on trumped-up drug charges. I had responded to Nicole all along as one writer to the next, commenting on the aesthetics and cosmetics of her sentence structure, attempting to bury the tragic and brutal context in some other part of my brain. Following Clough's advice, I never asked the women about their crimes. This was also one of the important lessons that the Walls to Bridges Program imparted to us as prison facilitators in training. And then there was my intuition that guided me to the precept that to ask the women about their "crimes" was a way to reduce them to past transgressions, or even to crimes that they might not have committed. It was also an avenue to extract sensational confessions.

Thus, when Nicole told me her story, I felt both intrigued and frightened. I felt overly sensitized to her proximity to me on that Friday afternoon: her starched white T-shirt tight against her body, her overarched eyebrows, and the very red lipstick she had begun to wear. When I praised her ability to alter her handwriting when speaking in different voices, she glared at me and spat in a tone that I had never heard: "I hate it when people analyze my handwriting." This was the only time I have ever felt uncomfortable in the incarcerated classroom. I became acutely aware that Nicole and I were alone—Nicole, who had burned down her home with her father inside at the age of fifteen. Due to her status as a juvenile, her family history of abuse, and the fact that this was her first serious offense, Nicole was extradited to her sister's home in Hawai'i.[11]

At home that evening I did something that I am not proud of. I took Nicole's dare to "look her up" and, yes, I googled her, splintering the bond between teacher and student. There was Nicole, smiling elatedly at the closed face of her boyfriend in court. The boyfriend was the physical perpetrator in the stabbing of her sister, who was in the military and pregnant. This cemented Nicole's life sentence. Under the court photograph was text that painted Nicole as a psychopath. I was unable to reconcile the smart, edgy Nicole from my class—the gifted writer—with that description, or with the young, almost cherubic face that peered up at me from the screen.

Nicole and Alana are in some ways exceptional students. They are critical of the system, and both are able to articulate their dissent succinctly. But out there in 'Olomana, the "jungle," as the women call it, they are careful not to reveal their frustration. Alana, in particular, has uncovered ways to negotiate the system. This is her second time in the facility, and she too has "high" charges of assault. It is only at the end of the term that she confides that she is an incest victim. Reflective of her up-front character and intellect, Alana says: "I always ask women in here directly, because I want to know if they are incest survivors—80 percent are—and if they are gay or just gay for the stay. I think most of the women are just lonely."

Both Nicole and Alana reject the women's auto/biographies with their predictable arc from trauma to healing. They also reject what they refer to as the tiresome process group with its tenet of religious conversion and its apparatus of brainwashing. In some ways both Alana and Nicole are too smart for process groups. Nicole vehemently resists any type of religious conversion: "Listen to this bullshit, I am in advanced ukulele and I can't even play because the teacher wants to convert me. It was worse in Georgia. I will never forget the traumatizing time when I was a juvenile and incarcerated in the state prison. A woman, ministering to us, cornered me in a room and refused to let me out until I was *saved*! I was a lot more sensitive then and this experience haunts me." Nicole brings in some of her old poetry that she wrote as a teenager in the Georgia prison. The words sit on lined pages—those antiquated pages from Bible school with rubber-stamped endorsements of God at the bottom of the page.

I know I have one more teaching term ahead of me, and the impending departure from the facility fills me with remorse and an intractable depression. I don't want to leave. These days, the only thing that makes sense to me is the work I do in the prison. The types of conversations that I share with the women inside feel more genuine than those I have on the outside.

Departure: A Lesson in Discipline

I am leaving for the day—heading to an awards ceremony organized by the local chapter of the American Association of University Women. I am late and have to take the bus, which departs from the Kailua side only twice an hour. As I make my way down the hill out of Maunawili cottage and head to the main bubble, the guard sees me coming, but rather than letting me pass, he directs a barrage of insults at the women inside. Through the glass, I see his legs splayed, his head nodding in contempt as he stuffs popcorn in his mouth. I knock at the window, timidly at first, but then more assertively. For more than twenty minutes, I knock as he refuses to acknowledge me. I can feel myself tremble, enraged at his dismissal and at the prospect of missing my speech. I know I wouldn't last a day inside.

This temporary moment of humiliation is a microcosm of the extensive humiliations that the inside women face on a daily basis. My sense of disempowerment reminds me of the time that Clough gets locked in the white prison van at a Prison Monologues performance. Clough, visibly shaken by her experience, shares that moment of panic and desperation in both of her creative writing classes. The women nod in a gesture of understanding, but it is hard to know what they feel inside. After all, unlike the inside women, Clough and I head home after our teaching day. We walk the long and winding path out of Maunawili, past the cats and the roosters on the hill. The door clangs behind us.

Thinking about my life, I'm almost free in a month. It's scary knowing I'm maxing out, getting out for good, no cushion to fall back on. It's up to me now, my life given back to me in my own hands. I've been down for 5 straight. It's almost surreal. I look back and think, "wow, I'm almost out!" I should be happy but it's scary—an oxymoron that delights and hurts at the same moment.

I'm an institutionalized addict, raised by ACOS I've known for 15 years—recycling in and out. Other inmates helped shape my beliefs, strengthening my criminal activity and instant gratification to get what I want. Surviving to get mine, survival of the fittest—like the wild.

It's a game I can be beaten at if I show my heart . . . a maze with many detours. A labyrinth any novice can get lost in. I hide my heart safe and secure. . . . Everyone has something to hide, something to protect. No one wants to hurt, to feel, to seem weak or vulnerable. It's a masquerade, a dance of masks, changing faces, side stepping [one's] true self, pushing away [one's] true worth.

Everyone's hiding from each other—all little girls inside, all broken in pieces . . . each afraid to be seen . . . the recognition in eyes that spark attraction. It's a tug of war. No one can hurt me this way. The sudden . . . gentle nudge to heal, to overcome, to grow, to change—the fight to the light, screaming in silence. . . .

My time is up. It's time for another chapter . . . my life beyond these gates, making the best of what's left of my life . . . freeing myself from the chains of the past, the handcuffs, the regrets. I will not look back. I do not long or yearn for anything here. . . . My future's so bright—I gotta wear shades!

~ Kailani, Women's Community Correctional Center

Performances of the Prison Monologues

The following is a list of the Prison Monologue performances I attended between 2012 and 2014:

- *Hulihia XIII* dedication in the Maunawili courtyard at wccc (September 2012)
- Talent show at wccc Martin Luther King Jr. celebration (2013)
- Roosevelt High School (March 2012 and March 2013)
- Two separate events at Chaminade University, Department of Criminology (March 2012 and March 2013)
- Office of Youth Services annual conference at the Ala Moana Hotel (April 2013)
- Oʻahu's Youth Leadership Conference at JW Marriott Ihilani Resort and Spa, Ocean Ballroom (February 2013)
- National League of American PEN Women Honolulu Branch Meeting at Alan Wong's Pineapple Room (February 2013)
- Bobby Benson Residential Treatment Program in Nānākuli (November 2012); Girl's Court (July 2013); Kapolei, Kaimukī, Farrington, and Sacred Hearts high schools (February to May 2013)
- Hawaiʻi Pacific University Conference (March 2013)
- Sixth Annual Distinctive Women in Hawaiian History Program He Hoʻolauleʻa No Nā Moʻolelo o Nā Wāhine, a Celebration of Women's History at Honolulu Hale (September 2012 and March 2013)
- Thirtieth Pacific Rim International Forum on the Rights of Persons with Disabilities at the Hawaiʻi Convention Center (April 2014) and an alumnae performance, "Voices from the Inside," at the Women Helping Women benefit at Kapiʻolani Community College (Summer 2014)

Prison Monologues Audition Guide

Pat Clough began the audition on February 16, 2013, with an overview of the Prison Monologues:

> The Big Picture: What are the Monologues? What is the purpose? How did it begin? From what?

She also disseminated a sheet with the following questions:

1: Why are you here?
2: Philosophy of the Prison Monologues: *Serving vs. Helping. Serving:* Knowing yourself—developing skills, insights, self-knowledge, offering your message because you know who you are, *you are humble. Helping* creates a dependency—your dependency on being recognized, seen, admired, needed, image more important than message (*not what I'm seeking*).
3: Motivation: What is it? What does it take to have the right motivation?
4: Initiative: What is it? How do you recognize it?
5: Curiosity: Why is it necessary?
6: Leadership: in the facility—you are now living your words through your actions.
7: Teamwork: You are no more or less important than the members of the team. What are the characteristics of a team player? List.
8: What does it take to be honest with ourselves?
9: What does it mean to have credibility?
10: What is the role of "timing?"

Rate yourself on your answers.

ACKNOWLEDGMENTS

1   Davis et al., *Abolition. Feminism. Now.*, 58.

INTRODUCTION

As I prepared the manuscript for this book, bell hooks passed away. I was introduced to her in Nellie McKay's African American Women Writers seminar at the University of Wisconsin–Madison. We all mourn hooks's passing and honor her indelible impact in this shattered world.

1   See R. Gilmore, *Golden Gulag.*
2   Barrett et al., "More Than Transformative," 18.
3   Barrett et al., "More Than Transformative," 18.
4   The Prison Policy Initiative has only recently added an interrogation of gender identity in its reporting. The 2023 report states: "The data available that are disaggregated by sex are also limited, in that they typically only differentiate between 'male' and 'female,' ignoring the reality that the gender identities of confined people (and all people, for that matter) are not limited to this binary. . . . This field of research has a long way to go before the data are consistently collected and reported by gender identity rather than an administrative categorization of 'male' versus 'female.'" Kajstura and Sawyer, *Women's Mass Incarceration: The Whole Pie 2023.*
5   The Sentencing Project, "Fact Sheet: Incarcerated Women and Girls."
6   United Nations Office on Drugs and Crime, "Women and HIV in Prison Settings."
7   Scholars and activists such as Beth Richie, Angela Davis, and Andrea Ritchie have contributed immeasurably to transporting public attention to the incarceration of women—particularly Black women.
8   For an exploration of the historical incarceration of Kānaka Maoli—Native Hawaiians—and its contemporary implications, see Keahiolalo-Karasuda, "The Colonial Carceral and Prison Politics in Hawai'i."

9 For relatively recent anthologies by and about incarcerated women that fill the gap and speak to women's communal writing practices, see Jacobi and Stanford, *Women, Writing, and Prison*; Solinger et al., *Interrupted Life*; Lawston and Lucas, *Razor Wire Women*; and Jacobi, "Twenty-Year Sentences."

10 The direct translation for *ho'oponopono* is "correct/mental cleansing: family conferences in which relationships were set right." This "setting right" is achieved through "prayer, discussion, confession, repentance, and mutual restitution and forgiveness." Pukui and Elbert, *Hawaiian Dictionary*. However, as an external reviewer for Duke University Press pointed out, it is problematic to collapse the Indigenous model of *ho'oponopono* with the Christian framework of forgiveness and reconciliation. Some Native Hawaiians are currently contesting the cultural appropriation of *ho'oponopono* in restorative justice circles.

11 I want to thank an external reviewer at Duke University Press who encouraged me to foreground this idea.

Note: I use diacritical marks—kahakō (macron) and 'okina—except in the case of texts derived from another source (quotation, proper name, or creative writing). For the name Kanaka Maoli, I use the macron when referring to the plural (Kānaka Maoli or Kānaka) but not when using the singular.

12 Penney, "Creating a Place of Healing and Forgiveness," 1. Here I use the word *inmate* because it is utilized in the publication.

13 Sawyer and Bertram, "Prisons and Jails Will Separate Millions of Mothers from Their Children."

14 "Working to Make Justice Healing and to Increase Peace," Hawai'i Friends of Restorative Justice newsletter (Summer 2022), University of Hawai'i at Mānoa. These devastating statistics echo the fact that in the continental United States, the mortality rate for Black mothers is three times that for white mothers.

15 Kates, *Moving beyond Prison*.

16 Richie, "Feminist Ethnographies of Women in Prison," 438.

17 In 1994, Congress ended a prominent federal effort to support higher education behind bars. People incarcerated in state and federal prisons became ineligible for Pell Grants through a provision of the omnibus crime bill that President Bill Clinton signed into law. The House, then controlled by Democrats, approved the provision on a vote of 312 to 116. In December 2020, lawmakers expanded access to Pell Grants once again to include students who are incarcerated, as long as they are enrolled in prison education programs that are approved by their state corrections departments or the Federal Bureau of Prisons, and that meet other requirements. This was a focus of many panels and conversations at the Eleventh National Conference on Higher Education in Prison that I attended in Denver, Colorado, in November 2021.

18 I have a view into the power and limits of the reinstatement of Pell Grants based on my current work in Illinois as a member of the Illinois Coalition for Higher Education in Prison (IL-CHEP) and in my work establishing a higher education in prison program between Knox College and Henry Hill Correctional Facility in Galesburg. IL-CHEP foregrounds the experience and knowledge of the inside community.

19 Harkins and Meiners, "Beyond Crisis." The authors argue that the "prison upris-
ings throughout the 1970s—from Pontiac to Attica—pushed for greater access to
relevant and quality education for people behind bars. These movements linked
educational access to broader aims of self-determination, racial justice, and prison
abolition and were connected to larger race radical freedom struggles of the period. In the wake of these legislative and activist demands, education programs
in prison flourished. By the 1990s, hundreds of college programs awarding
degrees were offered in correctional facilities across the country. . . . In 1994
the Violent Crime Control and Law Enforcement Act restricted access to Pell
Grants for incarcerated people. . . . As a result, roughly 350 college programs in
prison closed."

20 The Bard Prison Initiative, which houses the Consortium for the Liberal Arts in
Prison, currently comprises fifteen institutions, including Wesleyan University in
Connecticut, Grinnell College in Iowa, Goucher College in Maryland, and Bard
College in New York: https://bpi.bard.edu. For an insight into the Bard Prison
Initiative, see the documentary film *College Behind Bars*, directed by Lynn Novick
(PBS, 2019).

21 Patterson was joined by executive director Toni Bissen and Puanani Burgess of the
Puʻa Foundation, and University of Hawaiʻi psychologist Patrick Uchigakiuchi. In a
television interview at Hawaiʻi Pacific University, Bissen articulates that the initiative used the acronym SPACE (staff, programming, administration, community, and
environment)—all recipients for trauma-informed care training. The trauma initiative uses the framework of a *puʻuhonua* for women to "build their beloved community" and to transform their lives. According to a report by the National Center
for Trauma-Informed Care: "The field of trauma-informed care emerged in the past
20 years. Rather than focusing on treating trauma symptoms, trauma-informed care
is a philosophy for reorganizing service environments to meet the unique needs of
survivors and to avoid inadvertent re-traumatization. Trauma-informed practices
support resilience, self-care, and healing. In trauma-informed settings, everyone is
educated about trauma and its consequences, and everyone is mindful of the need
to make the environment more healing and less re-traumatizing for both program
participants and staff." Penney, "Creating a Place of Healing and Forgiveness," 3.

22 Penney, "Creating a Place of Healing and Forgiveness," 1.

23 See Kosasa, "Journey to Justice." I italicize the word *him* because in this interview
the warden uses the masculine pronoun.

24 Kosasa, "Journey to Justice."

25 I want to thank an external reviewer at Duke University Press who clarified the
specificity of Pacific Islander as a marker.

26 For an exploration of the complex manifestations of *hulihia* in our contemporary
political landscape, see Goodyear-Kaʻōpua et al., *The Value of Hawaiʻi 3: Hulihia,
the Turning*.

27 This quotation is taken from testimonial language utilized in publicity materials,
including by the State of Hawaiʻi, as well as in local newspapers.

28 Conversation with Pat Clough at a popular local café, Morning Brew, in Kailua,
May 15, 2017.

29   Patterson has achieved success at HYCF in his implementation of a *puʻuhonua* where Hawaiian healing modalities are integrated with therapeutic programming. With his innovative vision, Patterson has spurred a 75 percent reduction in incarceration, which eventuated in a repurposing of the HYCF "campus" and three hundred acres of agricultural land. See Office of Hawaiian Affairs, "A Correctional Center Becomes a Puʻuhonua."

30   At the start of the COVID-19 outbreak in early 2020, I had just begun teaching a creative writing class at SCI Phoenix in Pennsylvania—a maximum-security men's prison—as part of Villanova University's program at SCI Phoenix. Formerly the Graterford Program, the Villanova program is one of the oldest continuously running degree-granting prison education programs in the United States. The pandemic ushered in a complete halt to my class as the men went into lockdown—the inhumane way in which prisons have addressed the pandemic crisis.

31   The PEN Prison Writing Program is part of the larger PEN American Center, founded after World War I to "[dismantle] barriers to free expression and reach across borders to celebrate, through writing, our common humanity." PEN America, https://pen.org.

32   The International PEN Writing Program began in the 1920s.

33   Today, American prison writing programs are infiltrated with educators—a movement away from artists as cultural ambassadors to one in which educators are heralded as transmitters of knowledge. A plethora of universities have now connected with prison writing programs, and the recent trend is to offer credit-based courses toward degree acquisition for those inside. Another burgeoning development is the proliferation of Inside-Out programs throughout the nation and globally. See Pompa, "Drawing Forth, Finding Voice, Making Change." Simone Weil Davis, who brought Inside-Out to Canada, wrote "Inside-Out," a metatextual exploration of the Inside-Out Prison Exchange Program, which hosts campus-enrolled and incarcerated students together as classmates in postsecondary courses constructed around dialogue, collaboration, and experiential learning within a carceral setting. Similar to the praxis of theater, where the liminal and unexpected are transformative, Weil Davis celebrates the conspiracy of committing poetry, where a single poem can indeed alter our world. For another example of Inside-Out pedagogical praxis, see Shailor, *Performing New Lives*. I explore the ethics of pedagogical praxis in a prison classroom in chapter 1; as well as the summoning of a feminist-inspired and ethical critical literacy in the introduction.

34   Established in 2008, the Justice Arts Coalition (formerly the Prison Arts Coalition) serves as a national network for prison arts in the United States. Justice Arts Coalition, "Welcome to the Justice Arts Coalition (JAC)."

35   The inside writers Jack Abbott, Eldridge Cleaver, George Jackson, Angela Davis, and Assata Shakur, for example, held the nation-state culpable for its human rights abuses, particularly against Black and Latinx communities. Their prose, whether fictional, expository, or testimonial, can be articulated as "out-

law writing." Carceral writing can be read as diasporic writing: a writing of exile. Indigenous critical prison scholar Luana Ross and Canadian scholar Deena Rymhs—whose research on Indigenous writing focuses on issues of mobility and spatial politics—explore the pain of exile for marginalized communities that are already in exile: economically, spiritually, and culturally. Indigenous writers are doubly displaced, as they are frequently imprisoned on their Indigenous home-lands, in wasteland spaces, proximate to reservations.

36 Here I use the word *inmate* because it is implemented in the Prison Monologues' promotional materials.

37 The following description is included in publicity materials disseminated at the Prison Monologues presentation to the PEN Women Writers' meeting, which I attended in Honolulu in 2013: "In 2008, the creative writing classes hosted its first book dedication in the prison facility courtyard. [Then] Governor Linda Lingle [the sixth governor of Hawai'i from 2002 until 2010] was present and celebrated with the women writers who read their best work. She then challenged them to keep writing, keep learning, to become role models for their children. Acclaimed by TV and print media at the debut event, one reporter suggested that all O'ahu's high schools should see the production. 'Prison Monologues' was born."

38 "The Pacific Rim International Conference, considered one of the most 'diverse gatherings' in the world, encourages and respects voices from 'diverse' perspec-tives across numerous areas, including: voices from persons representing all dis-ability areas; experiences of family members and supporters across all disability and diversity areas; responsiveness to diverse cultural and language differences; evidence of researchers and academics studying diversity and disability; stories of persons providing powerful lessons; examples of program providers; and ac-tion plans to meet human and social needs in a globalized world." "Pacific Rim International Conference on Disability and Diversity 2017," https://www.hawaii .edu/calendar/manoa/2017/10/09/31053.html. See the Pacific Rim International Conference on Disability and Diversity website: https://pacrim.coe.hawaii.edu.

39 Here I refer to the criminal justice system, rather than the criminal legal system, to reflect the language utilized by the state. See Kosasa, "Journey to Justice." Also extracted from a conversation with Warden Patterson at the WCCC facility in 2013.

40 James, *The New Abolitionists*.

41 See Whitlock, *Soft Weapons*.

42 See AP News, "Hawaii Governor Withholds Funds for Corrections Oversight." In March 2021, Hawai'i lawmakers finally advanced a bill to grant additional funds for an all-volunteer corrections oversight commission that was accorded powers in 2019 but lacked sufficient funding to hire a staff. Governor David Ige withheld funds reportedly due to the economic recession that resulted from the COVID-19 pandemic. The additional funds have been supported by groups such as the American Civil Liberties Union of Hawai'i and the Community Alliance on Prisons. I sat in on a few of the commission's meetings, which are open to the community. There was much concern about how the State was handling the pan-demic and its deleterious effects on the inside community—both in Hawai'i and

in Arizona. The oversight commission is calling for a moratorium on the state Department of Public Safety's public-private partnership to fund a $525 million project to build a new Oʻahu jail complex in the Hālawa area.

43 See van Gelder, "Can Prison Be a Healing Place?"

44 A *loʻi* is a patch of land dedicated to growing kalo (taro). Hawaiians have traditionally used water irrigation systems to produce kalo. The *loʻi* is part of an *ahupuaʻa*, a division of land from the mountain to the sea. On reentry and transition planning circles, see Walker and Greening, *Reentry and Transition Planning Circles for Incarcerated People*.

45 For an extended analysis of recuperation of Indigenous resistance to American colonialism, evident in the 1897 petitions against forced annexation to the United States, see Noenoe K. Silva's *Aloha Betrayed*.

46 *Future of the Oʻahu Community Correctional Center* 14, "WCCC Expansion Planning Underway" (August 2017), https://dps.hawaii.gov/wp-content/uploads/2017/08/Hawaii-OCCC_newsletter_Vol14_v8.pdf. I interrogate the Department of Public Safety's linguistic utilization of "houses," which conflates the prison with a home, rather than the warehousing of inside people for profit. Likewise, "cottages" serves to feminize the carceral space.

47 Hina Mauka developed Ke Alaula—a unique, therapeutic community-treatment program based on traditional Hawaiian culture and values. The program is the result of a collaboration between the state's Department of Public Safety and the WCCC warden and his staff. While outcomes are still being compiled for this relatively new program, testimonials from staff, families of clients, and clients themselves show the transformation taking place: clients growing in self-esteem, clarity of purpose, and resolve to build happier, healthier, and more productive lives. See the prison's website: http://dps.hawaii.gov/wccc.

48 "The Bridge is a fifteen-bed open housing unit (no corrections officers are stationed there) providing transitional substance abuse services and assisting women in developing mind, body, and spiritual wellness to support their reentry. Many women in the program have jobs outside the facility. They also participate in community re-integration activities to reduce the rate of recidivism and parole violations." Penney, "Creating a Place of Healing and Forgiveness," 8.

49 Total Life Recovery is a "faith-based, gender specific program that addresses every area of a woman's life mentally, emotionally, spiritually and physically." Total Life Recovery, "Turning Stories into Life Changing Lessons." Note the utopic and redemptive language with which these programs are described.

50 In a 2013 interview with Dr. Eiko Kosasa at the facility, Warden Patterson made reference to these statistics, which he said are representative of national statistics on women and crime. Kosasa, "Journey to Justice."

51 "WCCC Improvements Moving Forward" is the fourth section of *Future of the Oʻahu Community Correctional Center* 26, "Improving Facilities on Oʻahu" (November 2020), https://dps.hawaii.gov/wp-content/uploads/2020/11/Hawaii-OCCC_newsletter_Vol26-v4.pdf-11-19-20-RN.pdf.

52 "WCCC Improvements Moving Forward."

53 Harkins and Meiners, "Beyond Crisis."

54 Penney, "Creating a Place of Healing and Forgiveness," 1.

55 Patterson was invited as a keynote speaker to the 2015 Criminal Justice Forum in British Columbia. In his keynote, "The Cycle of Trauma in the Criminal Justice System," Patterson addressed how he "transformed both a youth correctional facility and a women's prison from a modality of punishment to one of treatment using the methodology of trauma-informed care." He stated, "To enhance gender-specific programming for incarcerated girls, HYCF continues collaborating with Project Kealahou [the New Pathway in Hawaiian] to positively impact the girls at the facility. Project Kealahou is twofold. Advocates/counselors from the program work directly with the girls who have been the victims of trauma. Additionally, Youth Correctional Officers who work with the female population receive trauma-informed training to enhance their sensitivity and to broaden their skills and knowledge." See the Office of Youth Services website: https:// humanservices.hawaii.gov/oys/office/. Clearly, Patterson is invested in treatment over punishment.

Thanks to Warden Patterson's efforts, as of June 2022, there are no girls incarcerated in HYCF. See Healy, "Hawaii Has No Girls in Juvenile Detention." For a considered discussion of the racialized school-to-prison pipeline, see Meiners, *Right to Be Hostile*.

56 Prison Policy Initiative, *Hawai'i Profile*.

57 ACLU, *Blueprint for Smart Justice: Hawai'i*.

58 Chesney-Lind and Brady, "Prisons," 112.

59 There is much debate about carceral statistics and the percentage of Native Hawaiians in the state's prison population. I owe much gratitude to RaeDeen Keahiolalo-Karasuda's trailblazing work in Hawai'i's prisons. She argues that Native Hawaiians are underreported by the Department of Public Safety because people are comfortable with the approximate 40 percent assessment. Keahiolalo-Karasuda posits that Native Hawaiians constitute close to 60 percent of Hawai'i's prison population. Keahiolalo-Karasuda, "The Colonial Carceral and Prison Politics in Hawai'i," 4–6.

60 *The Disparate Treatment of Native Hawaiians in the Criminal Justice System*, 39. For these statistics, see Chesney-Lind and Bilsky, "Native Hawaiian Youth in Hawai'i Detention Center."

61 *The Disparate Treatment of Native Hawaiians in the Criminal Justice System*, 38.

62 Prison Policy Initiative, "Hawai'i Incarceration Rates by Race/Ethnicity, 2010." Calculated by the Prison Policy Initiative from the US Census 2010 Summary File. According to this report, many part Native Hawaiians identify as Samoan or another racial classification, rendering the accurate representation of Native Hawaiians incarcerated in the state opaque. Government and media publications frequently do not utilize accurate Hawaiian diacritics.

63 I thank Brandy Nālani McDougall for her spring 2016 lecture in her Introduction to Indigenous Studies seminar at the University of Hawai'i at Mānoa (in which I was an instructor) that addressed the conditions under which Native Americans

were released from prison in the 1970s. From 1973 to 1976, 3,406 Native American women were sterilized without their permission. The US government recently admitted to forcing thousands of Native American women to be sterilized. Garcia, "8 Shocking Facts about Sterilization in U.S. History."

64　This is according to Flanagin, "Reservation to Prison Pipeline." The much-touted fact that the US "justice" system is "broken" is countered by prison scholars and activists, who argue that the US racialized legal system is working exactly in accordance with its design.

65　Wang, "The U.S. Criminal Justice System Disproportionately Hurts Native People." In South Dakota, the state with the fourth-highest percentage of Native American residents, Native Americans constituted over 52 percent of the federal caseload in Fiscal Year 2021 but only 8.5 percent of the total population. The trend continues across states with similarly substantial Indigenous populations; for example, Native Americans constituted over 26 percent of the caseload in Montana and 34 percent in North Dakota.

66　Evershed and Davidson, "Indigenous Imprisonment Rates Still Rising."

67　According to a report by Binghamton University, "Popularly conceptualized as the model minority, Asian and Pacific Islanders are not exempt from the increasing prison population in the United States. Between 1990 and 2000, the Asian and Pacific Islander prisoner population skyrocketed by 250 percent—an unprecedented rise in the prison population in their history. In addition to increasing incarceration rates, deportation has also increased in dramatic numbers, particularly in the Asian and Pacific Islander community." Thach, *Incarceration*, 5.

68　Rojas, *Women of Color and Feminism*, 75.

69　Deer, "Sovereignty of the Soul."

70　According to the local newspaper, the *Honolulu Civil Beat*: "The five-member Hawaiʻi Correctional Systems Oversight Commission voted unanimously to urge the State Department of Public Safety to create an advisory committee to 'review, and if necessary revise the planning that has been done to date, and to actively participate in the planning process going forward.' Ted Sakai, a commission member and former director of the Department of Public Safety, said that the latest draft plan for a new jail at the old Animal Quarantine Station site in Hālawa Valley calls for building a facility that can hold 1,380 male inmates." Dayton, "Corrections Commission Wants to Pause Planning on New Oahu Jail."

71　*The Disparate Treatment of Native Hawaiians in the Criminal Justice System*, 41.

72　Hager and Kaneya, "The Prison Visit That Cost My Family $2,370."

73　When men from the Hālawa Correctional Facility were deported to a Texas prison, they were not able to fit in with the Mexican gangs. They formed the United Samoan Organization (USO), the largest Hawaiian gang on the mainland. When they returned to Hālawa, they transported undue aggression and violence to the local prison culture. Interview with Kat Brady, *Star Advertiser*, June 27, 2012. For a complex portrayal of Native Hawaiians finding a connection to their lost Hawaiian identities in a maximum-security private prison in the Arizona desert, see the film *Out of State* (2017) by Native Hawaiian filmmaker Clara Lacy.

Native Hawaiian cultural ambassador Kumu Hinaleimoana Wong-Kalu's restorative justice work at Hālawa is featured in the video OHAHawaii, "Healing in Hālawa with Kumu Hina." Kumu Hina, in a recent talk at a Peace and Justice Studies Association conference, had me rethink mainland as a colonial construct when she asked one of my Native Hawaiian students who grew up in Oregon: "Where is your mainland?" (heart/home).

74 Interview with Kat Brady, *Star Advertiser*.

75 Interview with Kat Brady, *Star Advertiser*.

76 Hawai'i State Legislature, S.B. 467 (Act 258), 2006, https://www.capitol.hawaii.gov /sessions/session2006/bills/SB467_cd1_.htm.

77 See Urbina, "Hawaii to Remove Inmates over Abuse Charges." According to a *Hawaii News Now* article, "Status on Hawaii Inmates in Mainland Prisons," "When Governor Neil Abercrombie assumed office last year, he said his priority was to tackle the state's prison overcrowding problem—that includes bringing home some 1,700 Hawaii prisoners locked up in mainland corrections centers." Several women in my class and Clough's classes, as well as some of the women I interviewed, reported that they preferred mainland prisons because they offer "better" and more varied programming, are cleaner, and expose them to another world (most of these women had never left Hawai'i).

78 Nationally, women constitute 7.5 percent of the prison population, while in Hawai'i, women constitute 14.3 percent of the prison population.

79 Penney, "Creating a Place of Healing and Forgiveness," 1.

80 Sawyer and Wagner, *Mass Incarceration*.

81 Chesney-Lind and Brady, "Prisons," 109.

82 Nellis, "Mass Incarceration Trends."

83 Sawyer and Wagner, *Mass Incarceration*.

84 Fellner, "Punishment and Prejudice."

85 The Sentencing Project, "Fact Sheet: Incarcerated Women and Girls."

86 The Sentencing Project, "Fact Sheet: Incarcerated Women and Girls."

87 Chesney-Lind and Jones, *Fighting for Girls*; Tonry, *Thinking about Crime*.

88 The Sentencing Project, "Report to the United Nations on Racial Disparities in the U.S. Criminal Justice System."

89 The Sentencing Project, "Fact Sheet: Incarcerated Women and Girls."

90 See Richie, *Arrested Justice*; Chesney-Lind and Pasko, *Girls, Women, and Crime*.

91 Carson, "Prisoners in 2019," table 10. See Davis, *Are Prisons Obsolete?*

92 See Chesney-Lind and Jones, *Fighting for Girls*; Owen, "In the Mix."

93 Ross, *Inventing the Savage*; Rymhs, *From the Iron House*, 13.

94 In 1865, the Thirteenth Amendment criminalized African Americans and ushered them into a "civic death." This normalized the legal and cultural disenfranchisement of African Americans in American society. Many theorists in the field of American crime and punishment witness the civic death of imprisonment as a continuation of slavery. See Perkinson, *Texas Tough*; M. Alexander, *The New Jim Crow*.

95 The following texts, which employ feminist perspectives on trauma theory, are primary influences on my argument that trauma studies intersects with prison

studies and women's life writing: Ahmed, *The Cultural Politics of Emotion*; J. Alexander, *Pedagogies of Crossing*; Conway, *When Memory Speaks*; Cvetkovich, *Depression*; De Salvo, *Writing as a Way of Healing*; L. Gilmore, *The Limits of Autobiography*; Henke, *Shattered Subjects*; Maier and Dulfano, *Woman as Witness*; Whitlock, *Soft Weapons*; Williams, *The Alchemy of Race and Rights*.

96 Simpson, *Mohawk Interruptus*, 83. "Hidden transcripts" is a reference to Scott, *Domination and the Arts of Resistance: Hidden Transcripts*.

97 Women's programming, particularly in creative writing, is sparse, and few scholars have paid attention to this topic. Anthologies such as Jacobi and Stanford, *Women, Writing, and Prison*; Lawston and Lucas, *Razor Wire Women*; Scheffler, *Wall Tappings*; and Weil Davis and Roswell, *Turning Teaching Inside Out* are the exceptions. Wally Lamb and Eve Ensler have conducted creative writing programs in the York Correctional Institution in Connecticut and the Bedford Hills Correctional Facility in New York, respectively. Nevertheless, the latter examples summon ethical considerations given that both Lamb and Ensler are celebrities and Ensler has been critiqued for employing "forced confessionals" in her writing classes, which feminist prison practitioners caution against due to their potential for traumatic reinjury. See Lamb, *I'll Fly Away*; Ensler, *What I Want My Words to Do to You*.

98 Fletcher, Shaver, and Moon, *Women Prisoners*.

99 Some of the notable scholars who view prisons refracted through race, gender, sexuality, and class include Michelle Alexander, Andrea Ritchie, Angela Davis, Beth Richie, Ruth Wilson Gilmore, and Meda Chesney-Lind.

100 Many of these theorists call for the downsizing of the industry, while others, like scholar-activists Angela Davis and Ruth Gilmore, agitate for the abolition of the prison-industrial complex—a position that I, too, endorse.

101 Scheffler, *Wall Tappings*; Lawston and Lucas, *Razor Wire Women*; Jacobi and Stanford, *Women, Writing, and Prison*.

102 For an example of pedagogical anthologies, see Lamb, *Couldn't Keep It to Myself*.

103 Lucas, "Identifying Marks: What the Razor Wire Hides," epilogue to Lawston and Lucas, *Razor Wire Women*, 301–3.

104 Formative prison autobiographies Davis, *Angela Davis*, and Shakur, *Assata*, contest the notion of imprisoned women as apolitical.

105 Rymhs, *From the Iron House*, 13. I explore the "second hearing" and secondhand witnesses in both chapters 1 and 4.

106 Rymhs, *From the Iron House*, 14.

107 I wish to thank Lorenn Walker for providing me with a writing room of my own during my 2019 visit to Hawai'i.

108 Smith and Watson, *Reading Autobiography*, 124.

109 Smith and Watson, *Reading Autobiography*, 125.

110 Jacobi and Stanford, *Women, Writing, and Prison*, 100–102.

111 Tuck, "Suspending Damage," 409.

112 Tuck, "Suspending Damage," 416.

113 Tuck, "Suspending Damage," 412.

114 Many prison ethnographers, academics, and practitioners articulate the difficulty in inhabiting the role of both ethnographer and teacher in an incarcerated space. In "Closed Doors: Ethical Issues with Prison Ethnography,"
John M. Coggeshall unveils the particular obstacles involved in both teaching
and conducting ethnography in a medium-security male prison in a place he
never names. Ultimately, Coggeshall discloses that he felt a moral ambivalence
toward his informants, the "inmates," and was encumbered by the necessity to
choose between the institution and his informants/students.

115 Other autoethnographies that inspire this monograph include Julie Taylor's
Paper Tangos for its use of poetics and the evocation of place, Karen McCarthy's
Mama Lola for its use of parallel voices of ethnographer and informant, and
Alice Goffman's *On the Run* for the complex issues it raises about class and racial
appropriation and ethics. For a methodological text on feminist ethnography,
see Ettorre, *Autoethnography as Feminist Method*.

116 Clough shared this with me in an email correspondence on June 18, 2017, after
she read the manuscript for this book. Her reading ushered in several email
exchanges, which I have incorporated into the final book.

117 Oliver, *Witnessing: Beyond Recognition*.

118 See Hinshaw and Jacobi, "What Words Might Do." Also see Weil Davis, "Inside-
Out," 163–75.

119 Hinshaw and Jacobi, "What Words Might Do." See also Collis, Davis, and Smith,
"Breaking Free while Locked Up," 171, in Hinshaw and Jacobi's special issue
of *Reflections* (19, no. 1). This tactical redistribution of power is inspired by
feminists committed to social justice. See Davis, *Are Prisons Obsolete?*; Mohanty,
Feminism without Borders.

120 Hinshaw and Jacobi, "What Words Might Do"; Weil Davis, "Inside-Out."

121 Weil Davis, "Inside-Out."

122 The interviews accompanied a consent form that was signed by all participants,
according to IRB requisites.

123 Girshick, *No Safe Haven*.

124 Duff and Garcia Coll, *Reframing the Needs of Women in Prison*, 16.

125 I applied for and received IRB approval on February 21, 2013, to conduct my
interviews at WCCC. On February 21, 2014, my IRB approval was renewed for an
additional year.

126 The number of women in the classes shifted over the term, with the beginning
class being more volatile. Midway, some women were dropped from the class
due to behavioral and administrative infractions. At times, there were issues
with "wives" taking the class together and disrupting the class community.

127 Clough's class terms run for ten weeks, and there are two terms per year.

128 Huikahi (literally "individual and community") is an Indigenous form of restorative justice. Women's Way is a parole reentry and drug treatment program.
Unfortunately, Tessa, who wrote humorous poems, such as "Fat Lips," and was
a fan of Angela Davis, was returned to WCCC after a couple months at Women's
Way due to a violation of its rules: the use of her cell phone. Tessa accompanied

me to Angela Davis's keynote address "Freedom Is a Constant Struggle," at the University of Hawai'i Mānoa Campus, on April 8, 2016.

129 At the time, Vailea, one of the original Prison Monologues women, was participating in the "outside" Prison Monologues group—Voices From the Inside, which included two other Prison Monologues alumnae. Voices From the Inside was active in addressing the broader community, performing for school groups and conferences.

130 After Vailea, Ivelisse, and Reiko were released from prison, the Prison Monologues lost its core members. Only Liezel remained. Clough established the Prison Monologues Lab, which Liezel led over the summer of 2014 when Clough left for California. I attended a few initial rehearsals and laboratory workshops. Up until early 2015, the group was still in training and had not reached the polish and cohesion of the more established Prison Monologues group. At the first lab rehearsal, Clough disseminated a Prison Monologues expectation guide that addresses credibility, timing, standards, investment, the role of writing, presentation skills, and practice. The guide includes a self-assessment related to teamwork, honesty, leadership, initiative, motivation, and the "serving versus helping philosophy."

131 Tengan, *Native Men Remade*; Franklin and Fuchs, "Shifting Ground." Irwin and Umemoto's *Jacked Up and Unjust* is a nine-year ethnographic collaboration with inner city and rural young people in Hawai'i who confront racism, sexism, poverty, and political negligence.

132 Whitlock, *Soft Weapons*, 119, 122.

1. PEDAGOGY AND PROCESS

1 Allyson wrote "Governmental Seduction" in response to the HBO series *Def Poetry*, which the students viewed in my Friday class in November 2015.

2 Allyson's poem began (as she articulated in class) as a personal ode of seduction that journeyed, perhaps not so strangely, into a critique of the nation-state. Here the erotic sits close to systemic tentacles of power.

3 I use the word *sacred* in this chapter to foreground the transformative nature of life writing in this particular class based on my observations, facilitation of the class, and, foremost, the testimony of the inside women in the interviews I conducted. The healing that occurs in this incarcerated classroom approximates liberation because of the transformational potential this community of writers has for the writers in the class. As the idea of the sacred carries a fraught genealogy, I use this word divorced from any religious context.

4 The idea of "self" is part of the rhetoric omnipresent in the Hina Mauka and Total Life Recovery programs. The women frequently refer to "self" without an article before it as though it is a psychological and epistemological containment.

5 I interrogate the notion of freedom as the inside women reminded me that communities on the outside are often not free psychologically, spiritually, or emotionally.

6   I am indebted to Kelly Oliver's argument about witnessing as a radical act that summons mutual vulnerabilities across hierarchical divides. Oliver, *Witnessing: Beyond Recognition.*

7   *Poseidon and the Bitter Bug* is the eleventh studio album by Indigo Girls, released on March 24, 2009, by Vanguard Records. The title is drawn from lyrics in their song "Fleet of Hope" ("You're all washed up when Poseidon has his day") and from "Second Time Around" ("I've been bitten by the bitter bug"). Some themes the Indigo Girls address are fate's deliverance of cruel blows, dashed dreams, and love gone wrong—all infused with social justice overtones.

8   The twelve-step programs are modified to fit a Hawaiian context, particularly Hina Mauka.

9   There has been much discourse around creative writing classes as sacred communities. Within creative writing pedagogy, there is debate about whether one can actually teach creative writing. See Adam Breckenridge's review "What's Right and Wrong with the Workshop." Questions that haunt creative writing studies and workshops include: "Can creative writing be taught? Can students ever really hope to imitate great writers? Does the creative writing process practiced in universities actually produce great writing . . . ?" As a participant in an academic creative writing graduate program, I ascribe to the power of the writing workshop and a corresponding sacred writing community, which can—depending on the bond between the authors in the class—allow for writerly risks and vulnerabilities that frequently are transformative for the writers.

10 Clough shared this with me in an email correspondence on June 22, 2017, after she read the manuscript.

11 Clough tells me that in all the years of her teaching creative writing at the facility, there was never a single meeting of "faculty" in the prison, which precluded any collaboration.

12 *Haole* means white or foreigner. In contemporary Hawai'i, it is almost exclusively used to mean white. Today the term is used both innocuously and in a racialized way. *Hapa* in Hawai'i is typically reserved for Kānaka Maoli who are of mixed race, but it has been appropriated by Asians without Hawaiian ancestry who are multiracial.

13 Many of the theater/literary/educational practitioners in prison classrooms attest to the fact that prison guards are frequently suspicious of and resentful that the "inmates" are receiving an education, which the guards have been denied. The promise of doing "hard time" without mollification is part of a retributive model, reinforced by the institutional ideology.

14 Koa is an Indigenous wood in Hawai'i. Many Indigenous forms are made from this exquisite wood, such as canoes and bowls (for utility and as art).

15 This is a play on words: *wai* means "water," and *waiwai* means "prosperity."

16 Likewise, reducing the translation of *Hulihia* to "transformation" speaks to the impossibility of transformation within the carceral logics/landscape. Some of the censorship in the journal occurs within the editorial process. The women's relationship with wives and performances of the queer self are not represented in *Hulihia.*

For the most part, romantic relationship as a theme is not included in *Hulihia* or the Prison Monologues. One reason for this could be the program's and Clough's belief in individualism as a requisite for change. The women frequently repeat in class that they are "codependent," a belief perpetuated in the process groups.

17   The women are aware of the deleterious physical space of the small classrooms inhabited by mold, and at times they complain when we are unable to utilize the large room with the computer lab because that space is occupied by the Kapiʻolani Community College (KCC) culinary class. The women come to the creative writing class with wistful food longings after smelling the scents emanating from the dishes of "real" food that the KCC chef creates with the women in his class. The fortunate women in the culinary classes have access to authentic ingredients that are unmarred by the designation "For inmates only!"

18   Clough shared this with me in an email correspondence sent on June 18, 2017, after she read the manuscript.

19   I am utilizing the idea of performance here both as a literal one and as a performative, less conscious derivative.

20   The Hawaiian Homes Commission Act—a land-leasing program—was instituted in 1921 to "rectify" the wrongs of imperialism and the theft of Hawaiian land from its Indigenous people. The act is intended to provide affordable homes for Native Hawaiian families. Waimānalo was designated as homestead land, reserved for Native Hawaiians. However, many Native Hawaiians have not been given leases because they can't afford to build a house on their own land.

21   There are numerous devastations as a result of tourism in Hawaiʻi, many of which are economic. The Whole Foods stores in Kailua and in Kahala, and more recently in Kakaʻako, are flooded with Japanese tourists, which drives up the prices in an already inflated market, targeting people who are health-conscious. The exorbitant prices alienate many local people, particularly Native Hawaiians. Whole Foods competes directly with the local farmers markets and local farmers. When I refer to encounters of imperialism, I have noted that the mostly young to middle-aged Japanese consumers exhibit acts of entitlement that accompany privilege: failing to clear or clean their own tables (assuming someone else will do it) and a general lack of awareness of people around them.

22   Clough testifies in class that she never alters the meaning of the writing but aims to make it "better."

23   Clough, email correspondence, June 18, 2017.

24   I begin to notice that the inside women are incongruously both well informed and isolated from current events in the contemporary world. Although they don't have access to the internet, they are informed about political events in their own and extended communities.

25   It has taken a while for me to read the cultural signage of the prison space. Only recently, in facilitating my own class, did I realize that not all of the women carry a minimum-custody status. "Talk story" is a prevalent expression used on the island. It implies a local way of perceiving reciprocal conversation and the fact that we are all informed by our genealogical stories.

26 The students inform me that they heard from Connie, who now lives in Portugal. She is trying to find a way to move to the United States to live with her daughter.

27 Clough, email correspondence, June 18, 2017.

28 Chesney-Lind and Bilsky, "Native Hawaiian Youth in Hawai'i Detention Center," 134, quoting Lili'uokalani, *Hawai'i's Story by Hawai'i's Queen*, 268.

29 Berry, "Beyond Hope," 2. See Berry, "Doing Time with Literacy Narratives."

30 Berry, "Beyond Hope," 163.

31 For a recent critique of college-in-prison writing programs and literary programs in prisons by inside writers and editors, see Barrett et al., "More Than Transformative"; Roy, "WordsUncaged"; and Martinez, "A Plea for Critical Race Theory Counterstory."

32 Sweeney, "Legal Brutality," 707.

33 According to the Academy of American Poets, "The highly structured villanelle is a nineteen-line poem with two repeating rhymes and two refrains. The form is made up of five tercets followed by a quatrain. . . . Contemporary poets have not limited themselves to the pastoral themes originally expressed by the free-form villanelles of the Renaissance, and have loosened the fixed form to allow variations on the refrains." "Poetic Form Part 2: Villanelle," The Poet's Billow—a Resource for Moving Poetry, June 21, 2012, https://thepoetsbillow.org/2012/06/21/poetic-form-part-2-villanelle/.

34 Clough, email correspondence, June 18, 2017.

35 Milward, review of *Justice as Healing*, 128.

36 Milward, review of *Justice as Healing*.

37 Adrienne Rich, quoted in Jacobi, "Speaking Out for Social Justice," 243. Rich writes: "Most often someone writing a poem believes in, depends on, a delicate, vibrating range of difference, that an 'I' can become a 'we' without extinguishing others, that a partly common language exists to which strangers can bring their own heartbeat, memories, images. A language that itself has learned from the heartbeat, memories, images of strangers." Rich, "Someone Is Writing a Poem."

38 Stanford, "Introduction," 8–9.

39 Feminist carceral-literacy practitioners are critical of Eve Ensler's work in the Bedford Hills maximum-security women's prison in New York State. The theorists point to the ethical transgression in eliciting forced confessionals from those inside, as well as its dangers, such as the potential for traumatic reinjury. See Hinshaw and Jacobi, "What Words Might Do." Also see Weil Davis, "Inside-Out."

40 Whitlock, *Soft Weapons*, 52.

41 Smith and Watson, *Reading Autobiography*, 207.

42 Kaplan, "Resisting Autobiography."

43 Ann Folwell Stanford, founder and former director of the DePaul Women, Writing and Incarceration Project and creative writing facilitator at a woman's prison, argues that we need to focus more adamantly on women's writing behind bars because "as long as prisons and prisoners remain relatively inaccessible, the

myth of prisoners' inherently predatory natures can remain in place to justify the brutality of incarceration." Stanford, "Introduction," 3.

44　In *Limits of Autobiography*, autobiography theorist Leigh Gilmore addresses the burden of marginalized writers' recording of trauma, when by virtue of their gender, race, and sexuality they are dispossessed of legitimate status with which to voice their crime.

45　Pompa, "Disturbing Where We Are Comfortable," 30.

46　Berry, "Doing Time with Literacy Narratives," 141.

47　One of these conundrums occurred in my Poetry and Performance Lab. Nicole, a gifted writer with impeccable grammar and syntax that intimidated some of the other writers, submitted lengthy, exquisite poems each week. The aesthetics of Nicole's writing utterly seduced me, yet the content of her writing was emotionally disturbing: a catastrophic narrative. I persisted in responding to Nicole as one writer to another with extensive comments that addressed the beauty of her writing. It wasn't until our one-on-one consulting session that I uncovered Nicole's life sentence. I realized that the cosmetics of her writing served as an anesthetization and aestheticization of unendurable pain, and I felt ambivalent about how to respond to her—beyond the surfaces of her writing. Here I thank Cynthia Franklin for her encouragement to problematize the dangers inherent in the normalization of trauma narratives in prison.

48　*Bollo* is a Hawaiian Creole English word for bald-headed.

49　Kristin Bumiller teaches an Inside-Out Prison Exchange seminar, "Regulating Citizenship," at the Hampshire Jail and House of Corrections.

50　Shelburne, "Two and a Half Hours a Week."

51　Fuchs, *The Text Is Myself*, 11.

52　Felman and Laub, *Testimony*.

53　Denzin, *Interpretive Autoethnography*.

54　Simon, Rosenberg, and Eppert, *Between Hope and Despair*, 8.

55　Berry, *Doing Time, Writing Lives*, 3.

56　Stanford, "Introduction," 3.

57　"The Stuck-Up Blues," by Allyson, came out of my Friday class in October 2015 in response to the students' viewing of *Def Poetry*. Allyson's institutional dissent mirrors the systemic dissent prevalent in the show, which reveals that the creative writing facilitator's selection of required texts directly influences student-generated writing.

2. "HOME"

A version of this chapter appeared as "Reimagining Home: Redemption and Resistance in Hawai'i Women's Prison Writing," *Signs: Journal of Women in Culture and Society* 46, no. 1 (2020): 201–27. Working with Miranda Outman—my editor at *Signs*—was a journey that impressed on me the collaborative nature of writing. I want to thank her for her discerning intellect and generative suggestions.

1   The poem "Home," by Joanne, is published in *Hulihia VII: Writings from Prison and Beyond: "Home" Edition*, the seventh volume of the prison's yearly publication.

2   Keahiolalo-Karasuda, "The Colonial Carceral and Prison Politics in Hawai'i," xi. See Keahiolalo-Karasuda, "A Genealogy of Punishment in Hawai'i," 149.

3   I was invited to participate in an outrigger canoe race on Moloka'i, an island where mostly Native Hawaiians live. From personal observation and the stories of my friend's family (*'ohana*) with whom I stayed and paddled, "everyone in Moloka'i is someone's aunty," and there is a marked absence of haole folk. Moloka'i is perhaps the least visited of the Hawaiian Islands besides the uninhabited and militarily occupied Kaho'olawe and the privately owned Ni'ihau, and in this way, it is liberated from tourism. From the 1860s to the 1960s, eight thousand people, mostly Native Hawaiians, were forcibly removed from their families and relocated to Kalaupapa—the "leper" colony—on the remote island of Moloka'i. This exile echoes a disciplining of nonwhite bodies, paralleling contemporary examples in the Ebola crisis, the Guantánamo Bay detention camp, and the remote concentration camp of the South Pacific island nation of Nauru, euphemistically named the Nauru Regional Processing Centre. Nauru is one of a number of contemporary concentration camps, including those at the US-Mexico border and in northern India, western China, and the Greek island of Lesvos. The Nauru Regional Processing Centre is administered by the Australian government—thus releasing the government of Nauru from any culpability. I thank Miranda Outman for conversations about the Nauru Regional Processing Centre.

4   Wong, "When the Last Patient Dies," quoting Dan Barry, "In Kalaupapa, Hawaii, a Story of Exile and Union," *New York Times*, November 30, 2008.

5   An example of the ways in which the Pacific particularizes the writing in *Hulihia VII* is that the women's words serve as political resistance, much as the way double meanings (*kaona*) were embedded in the choreography of hula. *Kaona* frequently existed as insider ways of knowing, which were useful when hula was banned by the colonist invaders for its "lasciviousness." Hula extends to more than the widely known dance form and is accompanied by *oli*—the Hawaiian chant for the purposes of lament, prayer, and genealogy.

6   See Braly, *On the Yard*.

7   I explore Clough's penchant for masculinist and individualistic American narratives such as Ernest Hemingway's *The Old Man and the Sea* (1951) and Robert Frost's "The Road Not Taken" (1916) in chapter 1. These texts are a curious choice, given her audience.

8   The Hawaiian "Ki'i 'ōlelo a me ho'oman'o" is copied directly from *Hulihia VII* and duplicates the ungrammatical nature of some of the English creative writing.

9   I use the word *inmate* here because it appears as such in the KPWP's publicity materials.

10 The Farrington ninth graders, under the guidance of their teacher, Mel Malele, "added their Pacific island voices to the writing contest," writes Clough in her introduction to *Hulihia VII*. Clough states the youth from ROC "found writing

about home . . . compatible with their mission. . . . [S]tudents . . . are leading clean-up efforts, bridging poverty, housing projects and Pacific island neighborhoods in an ambitious charge to restore pride in their 'home.' ROC's driving force consists of youth from Our Lady of the Mount, St. Augustine's Tongan community, and Mormon youth ministries." Embedded in this introduction is a thorny marriage between Pacific Island voices and communities and the church. It is also worth noting that Farrington services economically disenfranchised communities, from which many of the women at WCCC come. Thus, there is a recognition of home that is passed between the women and the students.

11 See Shakur, *Assata*; Davis, *Angela Davis*; and Jackson, *Soledad Brother*.

12 Cummins, in *The Rise and Fall of California's Radical Prison Movement*, identifies a tension between prescriptions for autobiographical work as moral pedagogy versus prisoners' resistant counternarratives at the height of the 1960s bibliotherapy movement. The literary boom in the prisons, argues Cummins, faded with the demise of the radical prison movement.

13 The term *apologia* refers to a writing form that is a defense. The testimonio genre, developed in Latin America, foregrounds a collective witnessing of the oppressed. As described by Sidonie Smith and Julia Watson, "In testimonio, the narrator intends to communicate the situation of a group's oppression, struggle, or imprisonment . . . and to call on readers to respond actively in judging the crisis" (*Reading Autobiography*, 282).

14 Stowe, "Making Sense of Letters and Diaries."

15 "Home," by Jessica C., in *Hulihia VII*, 22.

16 "Home," by Jessica C., in *Hulihia VII*, 22.

17 Tracy Huling, introduction to Scheffler, *Wall Tappings*, xiii.

18 Huling offers up the narrative of a correctional officer in New York who, after observing the intricacies and curves of their gardens, complains that women cannot plant in a straight line. This is testament to women's subversive practices of artistry.

19 Hamm, "The Prisoner Speaks," 738.

20 See Hamm, "The Prisoner Speaks," 738–39. Hamm references Franklin, *Prison Literature in America*.

21 *Oli* is a Hawaiian chant used to accompany hula and for the purposes of lament, prayer, and genealogy, to name a few. 'Ilima Stern was the assistant director to Clough in the early years of the KPWP.

22 The literal translation of the Hawaiian word *pa'ahao* is "locked in irons." The Hawaiian titles are grammatically incorrect and their translations are inexact, resonating with some of the English creative writing. I thank Kapali Lyon in the Department of Religion at the University of Hawai'i and an anonymous reviewer at Duke for alerting me to the mistranslations.

23 The incarceration is ambiguous because Clough critiques the nuns' stifling of the girls (herself) but concludes the stanza with "I loved them for it / But not then / Not then" (Clough, *Hulihia VII*, 46). The emphasis and repetition of "not then" implies an ambivalence to institutional discipline that the auteur appreciates in

hindsight. Clough collapses her personal experience with "correction" to the pervasive corrections that her students face within the facility.

24 The entry "Finding Home," by Pat Clough, is set off as it is the only one that is identified with a last name and the appellation "Teacher." In a sense, it is the singular poem that rejects anonymity. The poem is published in *Hulihia VII*, 46.

25 "Home?," by Kelly, in *Hulihia VII*, 14. I have retained the unorthodox and perhaps awkward line breaks to maintain an authenticity to the published piece, which is more prosaic than poetic.

26 The Home of Reawakening for Women is a residential, community-based reentry program run by TJ Mahoney & Associates, a nonprofit organization. Its mission is to empower women to successfully transition from prison to the community. I first met the former director of the Home of Reawakening for Women, Lorraine Robinson, through feminist criminologist Meda Chesney-Lind. In 2012, I led classes at the reentry program for women transitioning from WCCC and worked on a newsletter in concert with them.

27 "Where Is Home?," by Tiffany, in *Hulihia VII*, 4.

28 Based on our conversations, I gleaned that Tiffany was unhappy living without her wife, after her wife was released. They did not engage in a physical relationship while in prison, fearing administrative retaliation.

29 "Home," by Joanne, in *Hulihia VII*, 23.

30 These tales are reinforced in the institutional programming, such as the religiously driven Total Life Recovery (TLR) and Hina Mauka programs, explored in the introduction to this book. Many of the women in the writing program are concurrently TLR and Hina Mauka participants, and many interview conversations circle around the embracing of Jesus in their lives, which exists alongside their desire to explore self-discovery. Clough attempts to steer the writing away from the scriptural.

31 My readings of the poem in connection to personal trauma are confirmed in several interviews with the women, as well as in the narratives they shared in class and in serial poems.

32 "Home," by Brooke, in *Hulihia VII*, 17.

33 "The Home I Now Carry," by Pamela (a repeat taker of Clough's advanced writing class), in *Hulihia VII*, 44. Pamela, whose work has been published in many of the *Hulihia* volumes, informed me that her "Home" poems are her least favorite. After a class that I taught at the facility, I saw Pamela engaged in artwork in the education room—her hair in high braids with more gray than I remembered. Pamela presents a complicated and composite performance of selves: Caribbean, Native American, Scottish, and German. Pamela's mother died while Pamela was in prison, and her request to attend her mother's funeral on a mainland reservation was denied. Many of the inside women suffer the perpetual trauma of losing a loved one while incarcerated, as I explore in chapter 1. Pamela attributes her poem "My Committee of Voices," in *Hulihia IX*, to Clough's ability to challenge her through grief: "I will always be grateful to Ms. Pat for that."

34 "Home," by Melody, in *Hulihia VII*, 24.

35 I explore the censorship of the *Hulihia* texts in chapters 1 and 3, positing Clough and the institution within the colonizer/colonized mother/daughter dialogic.

36 An external reviewer for Duke University Press points out that using Hartman's work is problematic because enslavement is distinct from settler colonialism. I am grateful for this point, but I maintain that it is important to include mention of Hartman because her work on "home as wound" is relevant to inside women's writing on home/homeland. I do not wish to liken Hawai'i to the space of diaspora, but I believe the experience of dislocation, mourning, and perpetual grieving has resonance here.

37 "I'll Be Home," by Brandy, in *Hulihia VII*, 10.

38 L. Gilmore, *Limits of Autobiography*, 101–2. Gilmore notes that Kincaid sanctifies her mother as a "mythic" creature. See also Lorde, *Zami*, in which Lorde allows the poetic voice to intercede and disrupt linear narrative—her deployment of the myth.

39 L. Gilmore, *Limits of Autobiography*, 98.

40 "My Permanent Home, Heaven," by Taniela at ROC, in *Hulihia VII*, 41.

41 "Home," by Amourelle, in *Hulihia VII*, 34.

42 This line evokes Eastern State Penitentiary in Pennsylvania, one of the first prisons in the United States. Eastern State Penitentiary countered the then contemporaneous Auburn, New York, system, which was aimed at communal silence, instituting a separate system of rehabilitation. The line also evokes the founding fathers' edict of America as a "beacon on a hill" amid the surrounding wilderness. "Farm," by Karen, in *Hulihia VII*, 16.

43 The cover art for *Hulihia VII* is by local artist Louisa S. Cooper, which reflects Clough's commitment to summoning the resources of the local community.

44 According to a concept note (document s/2015/543) prepared by the delegation of New Zealand, the United Nations classifies fifty-two territories as Small Island Developing States, including thirty-seven member states, with a combined population of over fifty million people. See "Issues Facing Small Island Developing States 'Global Challenges' Demanding Collective Responsibility, Secretary-General Tells Security Council."

45 "Looking Back," by Jennifer, in *Hulihia VII*, 11.

3. THE STAGE AWAY FROM THE PAGE

1 In a conversation on January 4, 2016, Clough expressed that the informal presentations in the dorms and cottages were in some way the most moving. The women, published in *Hulihia*, shared their published work with their "sisters." The larger inside community of women was able to experience the Kailua Prison Project firsthand.

2 See the appendix for a list of the Prison Monologues performances I attended between 2012 and 2014.

3 The 'Aha Wahine Conference is a gathering of Native Hawaiian women from the community.

4 Whitlock, *Soft Weapons*, 119, 122.

5 This is a reference to Salman Rushdie's memoir on exile, *Shame*, by performance studies scholar Yana Meerzon, *Performing Exile, Performing Self*.

6 From 2012 to 2014, I attended more than twenty Prison Monologues "performances," an appellation that Clough resists, which included "presentations at schools, residential treatments, community colleges, conferences and events." This quote is extracted from the Kailua Prison Project's publicity and testimonial materials.

7 The direct quotes from Vailea are transcribed from the interview I conducted with her on May 6, 2013, in the intake room at WCCC.

8 My idea on the intersection of theater and the staging of human rights is informed by Paul Heritage in "Taking Hostages," 97.

9 Kosasa, "Journey to Justice." See Chesney-Lind and Bilsky, "Native Hawaiian Youth in Hawai'i Detention Center."

10 Kosasa, "Journey to Justice."

11 This conversation with Warden Patterson occurred in 2013 in the warden's office.

12 Partly due to the media's accolades of the Prison Monologues program across the state, as well as Patterson's positioning of the prison as a *pu'uhonua*, the former warden has been featured on TED Talks, as well as on public television. See TEDxTalks, "The Criminal Justice System."

13 For a discussion of storytelling and story listening within a twelve-step program, see Swora, "Narrating Community."

14 For an analysis of public conversion narratives, see Don Waisanen's review of *Identity's Strategy* by Dana Anderson.

15 Meerzon, *Performing Exile, Performing Self*, 299.

16 Meerzon, *Performing Exile, Performing Self*, 299.

17 The performative rendition includes excerpts from *Hulihia VIII: Monologues from Prison*. In this eighth volume of the prison journal, Clough published the performed monologues mostly verbatim.

18 Kaipo was an exception to the minimum-custody rule. Despite Kaipo's infractions in the facility, Clough advocated for her to be part of the new Prison Monologues due to her talent and appeal. Ultimately, Kaipo was not allowed to join the Prison Monologues, which attests to the primacy of the prison's rules.

19 Interview with Vailea, May 6, 2014.

20 I italicize the words that are emphasized by Clough, the speaker.

21 The first two quotes are from Schechner, "Ritual and Performance," 613. The expression "beloved community" is used frequently in the facility's promotional material, by Warden Patterson, and by the WCCC Total Life Recovery and Hina Mauka programs.

22 I have a master's degree in special education from Fordham University and worked with teenagers designated as having learning disabilities in New York City and in Hawai'i. At the University of Hawai'i at Mānoa, I supervised special education teachers attaining graduate degrees in the Department of Education.

23 Vailea tells me that there was a part of her that didn't want to leave the facility when she was finally released to furlough. In fact, she chose Bridges, the furlough

program located on the facility's grounds, rather than going to TJ Mahoney & Associates, a gender-responsive program in downtown Honolulu. In her interview, Vailea expresses her attachment to the Prison Monologues program: "I can't imagine my life without the Prison Monologues!"

24 "Food for thought" is a phrase that Clough uses frequently in class. In this introduction of the Prison Monologues to the lab, Vailea is forceful, proffering potential Monologuers a lecture with moral overtones.

25 See the appendix for the audition guide that Clough disseminated at the Prison Monologues audition on February 16, 2013.

26 Schechner, "Self-Inflicted Wounds."

27 *'Ohana*, the Hawaiian word for "family," is used by locals and exemplifies the value of the extended family and of aloha (peace, love, welcome).

28 Making Waves Films LLC is a documentary production company in Honolulu, established in 2005 by award-winning independent filmmaker Kimberlee Bassford. According to the company's promotional materials, its mission is to "produce social issues, cultural, historical, and environmental documentary films that advance social justice, strengthen our connections to one another and deepen understanding of the world."

29 Introductory performance text to part 1, "Who We Were." Simultaneously printed in Clough, *Hulihia VIII*, 2.

30 See Kunzel, *Criminal Intimacy*.

31 Liezel's poem "Who I Was" always headlines the Prison Monologues performances. Published in *Hulihia VIII*, 6.

32 The warden explains that the parole board requires women to go through the Hina Mauka program—a drug treatment program with a Hawaiian cultural and religious framework—two to three years before they leave the prison. After the women complete their time in Hina Mauka, they are required to complete a work furlough program—TJ Mahoney or Bridges—and then their parole.

33 This conversation with the warden took place in the administration building in 2013.

34 Interview with Vailea, May 6, 2014.

35 The Oʻahu Community Correctional Center is one of the three men's prisons on Oʻahu and the largest facility in the state. The women are frequently housed there on arrest before their transfer to WCCC, even though OCCC can be a dangerous place for the women. Danika, a trans woman, was raped there before her transfer to WCCC. As discussed previously, there are plans to expand WCCC to afford the transfer of all female "inmates" currently "housed" in the overcrowded, deteriorating OCCC.

36 This conversation with the warden took place in the administration building in 2013.

37 Interview with Vailea, May 6, 2014.

38 At that time, Vailea and Reiko worked with Toni Bissen, executive director of the Puʻa Foundation, a charitable organization that was established in 1996 "out of an apology, redress and reconciliation initiative of the United Church of Christ for its complicity in the 1893 overthrow of the Hawaiian Government." The foundation's vision is that "through pūʻā, the process of feeding, nourishing,

and strengthening, there will be the emergence of enlightened communities and society. To help in the passing from one to another generation the nourishment of our ancestral dignity from which we revitalize our national consciousness. Through such acts of humanity, new life springs forth. So shall it be with the Hawaiian people." The Pūʻā Foundation, "Vision, Mission and Focus."

39 At our last meeting at Morning Brew in Kailua, on May 15, 2017, Clough tells me that Vailea has a job at a car dealership and has been instrumental in getting jobs for some of the inside women who have now been paroled. Even though Vailea is not working directly with youth, she is giving back to her community.

40 "Ipo Lei Momi" (Precious pearl lei) is the name of a song by Kealiʻi Reichel. The word *haku* means "master, lord." Both Clough and I encourage the women to work in blank verse as direct rhyme tends toward the cliché, but it can be effective as irony when employed to critique institutional violence, as in Allyson's poem "Governmental Seduction," displayed in chapter 1.

41 This authenticity is both debated and heralded by historians and by literary and carceral theorists.

42 The reference to creating "our own entertainment" prefaces the infamous and typically well-received "SKIT: Don't You Know Who I Am?" The women always preface the skit with "So—if you think that all we do in prison is sit around and boo-hoo all day, well . . ."

43 Introductory performance text to part 3, "Reflections." Also published in *Hulihia VIII*, 24.

44 "SKIT: Don't You Know Who I Am?," in *Hulihia VIII*, 12–13.

45 "A Letter from My Daughter," in *Hulihia VIII*, 27.

46 *Kolohe* is the Hawaiian word for "mischievous" or "naughty."

47 Kunzel, *Criminal Intimacy*, 34.

48 Smith and Watson, *Reading Autobiography*, 138.

49 Smith and Watson, *Reading Autobiography*, 138. Here Smith and Watson cite life-writing scholar Paul John Eakin.

50 Former governor Abercrombie commuted Liezel's hefty fifteen-to-life sentence before he left office partly because her central and visible role in the Prison Monologues inscribed her as a model prisoner and template for rehabilitation.

51 *Living Local with the Baraquios*, "Prison Monologues."

52 See Shailor, *Performing New Lives*.

53 Bhabha, "The World and the Home," 148. The poet Derek Walcott addresses the rhizomatic complexity embedded in exilic performances—the desire to leave home when there and the desire to return when away. This bipolar affect toward home is representative of many exilic anxieties and is present in both the Prison Monologues performances and the prison as a "border-zone." See also Meerzon, *Performing Exile, Performing Self*, 125.

54 Katsaridou and Vío, "Theatre of the Oppressed as a Tool of Educational and Social Intervention," 344.

55 Katsaridou and Vío, "Theatre of the Oppressed as a Tool of Educational and Social Intervention," 337.

56 Jupp Kina and Fernandez, "Augusto Boal's *Theatre of the Oppressed*," 246.

57 Boal argued: "On stage the actor is an interpreter who, in the act of translating, plays false" (Boal, *The Rainbow of Desire*, 7).

58 Oliver, *Witnessing: Beyond Recognition*.

59 Clough shared this reminiscence with me during our last conversation at Morning Brew in Kailua, May 15, 2017.

60 Daphne's testimony, titled "Giving Back," appears in the publicity material for the Prison Monologues. csac stands for certified substance abuse counselor.

61 From the conference program, Pacific Rim International Conference on Disability and Diversity, Honolulu, May 20, 2014.

62 Meerzon, *Performing Exile, Performing Self*, 17.

63 In the acknowledgments to *Hulihia VIII*, Clough gives a shout-out to Iwalani Meyer, a student in her creative writing class who is "responsible for the beautiful cover drawing" (3).

64 On performativity, see Butler, *Bodies That Matter*, 232. The subversive uses of performativity are manifested through citation and re-citation of the performative. It is through the use of "ordinary language" in "non-ordinary" ways, or what Derrida would call "reinscription," that a term can break with discourse to engender insurrectionary potential. See Derrida, *Limited Inc.*, 7–12. "The iterability of the performance is generated from the citationality of the sign that allows one to 'make trouble' by citing or reciting the performative in ways that are contrary to or revealing of the instability of heteronormative hegemony." Young, "Judith Butler."

65 In chapter 4, I explore the alterations in the Prison Monologues as the core group was released from the facility and Clough began her Prison Monologues Lab.

66 In early 2012, I formed a friendship with one of the women from the original cast—Karen Newberry—whom I met at the parole reentry program Ka Hale Hoʻāla Hou No Nā Wāhine/The Home of Reawakening for Women. At the reentry program, Karen was my coeditor of the transitioning women's newsletter. A journalist in her previous life, Karen was a gifted writer. After her release, we maintained a close connection, meeting for social activities and poem swapping. For a while she worked at the Honolulu Harbor Fishery piers, communicating with chefs from around the world and scribing humorous poems about her interactions with them. Sadly, Karen passed away in the spring of 2016. Her jubilant messages about her reentry into life remain as haunting inscriptions in my inbox.

67 See Heritage, "Taking Hostages," 97.

68 Heritage provides the notorious case study of theater artist Ruth Escobar, whose theatrical staging in a Brazilian facility in 1980 was followed by a prison riot.

69 Heritage, "Taking Hostages," 99.

70 One of the first times that I substituted for Clough at wccc, the class ran over by a few minutes because I did not want to interrupt a woman's story. A fuming guard approached me and sharply rebuked me for detaining the women. I realized that this class was markedly variant from the classes I taught at the univer-

sity, and that "time" in the prison carried a poignancy and urgency quite distinct from that in classrooms on the outside.

71 Heritage, "Taking Hostages," 100.

72 Conclusion to the Prison Monologues from *Hulihia VIII*, 37.

4. LOVE LETTERS

An earlier version of this chapter appeared as "Love Letters: Performative and Biological Families in Hawai'i's Women's Prison," *Frontiers: A Journal of Women Studies* 39, no. 2 (2018): 171–205.

1 The students alternate in naming the Prison Monologues "performances," "speeches," "history," "secrets," "life stories," and "lectures," which inserts them within a pedagogical framework.

2 I use pseudonyms for all the high school students at Nānākuli and Kapolei High Schools to protect their identities. Giselle is a student in Christine Wilcox's English class at Nānākuli High School. I maintain the punctuation of words to reflect how the students wrote their letters. Giselle's letter has been edited for brevity.

3 According to Mahina's own written testimony to the Nānākuli teenagers.

4 As I explore the letters from Nānākuli and Kapolei High Schools on separate occasions, I intersperse testimonials collected from various readings. They carry a dysynchronous essence, characteristic of memory.

5 For an important discussion on Hawaiian epistemologies, see Meyer, "Our Own Liberation." One of the central Hawaiian epistemologies that I witness in exploring the Love Letters is what Manulani Aluli Meyer conveys as "Aloha knowledge or service to others." In her keynote address at the Connecting Education and Environment conference, Meyer posits aloha knowledge as the most important knowledge or intelligence. Aloha intelligence, as Meyer articulates, is the "knowledge with which Native Hawaiians meet life," a knowing that is inextricable from understanding. Meyer explains that the Hawaiian word *'ike* means "to see," and she invites us to see differently as our world implodes. In the Love Letters, the teenagers see the inside women variantly from the expected narratives of criminality. By seeing differently, they see and love the women, a radical act that Meyer argues rests at the core of Hawaiian epistemology. It's not about cognitive accumulation, she says, but about knowing/seeing/feeling.

6 Nānākuli High and Intermediate School was founded in 1967 and serves 954 students; Kapolei High School was founded in 2000 and serves 2,500 students. The Prison Monologues had a long-standing relationship with Nānākuli, and Clough developed a close working and personal relationship with Mrs. Wilcox, the chair of the English department. Some of the Nānākuli responses are connected to themes embedded in the English high school curriculum standards, such as student exploration of Logos, Pathos, and Ethos. On the back of the poems, the students identify how the presentations cohere with these precepts.

7   The leeward side of Oʻahu is the west side, which is far drier and hotter than the east side.

8   Muñoz, *Disidentifications*.

9   Giselle's letter came out of a Nānākuli class on March 10, 2014.

10 After the core group—Vailea, Ivelisse, Reiko, and Liezel—was no longer present, Clough formed a group in training, which she called the Prison Monologues Lab, appointing Liezel as the director in her absence. This group of Prison Monologues Lab women included Kailani and Mahina—women whom Clough knew well as they were students in her creative writing classes. Clough wanted Lahela as part of this group for her raw talent and stage presence, but Lahela did not have the correct custody status to join the group, as she frequently received administrative infractions.

11 See Tengan's *Native Men Remade* and Irwin and Umemoto's *Jacked Up and Unjust*, which counter colonial histories/narratives in Hawaiʻi.

12 Chesney-Lind and Bilsky, "Native Hawaiian Youth in Hawaiʻi Detention Center," 133. The authors discuss contemporary carceral practices in Hawaiʻi that discriminate against Native Hawaiian youth.

13 Chesney-Lind and Bilsky, "Native Hawaiian Youth in Hawaiʻi Detention Center," 133.

14 As a side note, Palau (Belau) and the Marshall Islands (as well as Guam) are part of the region of Micronesia; thus there is a distinction between the political state of the Federated States of Micronesia and the geographic region of Micronesia.

15 The Hawaiian sovereignty movement ushered in the revitalization of the Hawaiian language in the 1970s.

16 Keahiolalo-Karasuda, "The Colonial Carceral and Prison Politics in Hawaiʻi." Another example of cultural genocide was the banning of hula by the missionaries.

17 Auslander, *Theory for Performance Studies*, 1.

18 Butler, *Gender Trouble*.

19 Butler, *Gender Trouble*. See also Cvetkovich, *Archive of Feelings*, for her queer approach to trauma and her archiving of everyday trauma, beyond the catastrophic, as well as for the collapse of the public and the private.

20 See Simon, Rosenberg, and Eppert, *Between Hope and Despair*; Irwin and Umemoto, *Jacked Up and Unjust*; and Henke, *Shattered Subjects*.

21 Muʻumuʻu is a traditional Hawaiian dress. *Kine* or *da kine* is an expression in Hawaiian Creole English that usually functions as a placeholder name, similar to *whatsit* and *whatchamacallit*. The humorous illustrated dictionary *Pidgin to Da Max* defines *da kine* as "the keystone of pidgin [colloquialism for Hawaiian Creole English]. You can use it anywhere, anytime, anyhow. Very convenient."

22 In this case not, as Vailea has been released on parole.

23 The reference to a "benevolent community" borrows from Dr. Martin Luther King Jr.'s "beloved community." Dr. King summoned a world that is love-blind, rather than color-blind.

24 The central point the warden is making is that the school population is only 4 percent Pacific Islander and is not representative of the community of inside women.

25 See De Salvo, *Writing as a Way of Healing*.

26 *Mahalo* (thank you); *nui* (big, great); *loa* (long). The etymology has resonances in Hawaiian voyaging practices.

27 Some of my ideas here are informed by Analisa Oboe's article "The TRC Women's Hearings as Performance and Protest in the New South Africa."

28 At times the students are homeless, living as indigents on the beaches on the west side of Oʻahu.

29 See Weil Davis, "Inside-Out."

30 Shoshana Felman, literary scholar, has written extensively on the secondhand witness in her coauthored text with psychiatrist Dori Laub, *Testimony: Crisis of Witnessing in Literature, Psychoanalysis and History*.

31 Kahuku is on the windward side. According to the program's website, "Bobby Benson Center offers both Residential Treatment Services for youth (ages 13–17) and Continuum Of Treatment Services for 13 years and older" ("Bobby Benson Center," updated 2023, https://www.bobbybenson.org). "The residential treatment program offers a supportive environment in which teenagers and their families can acquire the knowledge and skills needed to overcome the cycle of drug and alcohol addiction" ("Risking Connections," updated 2023, https://www.bobbybenson.org/treatment).

32 See Shoshana Felman, "The Return of the Voice: Claude Lanzmann's *Shoah*," in Felman and Laub, *Testimony*.

33 See the appendix for a list of the Prison Monologues performances I attended between 2012 and 2014.

34 Meerzon, *Performing Exile, Performing Self*, 36.

35 The students do not use Hawaiian diacritical marks in their names, which Brandy Nālani McDougall informed me is a means of preserving the ways in which their families have always written their names, as well as allowing for multiple meanings that the diacritical markings preclude. The use of diacritical notation is a more recent practice employed by academics.

36 Christine Wilcox and I had an immediate connection. Our planned one-hour interview lasted for close to eight hours and migrated from the house I was staying at in Mānoa (the house of the former governor Neil Abercrombie and his wife, Nancie Caraway) to Wilcox's favorite Italian restaurant in the Mānoa marketplace. The lengthy interview was taped.

37 Wilcox wrote the letter to her students in March 2014.

38 Felman, "The Return of the Voice," in Felman and Laub, *Testimony*.

39 Johnson and Ferraro, "Research on Domestic Violence in the 90s."

40 Ferraro, *Neither Angels nor Demons*, 72.

41 Bechdel, *Fun Home*.

42 Cvetkovich, "Drawing the Archive in Alison Bechdel's *Fun Home*," 121.

43 Cvetkovich, "Drawing the Archive in Alison Bechdel's *Fun Home*," 121. Cvet-kovich notes that "Cathy Caruth's notion of 'unclaimed experience' has widely disseminated the association of trauma with unrepresentability and epistemic crisis." See *Trauma* (1995) and *Unclaimed Experience* (1996).

44 Here Julia Watson cites Bechdel, *Fun Home*, as the originator of the term "net-work of transversals." Watson, "Autographic Disclosures and Genealogies of Desire in Alison Bechdel's *Fun Home*," 30, citing Bechdel, *Fun Home*, 102.

45 Cvetkovich, *Depression*, 126. As many prison theorists have argued, the prison-industrial complex in America is directly related to the collateral effects of slavery and colonialism and is an instrument of genocide for "surplus" populations.

5. POSTRELEASE AND AFFECTIVE WRITERS

1 Brown and Marusek, "'Ohana Ho'opakele," 225.

2 Walker and Tarutani, "Restorative Justice and Violence against Women," 63–65. I maintain all of Reiko's testimony as it was published.

3 As in the case of a few of the Prison Monologues women, Reiko's long sentence was commuted in part due to the community work she participated in through the Kailua Prison Writing Project. In this way the KPWP functions as restorative justice and as a direct antidote to recidivism.

4 Barrett et al., "More Than Transformative," 18.

5 Barrett et al., "More Than Transformative."

6 Chartrand, "I'm Not Your Carceral Other," 62.

7 Summer is referring to poems in *Hulihia IX: Writings from Prison, Conversations with Myself*. "Pam" is Pamela, whose poetry is included in chapter 2.

8 See Davis et al., *Abolition. Feminism. Now*; Cullors, *When They Call You a Terrorist*.

9 Leia's poem is published in *Hulihia IX*.

EPILOGUE

1 My interview with Sarah Shotland took place on February 16, 2016.

2 Harkins and Meiners, "Beyond Crisis."

3 Harkins and Meiners, "Beyond Crisis."

4 Bergner, *God of the Rodeo*. The Louisiana State Penitentiary (also known as Angola, Alcatraz of the South, and The Farm) is a maximum-security prison farm operated by the Louisiana Department of Public Safety and Corrections. It is called Angola after the country the slaves of this former plantation originated from and is the largest maximum-security prison in the United States, with 6,300 prisoners and 1,800 staff. During the Civil War, the property served at different times as either a Union or a Confederate prison. "Louisiana State Penitentiary," Wikipedia, last modified July 28, 2017, https://en.wikipedia.org/wiki/Louisiana

_State_Penitentiary#Angola_Rodeo. For more on prison tourism in relation to the rodeo show, see Perkinson, "Angola and the Agony of Prison Reform"; Adams, "The Wildest Show in the South."

5   Gould, "Discipline and the Performance of Punishment," 1.

6   Simmons and Mos Def, *Def Poetry*, season 6.

7   Some of the men in the Minnesota Prison Writing Workshop concur with Ivelisse's emphasis on finding their voice. Their testimonials speak to the value of their writing program, such as the following comment from one participant: "I spent many years of my life with no voice. No way of saying what I needed to say or think that what I had to say had any merit. Through writing I've found a way to give voice to my thoughts, ideas, and feelings. What comes out in writing is what I struggle to say with my own mouth." Minnesota Prison Writing Workshop, "Student Testimonials."

8   Clough shared this with me in an email correspondence on June 22, 2017, after she read the manuscript for this book.

9   Lee Cataluna is a noted local Honolulu playwright, journalist, and novelist. She is best known for her witty stage plays and newspaper columns about Island life and her "dorky" childhood in Maui.

10 Tuck, "Suspending Damage."

11 I am grateful to American studies and prison scholars Elizabeth Colwill and Robert Perkinson, who debriefed me after this troubling meeting with Nicole and encouraged me in my work through their rich experiences and insights.

ACLU (American Civil Liberties Union). *Blueprint for Smart Justice: Hawaiʻi.* 2019. https://50stateblueprint.aclu.org/assets/reports/SJ-Blueprint-HI.pdf.

Adams, Jessica. "'The Wildest Show in the South': Tourism and Incarceration at Angola." *TDR: The Drama Review* 45 (2001): 94–108.

Ahmed, Sara. *The Cultural Politics of Emotion.* Edinburgh: Edinburgh University Press, 2004.

Akaka, Moanikeʻala, Maxine Kahaulelio, Terrilee Kekoʻolani-Raymond, and Loretta Ritte. *Nā Wāhine Koa: Hawaiian Women for Sovereignty and Demilitarization.* Edited and with an introduction by Noelani Goodyear-Kaʻōpua. Honolulu: University of Hawaiʻi Press, 2018.

Alexander, Jacqui M. *Pedagogies of Crossing: Meditations on Feminism, Sexual Politics, Memory, and the Sacred.* Durham, NC: Duke University Press, 2005.

Alexander, Michelle. *The New Jim Crow: Mass Incarceration in the Age of Colorblindness.* New York: New Press, 2012.

AP News. "Hawaii Governor Withholds Funds for Corrections Oversight." March 2, 2021. https://apnews.com/article/david-ige-correctional-systems-coronavirus -pandemic-honolulu-hawaii-44da297265a11448b637ab16529a426a.

Auslander, Philip. *Theory for Performance Studies: A Student's Guide.* New York: Routledge, 2007.

Barrett, Larry, Pablo Mendoza, Logan Middleton, Mario Rubio, and Thomas Stromblad. "More Than Transformative: A New View of Prison Writing Narratives." *Reflections* 19, no. 1 (Spring/Summer 2019): 13–32. https://reflectionsjournal.net/wp -content/uploads/2019/08/Reflections-19.1-Barrett-Mendoza-Middleton-Rubio -Stromblad.pdf.

Bechdel, Alison. *Fun Home: A Family Tragicomic.* New York: Houghton Mifflin, 2006.

Belknap, Joanne. *The Invisible Woman: Gender, Crime, and Justice.* Belmont, CA: Wadsworth, 1996.

Bergner, Daniel. *God of the Rodeo: The Search for Hope, Faith, and a Six-Second Ride in Louisiana's Angola Prison.* New York: Crown, 1998.

Berry, Patrick W. "Beyond Hope: Rhetorics of Mobility, Possibility, and Literacy." PhD diss., University of Illinois at Urbana-Champaign, 2011. http://hdl.handle.net /2142/24138.

Berry, Patrick W. "Doing Time with Literacy Narratives." *Pedagogy: Critical Approaches to Teaching Literature, Language, Composition and Culture* 14, no. 1 (Winter 2014): 137–60. doi:10.1215/15314200-2348938.

Berry, Patrick W. *Doing Time, Writing Lives: Refiguring Literacy and Higher Education in Prison.* Carbondale: Southern Illinois University Press, 2018.

Bhabha, Homi. "The World and the Home." *Social Text*, nos. 31–32 (1992): 141–53. doi:10.2307/466222.

Boal, Augusto. *The Rainbow of Desire: The Boal Method of Theatre and Therapy.* Translated by Adrian Jackson. New York: Routledge, 1995.

Braly, Malcolm. *On the Yard.* New York: New York Review of Books, 1967.

Breckenridge, Adam. "What's Right and Wrong with the Workshop: A New Collection of Essays Examines the Effectiveness of the Creative Writing Workshop." *Pedagogy* 11, no. 2 (Spring 2011): 425–30. https://muse.jhu.edu/article /431027.

Brown, Marilyn, and Sarah Marusek. "'Ohana Ho'opakele: The Politics of Place in Corrective Environments." *International Journal for the Semiotics of Law* 27 (2014): 225–42. doi:10.1007/s11196-012-9291-8.

Butler, Judith. *Bodies That Matter: On the Discursive Limits of "Sex."* New York: Routledge, 1993.

Butler, Judith. *Gender Trouble: Feminism and the Subversion of Identity.* New York: Routledge, 1990.

Carson, E. Ann. "Prisoners in 2019." Washington, DC: Bureau of Justice Statistics, October 2020. https://www.bjs.gov/content/pub/pdf/p19.pdf.

Caruth, Cathy, ed. *Trauma: Explorations in Memory.* Baltimore, MD: Johns Hopkins University Press, 1995.

Caruth, Cathy. *Unclaimed Experience: Trauma, Narrative and History.* Baltimore, MD: Johns Hopkins University Press, 1996.

Castro, E. L., and M. R. Gould. "What Is Higher Education in Prison?" *Critical Education* 9, no. 10 (2018): 1–16. doi:10.14288/ce.v9i10.

Chartrand, Vicki. "I'm Not Your Carceral Other." *Journal of Prisoners on Prisons* 25, no. 1 (2016): 62–66. doi:10.18192/jpp.v25i1.5031.

Chesney-Lind, Meda. *The Female Offender: Girls, Women, and Crime.* Thousand Oaks, CA: Sage, 1997.

Chesney-Lind, Meda, and Brian Bilsky. "Native Hawaiian Youth in Hawai'i Detention Center: Colonialism and Carceral Control." *Hūlili: Multidisciplinary Research on Hawaiian Well-Being* 7 (2011): 133–58. https://kamehamehapublishing.org/wp -content/uploads/sites/38/2020/09/Hulili_Vol7_7.pdf.

Chesney-Lind, Meda, and Kat Brady. "Prisons." In *The Value of Hawai'i: Knowing the Past, Shaping the Future*, edited by Craig Howes, John Osorio, and Jonathan Kay Kamakawiwoole, 109–16. Honolulu: University of Hawai'i Press, 2010.

Chesney-Lind, Meda, and Nikki Jones, eds. *Fighting for Girls: New Perspectives on Gender and Violence.* Albany: State University of New York Press, 2010.

Chesney-Lind, Meda, and Lisa Pasko. *Girls, Women, and Crime: Selected Readings.* Thousand Oaks, CA: Sage, 2004.

Clough, Pat, ed. *Hulihia VII: Writings from Prison and Beyond: "Home" Edition*. Kailua, HI: Women's Community Correctional Center, 2011.

Clough, Pat, ed. *Hulihia VIII: Monologues from Prison*. Kailua, HI: Women's Community Correctional Center, 2012.

Clough, Pat, ed. *Hulihia IX: Writings from Prison, Conversations with Myself*. Kailua, HI: Women's Community Correctional Center, 2013.

Coggeshall, John M. "Closed Doors: Ethical Issues with Prison Ethnography." In *Anthropologists in the Field: Cases in Participant Observation*, edited by Lynne Hume and Jane Mulcock, 140–52. New York: Columbia University Press, 2004.

Collis, Taryn, Felice Davis, and Jennifer Smith. "Breaking Free while Locked Up: Rewriting Narratives of Authority, Addiction, and Recovery via University-Community Partnership." In "Prison Writing," edited by Wendy Hinshaw and Tobi Jacobi, special issue, *Reflections* 19, no. 1 (Spring/Summer 2019): 165–85.

Conway, Jill Ker. *When Memory Speaks: Reflections on Autobiography*. New York: Alfred A. Knopf, 1998.

Creating Better Outcomes, Safer Communities: Final Report of the House Concurrent Resolution 85 Task Force on Prison Reform to the Hawaiʻi Legislature, 2019 Regular Session. December 2018. https://www.courts.state.hi.us/wp-content/uploads/2018/12/HCR-85_task_force_final_report.pdf.

Cullors, Patrisse Khan. *When They Call You a Terrorist: A Black Lives Matter Memoir*. New York: St. Martin's, 2018.

Cummins, Eric. *The Rise and Fall of California's Radical Prison Movement*. Stanford, CA: Stanford University Press, 1994.

Cvetkovich, Ann. *An Archive of Feelings: Trauma, Sexuality, and Lesbian Public Cultures*. Durham, NC: Duke University Press, 2003.

Cvetkovich, Ann. *Depression: A Public Feeling*. Durham, NC: Duke University Press, 2012.

Cvetkovich, Ann. "Drawing the Archive in Alison Bechdel's *Fun Home*." *Women's Studies Quarterly* 36, nos. 1–2 (Spring/Summer 2008): 111–28. doi:10.1353/wsq.0.0037.

Davis, Angela Y. *Angela Davis: An Autobiography*. Chapel Hill, NC: Algonquin Books, 1991.

Davis, Angela Y. *Are Prisons Obsolete?* New York: Seven Stories, 2003.

Davis, Angela Y., Gina Dent, Erica Meiners, and Beth Richie. *Abolition. Feminism. Now*. Chicago: Haymarket Books, 2021.

Dayton, Kevin. "Corrections Commission Wants to Pause Planning on New Oahu Jail." *Honolulu Civil Beat*, December 17, 2020.

Deer, Sarah. "Sovereignty of the Soul: Exploring the Intersection of Rape Law Reform and Federal Indian Law." *Restoration* 15, no. 1 (2018): 22–25. https://www.niwrc.org/sites/default/files/files/magazine/restoration.15.1.pdf.

Denzin, Norman K. *Interpretive Autoethnography*. 2nd ed. Los Angeles: Sage, 2014.

Derrida, Jacques. *Limited Inc*. Evanston, IL: Northwestern University Press, 1988.

De Salvo, Louise. *Writing as a Way of Healing: How Telling Our Stories Transforms Our Lives*. New York: HarperCollins, 1999.

The Disparate Treatment of Native Hawaiians in the Criminal Justice System. Office of Hawaiian Affairs, Justice Policy Institute, University of Hawaiʻi, and Georgetown

University, 2010. https://justicepolicy.org/wp-content/uploads/2022/04/10-09_rep_
    disparatetreatmentofnativehawaiians_rd-ac.pdf.
Duff, Kathleen M., and Cynthia Garcia Coll. *Reframing the Needs of Women in Prison:
    A Relational and Diversity Perspective* (Project Report, no. 4). Wellesley, MA: Stone
    Center, Wellesley College, 1995. https://www.wcwonline.org/vmfiles/PR4.pdf.
Ensler, Eve. *What I Want My Words to Do to You.* PBS, December 16, 2003.
Ettorre, Elizabeth. *Autoethnography as Feminist Method: Sensitising the Feminist "I."*
    London: Routledge, 2017.
Evershed, Nick, and Helen Davidson. "Indigenous Imprisonment Rates Still Rising,
    Figures Show." *Guardian,* December 11, 2014. http://www.theguardian.com/australia
    -news/datablog/2014/dec/11/indigenous-imprisonment-rates-still-rising-figures
    -show.
Faith, K. *Unruly Women: The Politics of Confinement and Resistance.* Vancouver, BC:
    Press Gang, 1993.
Fellner, Jamie. "Punishment and Prejudice: Racial Disparities in the War on Drugs."
    Human Rights Watch, May 2000. https://www.hrw.org/reports/2000/usa/.
Felman, Shoshana, and Dori Laub. *Testimony: Crisis of Witnessing in Literature, Psy-
    choanalysis and History.* New York: Routledge, 1991.
Ferraro, Kathleen J. *Neither Angels nor Demons: Women, Crime, and Victimization.*
    Boston: Northeastern University Press, 2006.
Flanagin, Jake. "Reservation to Prison Pipeline: Native Americans Are the Unseen
    Victims of a Broken US Justice System." *Quartz,* April 27, 2015. http://qz.com
    /392342/native-americans-are-the-unseen-victims-of-a-broken-us-justice-system.
Fleetwood, Nicole R. *Marking Time: Art in the Age of Mass Incarceration.* Cambridge,
    MA: Harvard University Press, 2020.
Fletcher, Beverly R., Lynda Dixon Shaver, and Dreama G. Moon, eds. *Women Prison-
    ers: A Forgotten Population.* Westport, CT: Praeger, 1993.
Franklin, Cynthia, and Miriam Fuchs. "Shifting Ground: Translating Lives and Life Writ-
    ing in Hawai'i." *Biography* 32, no. 1 (Winter 2009): vii–xxix. doi:10.1353/bio.0.0068.
Franklin, H. Bruce. *Prison Literature in America: The Victim as Criminal and Artist.*
    New York: Oxford University Press, 1989.
Freedman, Estelle B. *Maternal Justice: Miriam Van Waters and the Female Reform
    Tradition.* Chicago: University of Chicago Press, 1996.
Freedman, Estelle B. *Their Sisters' Keepers: Women's Prison Reform in America,
    1830–1930.* Ann Arbor: University of Michigan Press, 1981.
Fuchs, Miriam. *The Text Is Myself: Women's Life Writing and Catastrophe.* Madison:
    University of Wisconsin Press, 2004.
Garcia, Saudi. "8 Shocking Facts about Sterilization in U.S. History." *Mic,* July 10,
    2013. https://www.mic.com/articles/53723/8-shocking-facts-about-sterilization-in
    -u-s-history.
Gilmore, Leigh. *The Limits of Autobiography: Trauma and Testimony.* Ithaca, NY:
    Cornell University Press, 2001.
Gilmore, Ruth Wilson. *Golden Gulag: Prisons, Surplus, Crisis, and Opposition in Glo-
    balizing California.* Berkeley: University of California Press, 2007.

Girshick, Lori B. *No Safe Haven: Stories of Women in Prison*. Boston: Northeastern University Press, 1999.

Goffman, Alice. *On the Run: Fugitive Life in an American City*. Chicago: University of Chicago Press, 2014.

Goodyear-Kaʻōpua, Noelani, Craig Howes, Jonathan Kay Kamakawiwoʻole Osorio, and Aiko Yamashiro, eds. *The Value of Hawaiʻi 3: Hulihia, the Turning*. Honolulu: University of Hawaiʻi Press, 2021.

Gould, Mary Rachel. "Discipline and the Performance of Punishment: Welcome to 'The Wildest Show in the South.'" *Liminalities: A Journal of Performance Studies* 7, no. 4 (December 2011): 1–31. http://liminalities.net/7-4/angola.pdf.

Hager, Eli, and Rui Kaneya. "The Prison Visit That Cost My Family $2,370." *Marshall Project*, April 12, 2016. https://www.themarshallproject.org/2016/04/12/the-hawaii -prison-visit-that-cost-my-family-2-370.

Hamm, Theodore. "The Prisoner Speaks." Review of *Prison Writing in 20th-Century America* by H. Bruce Franklin. *American Quarterly* 51, no. 3 (1999): 738–44. doi:10.1353/aq.1999.0040.

Harkins, Gillian, and Erica R. Meiners. "Beyond Crisis: College in Prison through the Abolition Undercommons." *Lateral*, no. 3 (Spring 2014). doi:10.25158/L3.1.24.

Hawaii News Now. "Status on Hawaii Inmates in Mainland Prisons." April 27, 2012. https://www.hawaiinewsnow.com/story/17859056/status-on-hawaii-inmates-in -mainland-prisons/.

Healy, Claire. "Hawaii Has No Girls in Juvenile Detention. Here's How It Got There." *Washington Post*, July 25, 2022. https://www.washingtonpost.com/nation/2022/07/25 /hawaii-zero-girls-youth-correctional-facility/.

Henke, Suzette. *Shattered Subjects: Trauma and Testimony in Women's Life-Writing*. New York: St. Martin's, 1999.

Heritage, Paul. "Taking Hostages: Staging Human Rights." *TDR: The Drama Review* 48, no. 3 (Fall 2004): 96–106. doi:10.1162/1054204041667695.

Hinshaw, Wendy, and Tobi Jacobi, eds. "Prison Writing." Special issue, *Reflections* 19, no. 1 (Spring/Summer 2019). https://reflectionsjournal.net/wp-content/uploads /2019/08/Reflections-19.1-Full-with-Cover2.pdf.

Hinshaw, Wendy Wolters, and Tobi Jacobi. "What Words Might Do: The Challenge of Representing Women in Prison and Their Writing." *Feminist Formations* 27, no. 1 (Spring 2015): 67–90. doi:10.1353/ff.2015.0010.

hooks, bell. *Wounds of Passion: A Writing Life*. New York: Henry Holt, 1997.

Irwin, Katherine, and Karen Umemoto. *Jacked Up and Unjust: Pacific Islander Teens Confront Violent Legacies*. Oakland: University of California Press, 2016.

"Issues Facing Small Island Developing States 'Global Challenges' Demanding Collective Responsibility, Secretary-General Tells Security Council." United Nations Meetings Coverage and Press Releases, July 30, 2015. http://www.un.org/press/en /2015/sc11991.doc.htm.

Jackson, George. *Soledad Brother: The Prison Letters of George Jackson*. New York: Bantam Books, 1970.

Jacobi, Tobi. "Speaking Out for Social Justice: Institutional Challenges and Uncertain Solidarities." In *Women, Writing, and Prison: Activists, Scholars, and Writers Speak Out*, edited by Tobi Jacobi and Ann Folwell Stanford, 241–51. Lanham, MD: Rowman and Littlefield, 2014.

Jacobi, Tobi. "Twenty-Year Sentences: Women's Writing Workshops in US Prisons and Jails." In *Feminist Popular Education in Transnational Debates: Building Pedagogies of Possibility*, edited by Linzi Manicom and Shirley Walters, 111–27. New York: Palgrave Macmillan, 2012. doi:10.1057/9781137014597_7.

Jacobi, Tobi, and Ann Folwell Stanford, eds. *Women, Writing, and Prison: Activists, Scholars, and Writers Speak Out*. Lanham, MD: Rowman and Littlefield, 2014.

James, Joy, ed. *The New Abolitionists: (Neo) Slave Narratives and Contemporary Prison Writings*. Albany: State University of New York Press, 2005.

James, Joy. *Warfare in the American Homeland: Policing and Prison in a Penal Democracy*. Durham, NC: Duke University Press, 2007.

Johnson, Michael P., and Kathleen J. Ferraro. "Research on Domestic Violence in the 90s: Making Distinctions." *Journal of Marriage and the Family* 62, no. 4 (2000): 948–63. doi:10.1111/j.1741-3737.2000.00948.x.

Jupp Kina, Victoria, and Kelly Cristina Fernandes. "Augusto Boal's *Theatre of the Oppressed*: Democratising Art for Social Transformation." *Critical and Radical Social Work* 5, no. 2 (2017). doi:10.1332/204986017X14951776937239.

Justice Arts Coalition. "Welcome to the Justice Arts Coalition (JAC)." Updated 2022. https://thejusticeartscoalition.org/about/.

Kajstura, Aleks, and Wendy Sawyer. *Women's Mass Incarceration: The Whole Pie 2023*. Prison Policy Initiative. https://www.prisonpolicy.org/reports/pie2023women.html.

Kaplan, Caren. "Resisting Autobiography: Out-Law Genres and Transnational Feminist Subjects." In *De/Colonizing the Subject: The Politics of Gender in Women's Autobiography*, edited by Sidonie Smith and Julia Watson, 115–38. Minneapolis: University of Minnesota Press, 1992.

Kates, Erika. *Moving beyond Prison: Building a Women's Justice Network in Massachusetts*. Wellesley, MA: Wellesley Centers for Women, 2014. https://www.wcwonline.org/images/stories/researchandaction/pdf/rar_springsummer2014.pdf.

Katsaridou, Martha, and Koldobika Vío. "Theatre of the Oppressed as a Tool of Educational and Social Intervention: The Case of Forum Theatre." *Proceedings of the Fourth International Conference on Critical Education: Critical Education in the Era of Crisis*, edited by Grollios Georgios, Liampas Anastasios, and Pavlidis Periklis, 334–56. Thessaloniki: Aristotle University, 2014. https://www.researchgate.net/publication/332866084.

Keahiolalo-Karasuda, RaeDeen. "The Colonial Carceral and Prison Politics in Hawai'i." PhD diss., University of Hawai'i at Mānoa, 2008.

Keahiolalo-Karasuda, RaeDeen. "A Genealogy of Punishment in Hawai'i: The Public Hanging of Chief Kamanawa II." *Hūlili: Multidisciplinary Research on Hawaiian Well-Being* 6 (2010): 147–67. https://kamehamehapublishing.org/wp-content/uploads/sites/38/2020/09/Hulili_Vol6_7.pdf.

Kosasa, Eiko. "Journey to Justice: A Conversation with Mark Kawika Patterson and Eiko Kosasa Part 1." Women's Community Correctional Center, 2013. Posted by the Center of Hegemony Studies. https://vimeo.com/80406408.

Krog, Antjie. *Begging to Be Black*. Cape Town: Random House Struik, 2009.

Kunzel, Regina. *Criminal Intimacy: Prison and the Uneven History of Modern American History*. Chicago: University of Chicago Press, 2008.

Lacy, Clara. *Out of State*. Los Angeles Film Festival. June 18, 2017.

Lamb, Wally. *Couldn't Keep It to Myself: Wally Lamb and the Women of York Correctional Institution*. New York: Regan Books, 2003.

Lamb, Wally. *I'll Fly Away: Further Testimonies from the Women of York Prison*. New York: HarperCollins, 2007.

Lawston, Jodie Michelle, and Ashley E. Lucas, eds. *Razor Wire Women: Prisoners, Activists, Scholars, and Artists*. Albany: State University of New York Press, 2011.

Liliʻuokalani. *Hawaiʻi's Story by Hawaiʻi's Queen*. Boston: Lee and Shepard, 1898. doi:10.5479/sil.186608.39088003419595.

Living Local with the Baraquios. "Prison Monologues." YouTube, December 7, 2012. https://www.youtube.com/watch?v=LlzWtlLTIao.

Lorde, Audre. *Zami: A New Spelling of My Name*. New York: Crossing Press, 1983.

Maier, Linda S., and Isabel Dulfano, eds. *Woman as Witness: Essays on Testimonial Literature by Latin American Women*. New York: Peter Lang, 2004.

Martinez, Aja Y. "A Plea for Critical Race Theory Counterstory: Stock Story vs. Counterstory Dialogues Concerning Alejandra's 'Fit' in the Academy." In *Performing Antiracist Pedagogy in Rhetoric, Writing, and Communication*, edited by Frankie Condon and Vershawn Ashanti Young, 65–86. Fort Collins, CO: WAC Clearinghouse, 2017. doi:10.37514/ATD-B.2016.0933.2.03.

McCarthy, Karen. *Mama Lola: A Voudou Priestess in Brooklyn*. Berkeley: University of California Press, 1991.

Meerzon, Yana. *Performing Exile, Performing Self: Drama, Theatre, Film*. London: Palgrave Macmillan, 2012.

Meiners, Erica R. *Right to Be Hostile: Schools, Prisons, and the Making of Public Enemies*. New York: Routledge, 2010.

Meyer, Manulani Aluli. Keynote address, Connecting Education and Environment: Mobilizing Sustainability in Education Policy, Practice, and Research conference, June 11, 2016. University of Saskatchewan, Saskatoon, Canada. Available on YouTube at https://www.youtube.com/watch?v=DoGmHSwOpSA.

Meyer, Manulani Aluli. "Our Own Liberation: Reflections on Hawaiian Epistemology." *Contemporary Pacific* 13, no. 1 (Spring 2001): 124–48. doi:10.1353/cp.2001.0024.

Milward, David. Review of *Justice as Healing: Indigenous Ways*, edited by Wanda D. McCaslin. *Wicazo Sa Review* 22, no. 1 (Spring 2007): 127–31. doi:10.1353/wic.2007.0010.

Minnesota Prison Writing Workshop. "Student Testimonials." Updated 2022. https://www.mnprisonwriting.org/testimonial/.

Mohanty, Chandra Talpade. *Feminism without Borders: Decolonizing Theory, Practicing Solidarity*. Durham, NC: Duke University Press, 2003.

Muñoz, José Esteban. *Disidentifications: Queers of Color and the Performance of Politics*. Minneapolis: University of Minnesota Press, 1999.

Nellis, Ashley. "Mass Incarceration Trends." The Sentencing Project, January 25, 2023. https://www.sentencingproject.org/reports/mass-incarceration-trends/.

Oboe, Analisa. "The TRC Women's Hearings as Performance and Protest in the New South Africa." *Research in African Literatures* 38, no. 3 (Fall 2007): 60–76. doi:10.2979/RAL.2007.38.3.60.

Office of Hawaiian Affairs. "A Correctional Center Becomes a Puʻuhonua." *Ka Wai Ola*, July 22, 2022. https://kawaiola.news/hoonaauao/a-correctional-center-becomes -a-puuhonua/.

OHAHawaii. "Healing in Hālawa with Kumu Hina." YouTube, September 17, 2019. https://www.youtube.com/watch?v=5Np3nxJ9tOY.

Oliver, Kelly. *Witnessing: Beyond Recognition*. Minneapolis: University of Minnesota Press, 2001.

Owen, Barbara A. *"In the Mix": Struggle and Survival in a Women's Prison*. Albany: State University of New York Press, 1998.

Penney, Darby. "Creating a Place of Healing and Forgiveness: The Trauma-Informed Care Initiative at the Women's Community Correctional Center of Hawaiʻi." Alexandria, VA: NCTIC, 2013. https://www.nasmhpd.org/sites/default/files/7014 _hawaiian_trauma_brief_2013(1).pdf.

Perkinson, Robert. "Angola and the Agony of Prison Reform." *Radical Philosophy Review* 3, no. 1 (2000): 8–19. doi:10.5840/radphilrev2000312.

Perkinson, Robert. *Texas Tough: The Rise of America's Prison Empire*. New York: Picador, 2010.

Pompa, Lori. "Disturbing Where We Are Comfortable: Notes from Behind the Walls." *Reflections* 4, no. 1 (2004): 24–34.

Pompa, Lori. "Drawing Forth, Finding Voice, Making Change: Inside-Out Learning as Transformative Pedagogy." In *Turning Teaching Inside Out: A Pedagogy of Transformation for Community-Based Education*, edited by Simone Weil Davis and Barbara Sherr Roswell, 13–25. London: Palgrave Macmillan, 2013.

Prison Policy Initiative. "Hawaiʻi Incarceration Rates by Race/Ethnicity, 2010." May 2014. https://www.prisonpolicy.org/graphs/2010rates/HI.html.

Prison Policy Initiative. *Hawaiʻi Profile*. Updated 2023. https://www.prisonpolicy.org /profiles/HI.html.

The Pūʻā Foundation. "Vision, Mission and Focus." Updated 2014. https://www .puafoundation.org/vision.

Pukui, M. K., and S. H. Elbert. *Hawaiian Dictionary: Hawaiian-English/English-Hawaiian*. Honolulu: University of Hawaiʻi Press, 1986.

Rich, Adrienne. "Someone Is Writing a Poem." In *What Is Found There: Notebooks on Poetry and Politics*. New York: Norton, 1993.

Richie, Beth E. *Arrested Justice: Black Women, Violence, and America's Prison Nation*. New York: NYU Press, 2012.

Richie, Beth E. "Feminist Ethnographies of Women in Prison." *Feminist Studies* 30, no. 2 (Summer 2004): 438–50. doi:10.2307/20458973.

Rojas, Maythee. *Women of Color and Feminism*. Berkeley, CA: Seal Press, 2009.

Ross, Luana. *Inventing the Savage: The Social Construction of Native American Criminality*. Austin: University of Texas Press, 1998.

Roy, Bidhan Chandra. "WordsUncaged: A Dialogical Approach to Empowering Voices." In *Prison Pedagogies: Learning and Teaching with Imprisoned Writers*, edited by Joe Lockard and Sherry Rankins-Robertson, 32–48. Syracuse, NY: Syracuse University Press, 2018. doi:10.2307/j.ctt20p5732.8.

Rymhs, Deena. *From the Iron House: Imprisonment in First Nations Writing*. Toronto: Wilfrid Laurier University Press, 2008.

Sawyer, Wendy, and Wanda Bertram. "Prisons and Jails Will Separate Millions of Mothers from Their Children in 2022." Prison Policy Initiative, May 4, 2022. https://www.prisonpolicy.org/blog/2022/05/04/mothers_day/.

Sawyer, Wendy, and Peter Wagner. *Mass Incarceration: The Whole Pie 2023*. Prison Policy Initiative. https://www.prisonpolicy.org/reports/pie2023.html.

Schechner, Richard. "Ritual and Performance." In *Companion Encyclopedia of Anthropology*, edited by Tim Ingold, 613–47. London: Routledge, 1994.

Schechner, Richard. "Self-Inflicted Wounds: Art, Ritual, Popular Culture." In *Performed Imaginaries*, 139–57. London: Routledge, 2015.

Scheffler, Judith A., ed. *Wall Tappings: An International Anthology of Women's Prison Writings, 200 A.D. to the Present*. New York: Feminist Press, 2002.

Scott, James. *Domination and the Arts of Resistance: Hidden Transcripts*. New Haven, CT: Yale University Press, 1990.

The Sentencing Project. "Fact Sheet: Incarcerated Women and Girls." Updated May 12, 2022. https://www.sentencingproject.org/publications/incarcerated-women-and-girls/.

The Sentencing Project. "Report to the United Nations on Racial Disparities in the U.S. Criminal Justice System." April 19, 2018. https://www.sentencingproject.org/reports/report-to-the-united-nations-on-racial-disparities-in-the-u-s-criminal-justice-system/.

Shailor, Jonathan, ed. *Performing New Lives: Prison Theatre*. London: Jessica Kingsley, 2011.

Shakur, Assata. *Assata: An Autobiography*. Chicago: Lawrence Hill Books, 1999.

Shelburne, Elizabeth Chiles. "Two and a Half Hours a Week." *Amherst Magazine*, Summer 2008. https://www.amherst.edu/amherst-story/magazine/issues/2008_summer/prison.

Silva, Noenoe K. *Aloha Betrayed: Native Hawaiian Resistance to American Colonialism*. Durham, NC: Duke University Press, 2016.

Simmons, Russell, and Mos Def. *Def Poetry*. Season 6. Simmons/Lathan TV, Home Box Office. Produced by Kamilah Forbes and Allen Kelman, directed by Stan Lathan. New York: HBO Video, 2007.

Simon, Roger I., Sharon Rosenberg, and Claudia Eppert, eds. *Between Hope and Despair: Pedagogy and the Remembrance of Historical Trauma*. Boston: Rowman and Littlefield, 2000.

Simonson, Douglas, Ken Sakata, and Pat Sasaki. *Pidgin to Da Max*. Honolulu: Bess Press, 1981.

Simpson, Audra. *Mohawk Interruptus: Political Life across the Borders of Settler States*. Durham, NC: Duke University Press, 2014.

Smith, Sidonie, and Julia Watson, editors. *De/Colonizing the Subject: The Politics of Gender in Women's Autobiography*. Minneapolis: University of Minnesota Press, 1992.

Smith, Sidonie, and Julia Watson. *Reading Autobiography: A Guide for Interpreting Life Narratives*. 2nd ed. Minneapolis: University of Minnesota Press, 2010.

Solinger, Rickie, Paula C. Johnson, Martha L. Raimon, Tina Reynolds, and Ruby C. Tapia, eds. *Interrupted Life: Experiences of Incarcerated Women in the United States*. Berkeley: University of California Press, 2010.

Stanford, Ann Folwell. "Introduction: Not Much Silence Here." In *Women, Writing, and Prison: Activists, Scholars, and Writers Speak Out*, edited by Tobi Jacobi and Ann Folwell Stanford, 1–18. Lanham, MD: Rowman and Littlefield, 2014.

Stanley, Eric, and Nat Smith, eds. *Captive Genders: Trans Embodiment and the Prison Industrial Complex*. 2nd ed. Chico, CA: AK Press, 2015.

Stowe, Steven. "Making Sense of Letters and Diaries." *History Matters: The US Survey Course on the Web*, July 2002. http://historymatters.gmu.edu/mse/letters /letters.pdf.

Sweeney, Megan. "Legal Brutality: Prisons and Punishment, the American Way." *American Literary History* 22, no. 3 (Fall 2010): 698–713. doi:10.1093/alh/ajq042.

Swora, Maria G. "Narrating Community: The Creation of Social Structure in Alcoholics Anonymous through the Performance of Autobiography." *Narrative Inquiry* 11, no. 2 (2001): 363–84. doi:10.1075/ni.11.2.06swo.

Taylor, Julie M. *Paper Tangos*. Durham, NC: Duke University Press, 1998.

TEDxTalks. "The Criminal Justice System: A Place of Healing: Mark Patterson at TEDxHonolulu." YouTube, November 2, 2012. https://www.youtube.com/watch?v =8uCC3DedyfU.

Tengan, Ty P. Kāwika. *Native Men Remade: Gender and Nation in Contemporary Hawai'i*. Durham, NC: Duke University Press, 2008.

Thach, Johnny. *Incarceration: Asian and Pacific Islanders*. Binghamton, NY: Binghamton University, 2012. https://issuu.com/johnnythach/docs/incarcerationapi.

Tonry, Michael H. *Thinking about Crime: Sense and Sensibility in American Penal Culture*. New York: Oxford University Press, 2004.

Total Life Recovery. "Turning Stories into Life Changing Lessons." Updated 2011. http://totalliferecovery.org.

Trask, Haunani-Kay. *From a Native Daughter: Colonialism and Sovereignty in Hawai'i*. Rev. ed. Honolulu: University of Hawai'i Press, 1999.

Trask, Haunani-Kay. *Night Is a Sharkskin Drum*. Honolulu: University of Hawai'i Press, 2002. http://www.jstor.org/stable/j.ctvvn78j.

Tuck, Eve. "Suspending Damage: A Letter to Communities." *Harvard Educational Review* 79, no. 3 (Fall 2009): 409–28. doi:10.17763/haer.79.3.n0016675661t3n15.

Tuck, Eve, and K. Wayne Yang. "Decolonization Is Not a Metaphor." *Decolonization: Indigeneity, Education, and Society* 1, no. 1 (2012): 1–40. https://jps.library.utoronto .ca/index.php/des/article/view/18630/15554.

United Nations Office on Drugs and Crime. "Women and HIV in Prison Settings." September 2008. https://www.unodc.org/documents/middleeastandnorthafrica /drug-prevention-health-publications/WOMEN_AND_HIV_IN_PRISON _SETTINGS.pdf.

Urbina, Ian. "Hawaii to Remove Inmates over Abuse Charges." *New York Times*, August 25, 2009.

van Gelder, Sarah. "Can Prison Be a Healing Place?" *YES! Magazine*, Beyond Prisons Issue, no. 58 (Summer 2011): 38–39. https://www.yesmagazine.org/wp-content /uploads/2022/01/58-Prisons.pdf.

Waisanen, Don. Review of *Identity's Strategy: Rhetorical Selves in Conversion* by Dana Anderson. *Rhetoric and Public Affairs* 12, no. 1 (Spring 2009): 145–47. doi:10.1353/ rap.0.0098.

Walker, Lorenn, and Rebecca Greening. *Reentry and Transition Planning Circles for Incarcerated People*. Honolulu: Hawai'i Friends of Justice and Civic Education, 2011.

Walker, Lorenn, and Cheri Tarutani. "Restorative Justice and Violence against Women: An Effort to Decrease the Victim-Offender Overlap and Increase Healing." In *Therapeutic Jurisprudence and Overcoming Violence against Women*, edited by Debarati Halder and K. Jaishankar, 63–84. Hershey, PA: IGI Global, 2017. doi:10.4018/978-1-5225-2472-4.ch005.

Wang, Leah. "The U.S. Criminal Justice System Disproportionately Hurts Native People: The Data, Visualized." Prison Policy Initiative, October 8, 2021. https://www .prisonpolicy.org/blog/2021/10/08/indigenouspeoplesday/.

Watson, Julia. "Autographic Disclosures and Genealogies of Desire in Alison Bechdel's *Fun Home*." *Biography* 31, no. 1 (Winter 2008): 27–58. http://www.jstor.org/stable /23540920.

Weil Davis, Simone. "Inside-Out: The Reach and Limits of a Prison Education Program." In *Turning Teaching Inside Out: A Pedagogy of Transformation for Community-Based Education*, edited by Simone Weil Davis and Barbara Sherr Roswell, 163–75. London: Palgrave Macmillan, 2013. doi:10.1057/9781137331021_18.

Weil Davis, Simone, and Barbara Sherr Roswell, eds. *Turning Teaching Inside Out: A Pedagogy of Transformation for Community-Based Education*. London: Palgrave Macmillan, 2013. doi:10.1057/9781137331021.

Whitlock, Gillian. *Soft Weapons: Autobiography in Transit*. Chicago: University of Chicago Press, 2007.

Williams, Patricia. *The Alchemy of Race and Rights: Diary of a Law Professor*. Cambridge, MA: Harvard University Press, 1992.

Wong, Alia. "When the Last Patient Dies." *Atlantic*, May 27, 2015. http://www .theatlantic.com/health/archive/2015/05/when-the-last-patient-dies/394163.

Young, Stephen. "Judith Butler: Performativity." *Critical Legal Thinking: Law and the Political*, November 14, 2016. http://criticallegalthinking.com/2016/11/14/judith -butlers-performativity.

Zapotosky, Matt. "In Executive Actions, President Trump Vows Crackdown on Violent Crime. Is America as Unsafe as He Thinks?" *Washington Post*, February 9, 2017.